CORPORATE INTERIORS No.3

CORPORATE INTERIORS
No.3

Edited by
Stanley Abercrombie

Designed by
Harish K. Patel

Visual Reference Publications Inc., New York

Copyright © 2000 by Visual Reference Publications Inc.

All rights reserved. No part of this book may be reproduced in any form or by any electronic or mechanical means, including information storage and retrieval systems, without permission in writing from the publisher.

Visual Reference Publications Inc.
302 Fifth Avenue
New York, NY 10001

Distributors to the trade in the United States and Canada
Watson-Guptill
1515 Broadway
New York, NY 10036

Distributors outside the United States and Canada
HarperCollins International
10 East 53rd Street
New York, NY 10022-5299

Library of Congress Cataloging in Publication Data:
Corporate Interiors

Printed in Hong Kong
ISBN 1-58471-00-4

Book Design: Harish Patel Design Associates, New York

CONTENTS

Introduction by Lester Dundes	7
Alan Gaynor + Company, P.C.	9
AREA	17
Berger Rait Design Associates, Inc.	25
Bergmeyer Associates, Inc.	33
Brayton & Hughes Design Studio	41
Brennan Beer Gorman Monk / Interiors	49
Burt Hill Kosar Rittelmann Associates	57
Callison Architecture, Inc.	65
CMSS Architects	73
DMJM Rottet	81
Felderman Keatinge Associates	89
Gary Lee Partners	97
Gensler	105
Griswold, Heckel & Kelly Associates, Inc.	113
The Hillier Group	121
HKS Inc.	129
IA, Interior Architects Inc.	137
Juan Montoya Design Corporation	145
Keiser Associates, Inc.	153
Kling Lindquist	161
Lehman-Smith+McLeish PLLC	169
Little & Associates Architects	177
Looney Ricks Kiss	185
LPA, Inc.	193
Mancini • Duffy	201
Mitchell Associates	209
Mojo • Stumer Associates P.C.	217
Montroy Anderson, Inc.	225
Oliver Design Group	233
O'Donnell Wicklund Pigozzi and Peterson Architects Inc.	241
Quantrell Mullins & Associates Inc.	249
Ridgway Associates Planning & Design	257
RMW Architecture + Design	265
RTKL Associates Inc.	273
Sasaki Associates, Inc.	281
SCR Design Organization, Inc.	289
Silvester Tafuro Design, Inc.	297
Skidmore, Owings & Merrill LLP	305
Staffelbach Design and Associates Inc	313
Sverdrup CRSS	321
Swanke Hayden Connell Architects	329
Ted Moudis Associates	337
van Summern Group	345
WPG Design Group	353
Future Proofing The Work Space	361
Project Index	432

Introduction What does Corporate America look like?

And who makes it look that way?

This is the third annual volume of a book that was conceived to answer these questions and to fill an important need. While there is a superabundance of media, both books and magazines, that show all types of residential design, there has not been — until now — an annual reference volume that can provide the business community with an overview of current developments in the design of corporate work spaces.

That's why, three years ago, I decided to publish Corporate Interiors. In the magazine Interior Design, which I published for many years, design professionals could see many such projects. But the corporate executive faced with the task of choosing a design firm and wanting to get some idea of who the best firms were ... where they were ... and what kind of work they were doing ... had nowhere to go.

The forty-four top firms invited to participate in this book have chosen to show examples of their work that are generally visually striking, but that is only part of the story told here. Today's interior design is much more than a pretty face. The projects here also encompass a large range of problem solving, including the analysis of needs, the selection of appropriate real estate, the efficient utilization of space, the provision for maximal productivity, the consideration of ergonomic factors, and the provision for increasingly critical demands for the technical backup of voice, image, and data transmission.

In addition to the case studies that dominate the book, you will find (beginning on page 384) Roger Yee's perceptive essay on the nature of the modern office, casting his experienced eye on directions where that office will be going in the next decade. And, in the back of the book, you will find information from companies making products you will want to discuss with your design team.

Finally, while looking at the projects shown here, it is important to remember that space has been limited and that what you are seeing is only a small fraction of each design firm's capabilities. No firm's story can be fully told without personal interviews and presentations, so take advantage of the addresses and 'phone numbers that preface each section and ask to see more. In addition, our brochure, "About Choosing a Design Firm," is yours for the asking; simply write me at: CORPORATE INTERIORS
c/o Visual Reference Publications, Inc.
302 Fifth Avenue, New York, NY 10001.

Lester Dundes
Publisher

Alan Gaynor + Company, P.C.

434 Broadway
New York
New York 10013
212.334.0900
212.966.8652 (Fax)
www.gaynordesign.com

Alan Gaynor + Company, P.C.

Offices for watersdesign.com
New York, New York

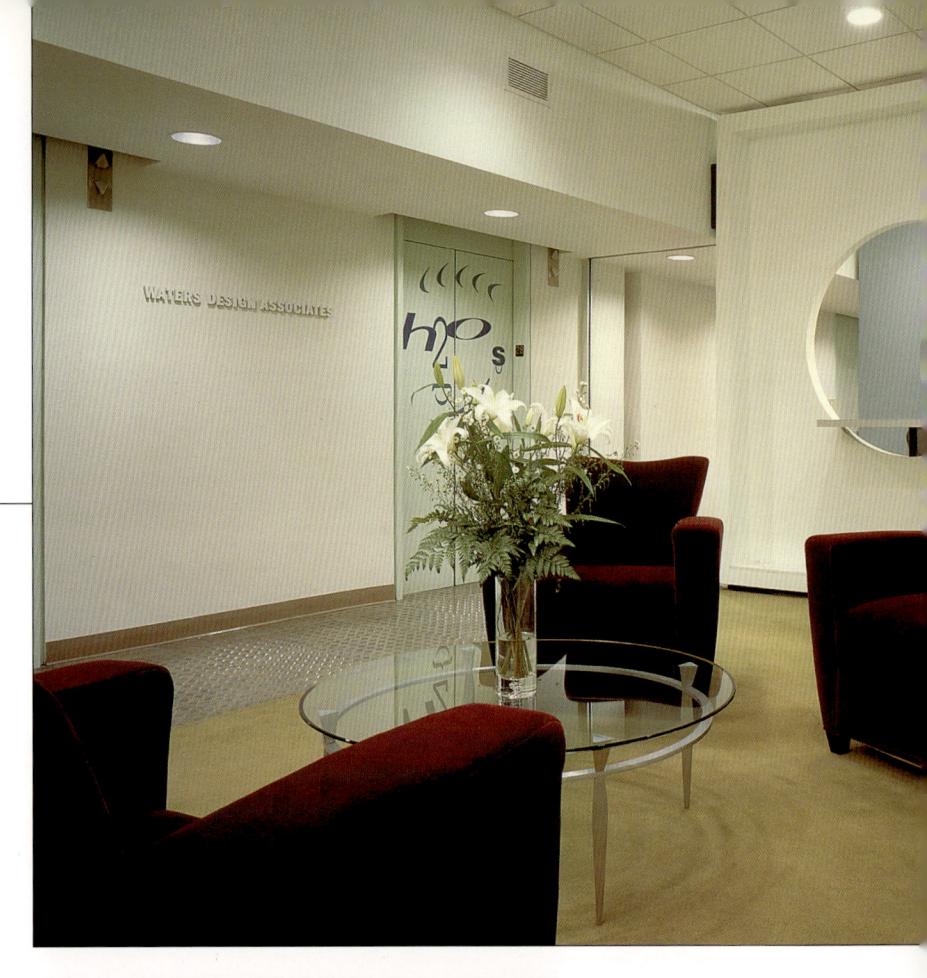

Right: Seating group in elevator lobby.
Below: The main design studio.
Below, right: The "wave" ceiling over a work area.
Photography: Roy J. Wright.

Above, right: Boardroom.
Right: Another view of the main design studio.
Below: Corridor with battered walls.

watersdesign.com formally known as Waters Design Associates, is a communications and graphic design firm that has recently experienced explosive growth. The firm hired Alan Gaynor + Co. to assist in selecting their new site, then to design it. The choice was 20,000 sq. ft. of rentable space on the 28th floor of a downtown Manhattan building, and functional requirements for the 40 employees included a well-lighted open-plan design studio environment, a spray booth, formal and informal meeting rooms, lunchroom, kitchen, reception area, and a sophisticated server/network facility to support digital graphic design work. The Gaynor team took the "waters" name as metaphor for their design concept, dividing program areas into "land" (represented by a color palette of warm earth reds and browns) and "water" (suggested by teals, greens, and silvery grays). Over the main design studio, angled ceiling planes shield indirect light sources and suggest "waves," and, taking the theme to more subtle levels, more indirect lighting reflected from prominent structural columns is said to suggest "lighthouses." Furnishings are contemporary, their spacing open and fluid, and the custom-designed boardroom table has a removable center panel for access to electrical and communications outlets.

11

Alan Gaynor + Company, P.C.

Harvest Partners
New York, New York

Above: Support staff area along carpeted corridor.
Left: Workstations for the support staff.
Bottom, left: Reception area, with view into boardroom.

For this financial services firm, Alan Gaynor + Co. designed a relocation to a full 20,000 sq. ft. floor of the Banker's Trust Building at 280 Park Avenue. Because future expansion beyond the present staff of 33 is expected, the initial layout includes a short-term sub-tenant space that can easily be converted for future use by Harvest Partners. The rest of the floor is occupied by large private offices at the building perimeter in a conventional plan, with interior spaces used for the support staff at amply scaled open workstations, a formal boardroom, reception area, pantry, copier room, and other support spaces. A traditional look was appropriate for this high-end, well-established financial consultancy, and such a look was achieved with simple means - such as stepped ceiling planes built from layered sheetrock - but with touches of elegance, such as generous amounts of mahogany in the furnishings, doors, moldings, and cabinetry. Flooring is wood in the reception area, wool carpets elsewhere, and pendant frosted glass lighting fixtures supplement the gentle cove lighting and incandescent downlights. The color scheme is generally warm, with the richness of the mahogany complemented by greens and beiges.

Above: *The formal conference room.*
Photography: *Roy J. Wright.*

Alan Gaynor + Company, P.C.

Carl Marks & Company
New York, New York

Right and below: Two views of the dramatically cantilevered stairway.
Photography: Paul Warchol.

Below: Over the reception area on the 27th floor, a sculpturally curved lighting soffit.

Carl Marks & Company, an investment banking and real estate firm, had leased 25,300 sq. ft. of space at a premier building on New York's East 57th Street. The space was divided into one full floor of 15,000 sq. ft. and a partial one of 10,300, and the most intriguing aspect was a partially skylit 27-ft.-high space shared by both the 26th and 27th floors. Adding a mezzanine level for additional floor area was prohibited, but Alan Gaynor + Co. turned the space into a great visual and functional asset by inserting a new stair with open risers and with its treads dramatically cantilevered from the structural column around which it is wrapped. Adjacent to the stair is a double-height curtain wall of glass, bringing daylight to the interiors of the work spaces beyond. In addition to the stair, the atrium space is used for open workstations for part of the firm's support staff, and its suspended ceiling carries electrical, mechanical, and sprinkler services. Other facilities include an elevator lobby and reception area, private offices, a boardroom, a library, private toilets, and a series of pantries for employee use. These facilities are organized around a curving corridor that follows the shape of the building envelope, and its curved

Left: Skylight over the Carl Marks support staff area, with curtain wall beyond and stair at left.
Below: The marble-faced elevator lobby.

form is visually reinforced by a wedge-shaped lighting cove formed of sheetrock and projecting downward from the ceiling, a dramatic device that leads visitors to its termination, the even more dramatic atrium and stair. Colors are warm throughout, and materials a rich interplay of industrial and natural. The panes of the glass curtain wall are framed with cherry mullions and supported by steel tubes and angles, and, similarly, the structural T-angles supporting the stair treads are steel, and the treads and platforms they carry are of cherry-stained ash. Some flooring is marble, and the elevator lobby creates a strong first impression with cherry paneling and floor and column facing of marble. In addition to the design, Alan Gaynor + Co. assisted with the site selection and provided a full range of services, including space planning, detailing of custom woodwork, furniture specification, and construction supervision.

AREA

550 South Hope Street
18th Floor
Los Angeles
California 90071
213.623.8909
213.623.4275 (Fax)
info@areadesign.com

AREA

Brobeck, Phleger & Harrison LLP
Irvine, California

Right: Double-height reception area with conference center beyond.
Below: The reception area, looking back towards reception desk.
Photography: Jon Miller ©Hedrich-Blessing.

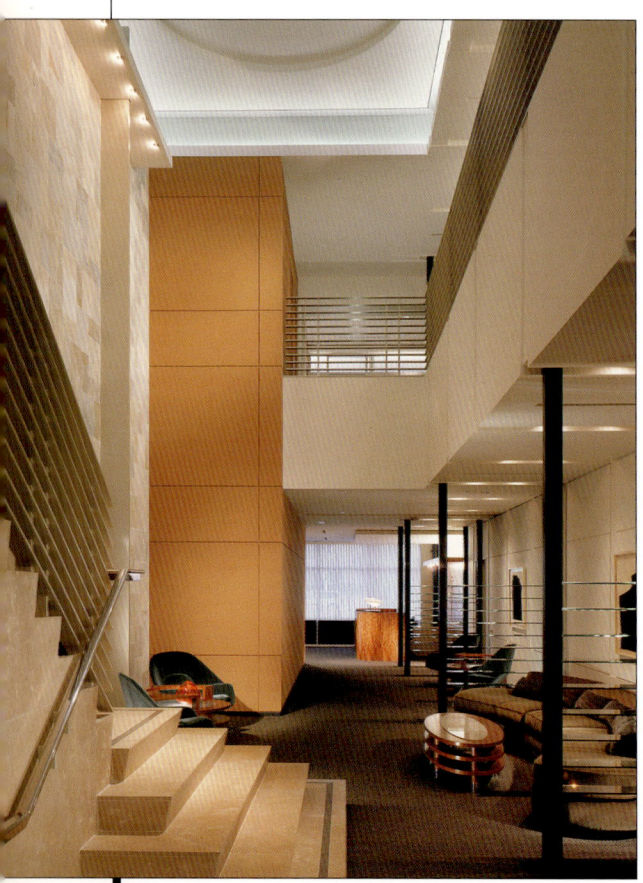

The law firm Brobeck, Phleger & Harrison LLP recently moved from a high-rise in Newport Beach, CA, to a two-story concrete "tilt-up" structure in Irvine, losing their view but bringing themselves closer to many of their clients — research, development, and high-tech industries. AREA was asked to customize the new 36,000-sq.-ft. quarters for the firm's specific corporate culture — one respecting its tradition, but with a "roll up your sleeve" attitude towards business — and to develop a park-like garden setting with a terrace accessible from the employee lounge. Concrete perimeter walls were left exposed, and structural columns and mechanical lines were also exposed and painted black. But contrasting tellingly with this rough shell are handsomely finished interior appointments, such as reception area walls and secretarial stations finished in highly figured African Sassandra, and reception desk and printer stations with accents of Hawaiian Koa veneer. Within the two-story reception area, used also for group functions, the prominent stair of French limestone is backed by a wall of rough-cut quartzite ashlar. AREA's technological expertise was applied here in the provision of state-of-the-art communication networks, ergonomic workplace amenities, and easy retrieval and transfer storage systems. A storage corridor of open shelving behind the secretarial stations, for example, provides ample storage in close proximity to both secretaries and attorneys. A continuous glass clerestory at private offices and louvered glass screens aid the flow of light and, along with "modern classic" furniture selections, evoke images of early modern architecture.

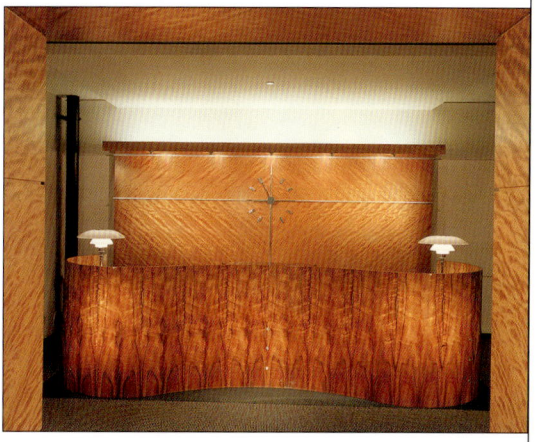

Right, top of page: Secretarial corridor.
Right, center: The reception desk.
Right: Main conference room.

19

AREA

Brillstein-Grey Entertainment
Beverly Hills, California

Above: *The main entrance.*
Far left: *Private toilet.*
Left: *An assistant's station with art work.*
Left, below: *Reception area seating.*
Photography: *Jon Miller © Hedrich-Blessing.*

Brillstein-Grey Entertainment has enjoyed a recent swell of success in managing entertainment personalities and producing motion pictures and television. Its new 12,000-sq.-ft. facility on Wilshire Boulevard in Beverly Hills needed to make its clients feel professionally represented, yet also provide them with a comfortable "down Home" atmosphere. This was achieved with a careful balancing of residential and commercial finishes and appointments. The reception area establishes the desired tone, for example, with plush furniture and Persian rugs over a floor of Chinese slate. In this space, wood and metal screens shield an undesirable view, but still allow the advantages of natural light. Throughout the installation, a warm, friendly character derives from the use of fiddleback and block-mottled African Makore woods, their color complemented by bright blue upholstery, pillow covers, and wall panels. The art collection adds a touch of lighthearted whimsy. AREA's space planning concept puts the assistants in an open band of space relating to the private offices of the managers and producers, and behind this band is a concealed-door storage wall providing ample space for files and scripts. The storage wall is given visual interest by a grid of painted wood battens, and the adjustable lamps at each workstation in the band add a warm glow, supplemented by continuous ambient fixtures above the files.

Left: An executive office.
Below, left: Overall view of the reception area.
Below: A group of assistants' workstations.

AREA

Nickelodeon
Burbank, California

Right: A nine-hole miniature golf course adjoins a picnic area.
Below: Part of the 150-ft.-long reception area, also a gathering place for employees.
Photography: Jon Miller © Hedrich-Blessing.

Above, right: "Living room area for team interaction.
Below, right: Beyond the guard desk at the end of the reception area, a basketball court also used as a screening room.
Below: View toward reception featuring Nick's signature "splat" as a piece of furniture.

The client's mission statement for the design firm AREA was, in this case, rather unusual: Make it look like a cartoon. Yet that directive was appropriate, for Nickelodeon's "Nicktoons" is the first animation studio to be built in the Los Angeles area in 35 years and the only television animation studio in the world. The raw material was a collection of five old warehouse buildings linked by an alleyway that AREA enclosed, transforming it into an art gallery for the Nickelodeon animators. Altogether, the thoroughly renovated facility now totals 70,000 sq. ft. Its main reception area is adjoined at one end by a large conference room and at the other by a gymnasium with a basketball court, which can also function as a screening room. When sliding doors are opened, the total length is an expansive 150 ft., and within it are a sound stage with windows to allow viewing by visitors and, behind a curved orange wall, a green room/employee lounge. The space, which also serves as an assembly space for all 350 employees and company guests, is entered over a bridge flanked by two green "infinity mirrors," and it connects to a mezzanine level by a staircase with parapet shaped like "dripping green slime." The rest of the facility is divided into a production technology core and five production groups. Each of these groups is

Far left: conference room used for teleconferencing.
Left: The cappuccino bar under an undulating stair.
Bottom of page, left: The slime chair provides access to the mezzanine.
Below: Mezzanine living room with "blimp" conference room at rear.

defined by an identifying color and a geometric shape, used in ceiling ribbons and carpet patterns to lead visitors to their destinations and used again within the production unit spaces. Each of these spaces includes workstations and also a "living room" where animators gather for informal team meetings beneath a suspended ceiling shape that gives the room intimacy and identity. Adding to the sense of unreality, the furniture was all custom designed based on models from the 1950s and from the Nickelodeon cartoons; seating is slightly overscaled, and upholstery fabrics lend "bathrobe comfort" to encourage casual lounging. Throughout the public areas, colors are vibrant, even electric, but the AREA designers have taken care to treat the interiors of private offices and workstations with neutral tones so that the animators can work with their own colors without the distraction of others nearby. And for "letting off steam" in this high-pressure creative environment, employees are offered a landscaped terrace with tables and umbrellas and a nine-hole miniature golf course.

Berger Rait Design Associates, Inc.

411 Fifth Avenue
New York
New York 10016
212.993.9000
212.993.9001 (Fax)
www.bergerrait.com

Berger Rait Design Associates, Inc.

**Merrill Lynch Business Financial Services
Chicago, Illinois**

Right: Elevator lobby and reception.
Below: Cross-floor view with connecting stair.
Photography: Christopher Barrett, Hedrich-Blessing

Right: Stair-to-atrium view featuring vaulted ceiling.
Bottom of page, center: Employee lunchroom.

Perched high within historic 222 North LaSalle overlooking the Chicago River and Wacker Drive, Berger Rait Design Associates, Inc. was commissioned to design the new regional headquarters for the Business Financial Services Division of Merrill Lynch. The program requirements necessitated two full floors of 70,000 square feet. Architecturally unique to this interior space is a three story atrium located asymmetrically to the building floor plate. A new monumental staircase between floors and a suspended perforated aluminum barrel vaulted ceiling system, spanning 40 feet, became the focal point of the project. The project space requirements included over 100 executive private offices and open plan workstations for a support staff of 300 employees. The ability to conduct sophisticated business meetings with visiting clientele and other Merrill Lynch Midwest financial support groups was accomplished by providing conference and meeting rooms with state of the art videoconferencing and teleconferencing systems. Traditional materials such as marble, cherrywood veneers and glass are detailed to display a contemporary design statement. Throughout the entire project area, indirect lighting sources provide comfortable and ergonomically sensitive lighting solutions in all task areas. Accent lighting is used dramatically in public and circulation spaces including a playful employee lunch room located adjacent to the atrium.

Berger Rait Design Associates, Inc.

Gruntal & Co.
New York, New York

Top of page, left: View from entrance into reception area.
Above: The boardroom.
Left: The president's office.
Photography: Peter Paige.

Designed for investment advisors, Gruntal & Co., 210,000 sq. ft. and occupying on five floors of a Wall Street high-rise. Imaginative planning was needed to break up long corridors and to bring natural light from the perimeter into the deep interior spaces. Changes in color, form, and texture were the solution to the first problem, and a generous use of glass doors and glass office fronts alleviated the second. Another challenge came from the client's organizational changes during the design process, requiring a thorough re-stacking of departmental layouts. These layouts include both conventional perimeter offices and open plan areas, and there are also a boardroom, a trading room, and a complement of support services. Wood doors and accent panels add warmth, and marble is used for flooring in the main reception area and for wall cladding and at the new connecting stair. Construction work began with a gut renovation and rebuilding of the entire space, and design work was done by Berger Rait in collaboration with Neville Lewis.

Above: General office area.
Left: Executive waiting area.
Below, left: The trading floor.
Below, right: The connecting stair.

29

Berger Rait Design Associates, Inc.

Draft Worldwide
New York, New York

Right: Elevator lobby, looking towards reception.
Below: Open stairs connecting floors.
Photography: Peter Paige.

Right: Coffee bar and reception area.
Below: Main conference room, with reception area beyond.

Having assisted Draft Worldwide, a direct marketing and advertising agency, in its pre-lease planning process, Berger Rait continued with a full range of interior design services for the company. Facilities required included private offices, open work stations for the administrative, support, and creative staffs, a reception area, a boardroom, a coffee bar for employees and their visitors, and a large variety of conference/meeting facilities and well-equipped rooms for client presentations. Executive offices are large, with comfortable seating areas and furniture for small meetings. Two of the client's overall goals for the design were the creation of optimal traffic patterns among the four floors of approximately 30,000 sq. ft. each and the establishment of a strong presence within a large multi-tenant building. Both goals were accomplished with a new internal stair, monumental in scale, but — with a gentle rise and open treads — light and graceful in appearance. The stair is prominently located next to the reception area, and both are adjacent to a window wall with dramatic views of Manhattan. Nearby also is the coffee bar, an attractive and popular amenity. Lighting throughout is an efficient mixture of fluorescent and incandescent, and the materials include terrazzo flooring, glass walls within metal frames, and accent panels of natural wood. The total square footage is 110,000, and it accommodates Draft Worldwide's 500 employees.

Above, right: Outside the main conference room, a corridor and banquette.
Right: An executive office for Draft Worldwide.

Bergmeyer

Bergrmeyer Associates, Inc.
Architecture and Interiors
286 Congress Street
Boston
Massachusetts 02210
617.542.1025
617.338.6897 (Fax)
www.bergmeyer.com

Bergmeyer

Bergmeyer

The Clarks Companies, N.A.
Newton, Massachusetts

Having already developed a prototype retail store for Clarks, the well-known British shoe manufacturer, Bergmeyer was asked to design this 24,000-sq.-ft. facility for the company's North American corporate headquarters. The specific site for the headquarters was a renovated mill building in a Boston suburb, and the designers retained its original hardwood flooring, timber framing, and high ceilings, sandblasting some elements for a cleaner appearance. In addition to private offices and open work areas for 60 employees, a key part of the program was the "branding room." Adjacent to the reception area, and centrally visible to the open office; this is a specialized conference room where the client's products are displayed to independent retailers. There are also workshops and design studios for the development of new prototypes. The interior design is sympathetic to the product and its identity, employing materials and details that also appear in the company's stores and trade show booths and presenting the balance of technology and fine craftsmanship that exemplifies the Clarks brand.

Above: The shell of the renovated mill building has been retained.
Above, left: The reception desk of wood and leather; beyond it, the "branding room."
Left: A cluster of open workstations.
Photography: Lucy Chen.

Bergmeyer   **MacTemps**
Boston, Massachusetts

Right: The reception area sets a spirited tone.
Right, below: The kitchen and impromptu meeting area.
Photography: Lucy Chen.

MacTemps is an international agency for temporary staffing and career placement, providing computer-proficient candidates to the marketplace. This 22,000-sq.-ft. renovation on four floors accommodates 100 MacTemps employees in a creative and egalitarian work environment. Leaving ceilings and other elements in a partially finished state and retaining evidence of numerous layers of earlier construction, the new office answers the client's request for a space "casual, colorful, and fun" without breaking the budget. Drywall partitions stop short of the exposed ceiling joists, HVAC and other services are left exposed, and fabrics and colors have been employed that are more typical of restaurant and bar design than of office design. In the company's spirit of democracy, private offices were eliminated.

35

Bergmeyer

Lehman Millet Incorporated
Boston, Massachusetts

Right: Main lobby.
Below: View from conference room toward reception area.
Photography: Lucy Chen.

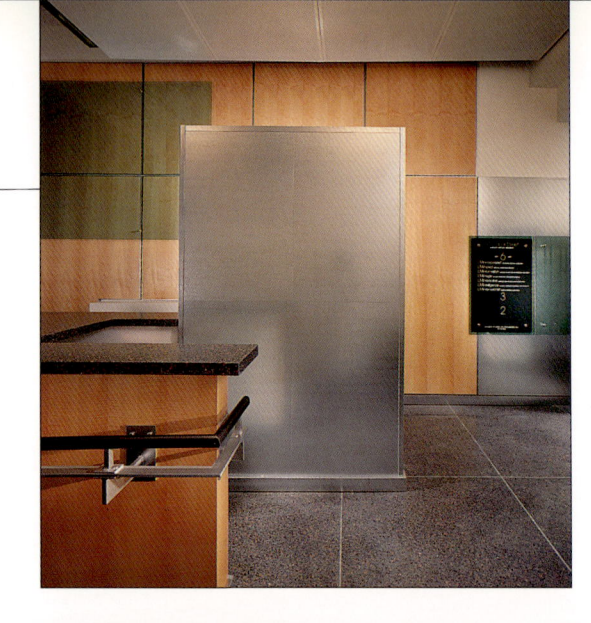

Right: President Bruce Lehman's office overlooking the atrium.
Below, right: The lunch room and kitchen with ceramic glass cooktop.

This renovation of a historic mercantile building in Boston's Bulfinch Triangle was designed for the 60 employees of Lehman Millet Incorporated (LMI), a medical marketing communications firm. It occupies three floors of approximately 7,000 sq. ft. each. For all its history, the building had the disadvantage of a long plan with windows only along the two narrow ends; this the designers alleviated by inserting a central skylit atrium that contains a new cantilevered stair of structural steel with concrete treads. The rest of the space was gutted to the basic structural elements: brick bearing walls, some of which have been left exposed and painted white; wood joist floor systems, and a central row of structural columns, cast iron on the lower floors and wood on the upper floors. The main lobby introduces the new materials that are used throughout: galvanized sheet steel, blonde sycamore paneling, white Surell solid surfacing material by Formica, and black terrazzo. The offices of LMI's president

Bruce Lehman and chairman Gerry Millet look out to the atrium on the next-to-top floor, putting them at the heart of the company's activity. On the floor above, beneath a peaked roof with multiple skylights, are two of the facility's most unusual spaces; the first is a large conference room that can be enclosed with a pair of anodized aluminum and glass garage doors and that is affectionately nicknamed "the garage"; the second, nearby, is a lunchroom and kitchen with a ceramic glass cooktop anchored to a stainless steel work island; above the island is a suspended stainless steel pot rack designed by chairman Millet himself. Indirect light in the workspaces is complemented by track lighting in the public areas, and furnishings throughout are resolutely modern.

Above, right: LMI's conference room is dubbed "the garage."
Right: The atrium stair. The kitchen is visible on the upper level.

Bergmeyer

**Sharf Information Center
Museum of Fine Arts, Boston
Boston, Massachusetts**

For Boston's venerable Museum of Fine Arts, this renovation of the information center was small (1,200 sq. ft.) but critical. Five existing circulation paths through the space had to be maintained, with room for large works of art to be moved through; the gallery entrance had to remain prominent, and its art had to remain dominant; but it was essential also to direct visitors' attention to the information desk, staffed by two, and to the information wall where questions are answered on video screens. The desk was built in a curve and placed to one side of the principal axis, and the video wall was placed opposite. Careful lighting design reinforces the placement of elements, and materials include cherry, stainless steel, and marble.

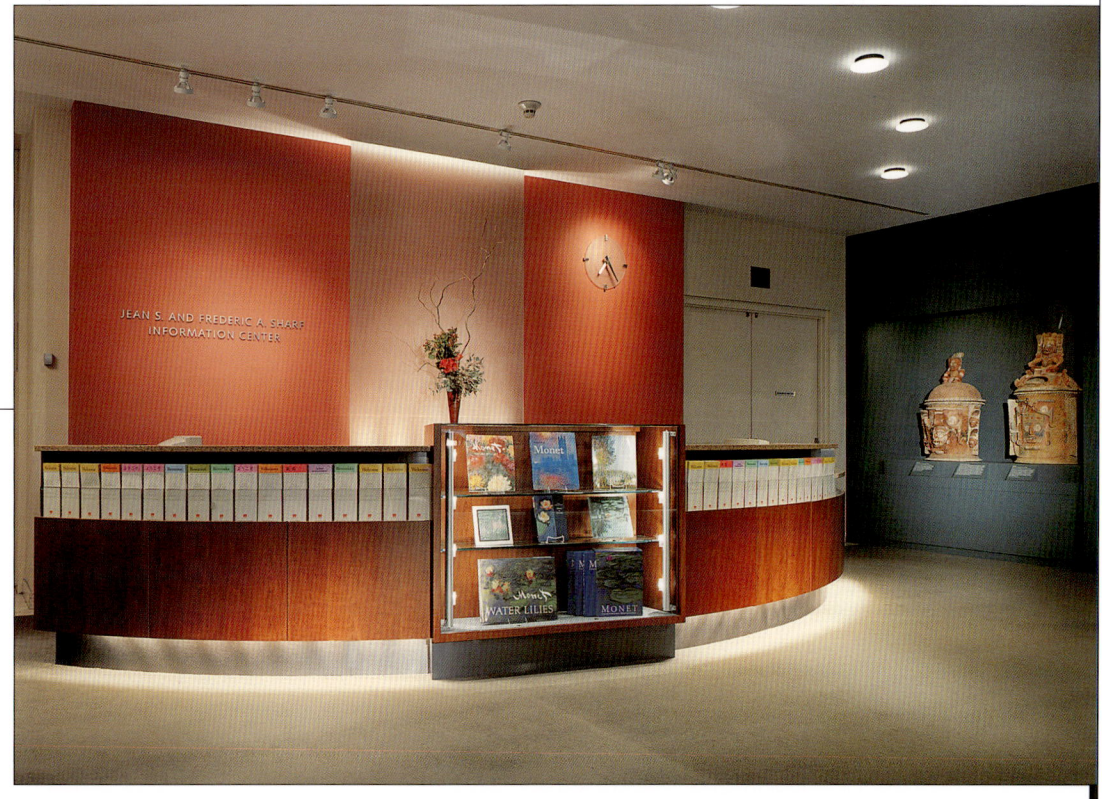

Right, above: The video information wall.
Right: The curved reception and information desk.
Photography: Lucy Chen.

Bergmeyer

Segrets Showroom
New York, New York

Above: The conference room and showroom.
Left: The reception and visitor waiting area.
Photography: Paul Ferrino.

Segrets is a designer and manufacturer of women's apparel, presenting European products to the American market. For Segrets, Bergmeyer renovated this 3,000-sq.-ft. facility, providing the requested "high-end, up-market" character on a limited budget. Showroom space was the heart of the matter, but also provided are a reception area, private offices, workstations, and an employee break area. Colors are light and neutral, reflecting the colors of the merchandise, furnishings are contemporary, spatial organization is open and flexible, and lighting is flexible as well. Wall surfaces have been left plain as a foil for the displays, but flooring is a complex combination of natural maple, buff-colored carpet, and black marble.

Brayton & Hughes
Design Studio

250 Sutter Street
Suite 650
San Francisco
California 94108
415.291.8100
415.434.8145 (Fax)

**Brayton & Hughes
Design Studio**

**Executive Offices
Menlo Park, California**

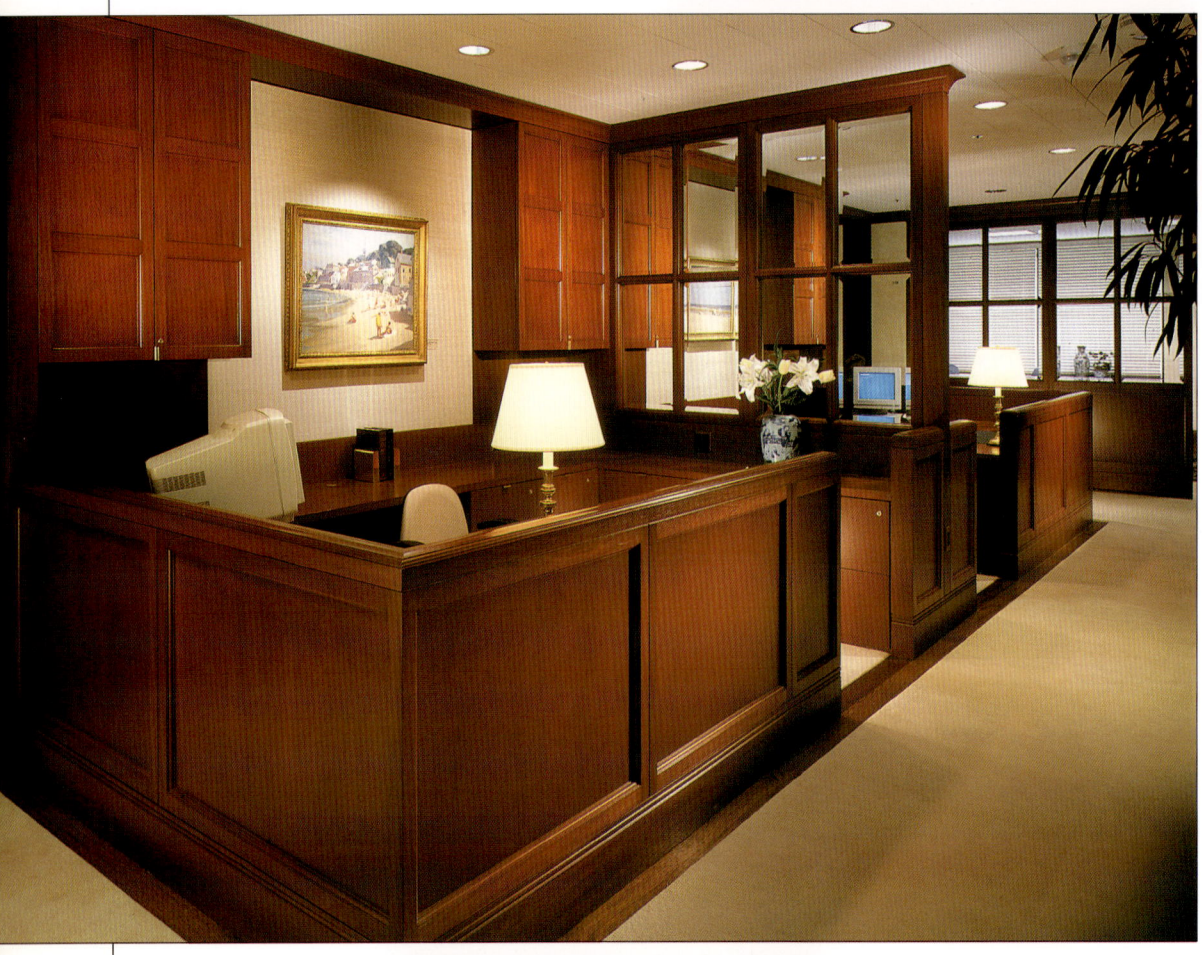

Top of Page: Main reception area.
Above: Administrative support workstations.
Left: Formal dining room.

These offices for an investment management firm occupy 15,000 sq. ft. on the top floor of a new building in Menlo Park, CA. They accommodate a total staff of 30, including nine partners in perimeter offices, each with a secretarial station opposite. There are also offices for the office manager, the accounting staff, the full-time cooking staff, and the security personnel. Other program requirements were for a reception area and guest lounge, a gallery for the firm's museum-quality collection of landscape paintings, a board room and extensive conference facilities, private rest rooms and shower, and support elements such as records storage and copy rooms. The space is organized along two axes that intersect at a central rotunda, which houses the formal executive dining area. The traditional formality of the layout is continued in the materials palette employed throughout: panels of beveled glass in mahogany frames, walls of Venetian plaster or upholstered silk, and (except in the corridors) floors of mahogany partly covered with antique rugs. Furnishings include English partners' desks and Regency antiques and reproductions. But some touches of luxury here are products of modern technology, such as the doors to private offices, which slide automatically into pockets when their motion sensors are approached.

Below: *Circulation in the private office area. Part of the formal dining room is seen at right.*
Photography: *John Sutton.*

**Brayton & Hughes
Design Studio**

**Pillsbury Madison Sutro
Law Offices
Palo Alto, California**

This two-floor, 53,000-sq.-ft. facility in the Stanford Business Park was built-to-suit for the Pillsbury Madison Sutro law firm. Before and after construction, Brayton & Hughes contributed a wide range of services: programming, space planning, interior architecture and design, furniture selection, and special lighting design. While some key areas are spatially generous — the double-height reception area, for example — the typical attorney per square foot ratio has been held here to less than 500 sq. ft., and this model has been applied across the board, with no larger offices as rewards for seniority. This standardization was a major client decision, reflecting the firm's youthful demographics and its perception that its clientele shared similar ideas of organization. Within these limited areas, however, the designers have provided furnishings with unusual storage capacity, a high degree of ergonomics, and almost a third more than the usual amount of work surface area. The firm's library and file area was also effectively downsized with the introduction of increased information technology and the outsourcing of some record storage and printing functions. Did the Brayton & Hughes design bring productivity as well as style? The law firm reports that in its new quarters its overhead is down, thanks to the increased density, and that its efficiency and billings are up 30 percent.

Top of page: Stair from reception area to second floor.
Left, above: Hallway with glass panels near ceiling for light transmission.
Left: Typical support staff workstations.
Right: Reception area.
Photography:
John Sutton.

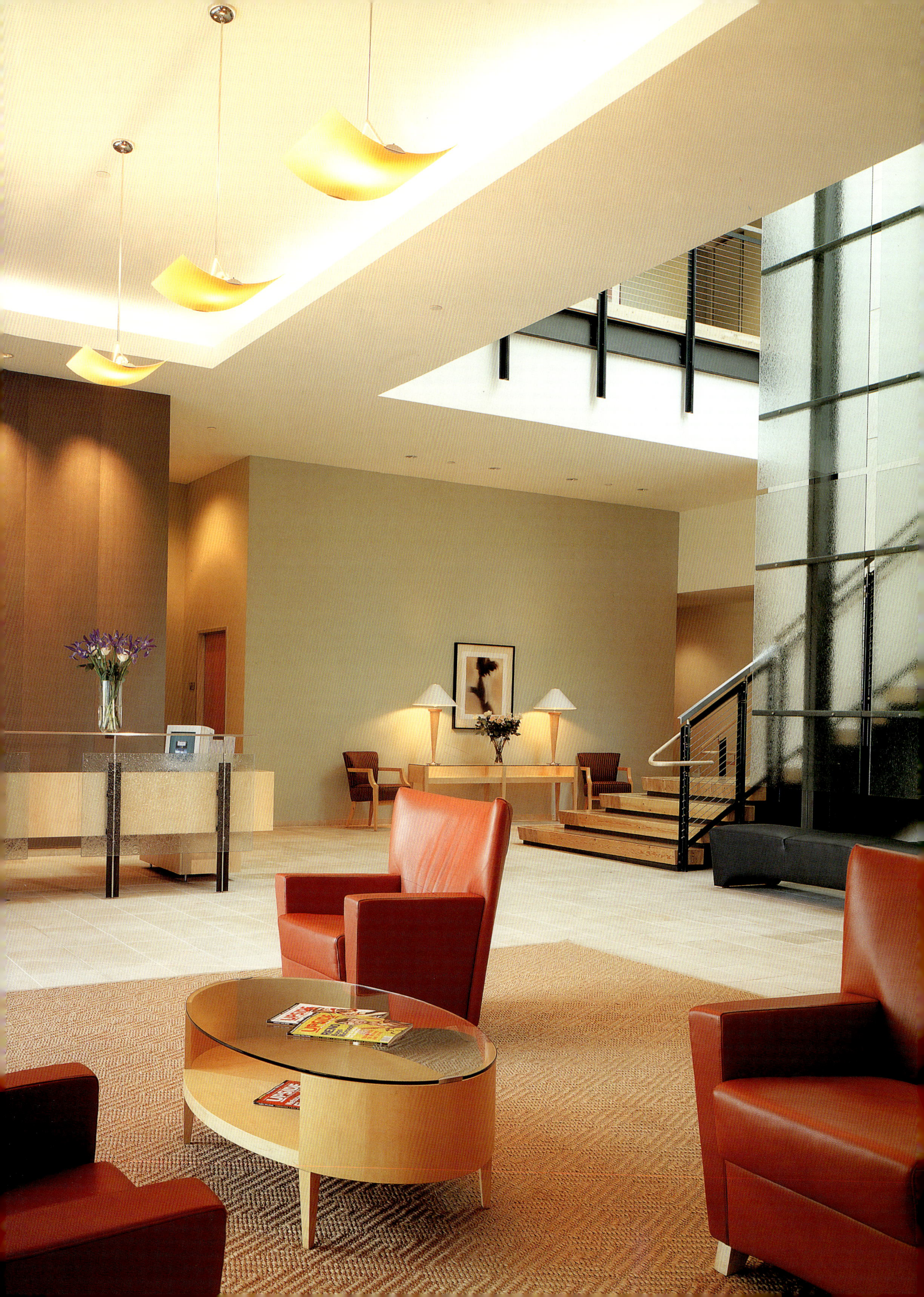

**Brayton & Hughes
Design Studio**

Forbes
Silicon Valley Bureau
Burlingame, California

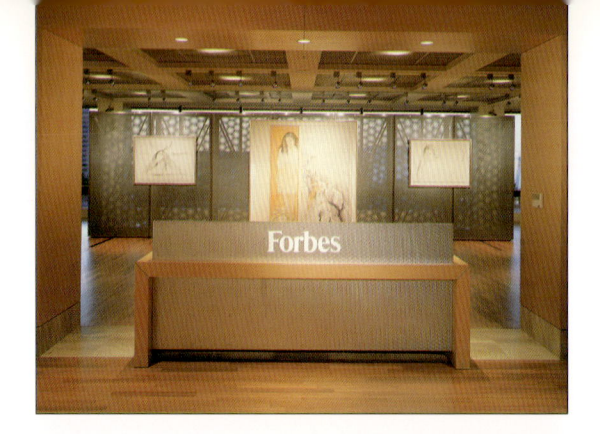

Opposite page, top: Reception desk.
Large photo, below: Art gallery doubles as entertaining space.
Photography: John Sutton.

Below, top photo: Product display case.
Below, bottom photo: The gallery's movable wall.

This 20,000-sq.-ft. headquarters near the San Francisco airport consolidates the Forbes publishing operations in the area and increases its visibility. Private spaces for writers and editors, team spaces for advertising staffs, and open studio spaces for graphic designers are supplemented with a generous gallery/hospitality area, its size modified as needed by a movable display wall. Christopher Forbes, Vice Chairman of Forbes, has described the design as "a triumph," and adds that "the public spaces are absolutely stunning and, perhaps even more importantly, everyone loves their offices." In confirmation of his enthusiasm, Brayton & Hughes is now at work on Phase Two of the project, including hospitality suites, executive lounges, and a Web broadcasting studio.

Brayton & Hughes
Design Studio

RCM Capital Management
Executive Offices
San Francisco, California

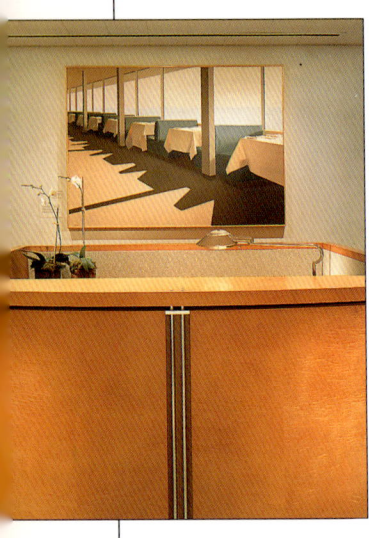

Left: Detail of reception desk.
Right: Looking into the main conference room.
Right, below: The main reception area.
Photography: JChas McGrath.

The offices designed by Brayton & Hughes's for this investment management firm are located on three floors of San Francisco's Embarcadero Center IV. The total of 55,000 sq. ft. accommodates 320 employees, including principals and key executives in perimeter offices and support and research staff in a variety of private offices and semi-private work stations. Also required were reception areas, two trading rooms, conference rooms, a computer room with raised floor, a research library, copy and printer areas, and — the nerve center of the operation — the "war room." A three-story internal stair links all levels and terminates at the "war room" on the topmost floor. Major assets of the space are its light quality and its dramatic view of the bay, and the design maximizes both with its layout and its transparency: many walls and pivoting doors are glazed, and partitions terminate in glass fins. More opaque surfaces include zinc panels, walls and cabinetry of figured maple, painted drywall, and Venetian plaster.

Brennan Beer Gorman
Monk / Interiors

515 Madison Avenue
New York
New York 10022
212.888.7667
212.935.3868 (Fax)

1030 15th Street NW
Suite 900
Washington DC 20005
202.452.1644
202.452.1647 (Fax)

Brennan Beer Gorman Monk / Interiors

Tishman Speyer Properties
520 Madison Avenue
New York, New York

Left: Glazing on office walls and workstation partitions allows passage of light in the offices.
Above: Steelcase montage glass partitions define the accounting staff's private offices.
Photography: Peter Paige.

BBGM recently completed two projects for Tishman Speyer Properties: 520 Madison Avenue and The Chrysler Building. On the 31st floor of William Van Alen's 1930 Manhattan landmark, the Chrysler Building, is the sales office for the building's new owner, Tishman Speyer Properties. The design challenge to Brennan Beer Gorman Monk / Interiors (BBGM) was to utlilize modern furnishings and an open floor plan while retaining the spirit of the "moderne" tower. Because the 31st is a setback floor, there was a relatively narrow depth from building core to perimeter, and because of large existing ductwork, some of the ceiling heights were low. To compensate for the latter, BBGM exposed the ceiling slab at the perimeter of the building, emphasizing the added height with

Tishman Speyer Properties
Chrysler Building
New York, New York

Right: Glass-front offices along the interior core wall.
Below: Reception desk and corner waiting area.

Right: Passage from a secondary entrance to the Sales Center.
Right, below: Executive suite beyond a curved glass wall.

uplighting. The vintage building also presented the designers with an unusually close structural grid, antithetical to open planning, and its module has been integrated with partition spacings and furniture modules. Furniture has been selected for its simplicity, and a straightforward planning approach has prevailed. Light penetration throughout has been maximized with sliding office doors of ribbed glass, and curving walls, their undulations accented by wall sconces, add a sense of fluidity. For the color scheme and materials palette, the BBGM designers took their cue from the building itself. Metal hardware and trim, for example, match the famous riveted-chrome gargoyles visible on the parapet just outside, and the 16x16 tiles of villebois jaune limestone in the reception area blend with the terrazzo and marble of the existing elevator lobby. The new 8,000-sq.-ft. sales center was completed on a 16-week schedule from beginning of design through completion of installation, and at a construction cost of about $60. per sq. ft. The client also retained BBGM to revitalize its 30,000 sq. ft. Finance department space, located at 520 Madison Avenue. Challenges presented to the design team included a hierachical office plan, high partitions and limited natural light. BBGM implemented an elegant, yet relaxed open plan work environment while maintaining a limited number of private offices for senior executives. Frosted glass partitions allow natural light penetration, increasing visibility and lessening the apparent hierarchy.

53

Brennan Beer Gorman Monk / Interiors

Pfizer, Inc.
New York, New York

Flexibility for the changing needs of the many departments of the Pfizer Pharmaceuticals Group drove the design of this 170,000-sq.-ft. space at Pfizer's 42nd Street offices in Manhattan. The first step, of course, was to determine what the changing needs might be, and to this end extensive employee interviews were conducted to determine present and future work needs, habits, adjacencies, and space utilization requirements. Only then did BBGM's space planning proceed.

Right, above: An executive office with wall unit and desk. **Right:** Reception area with vaulted ceiling. **Opposite:** Corridor between private offices and open workstations. **Photography:** Paul Warchol.

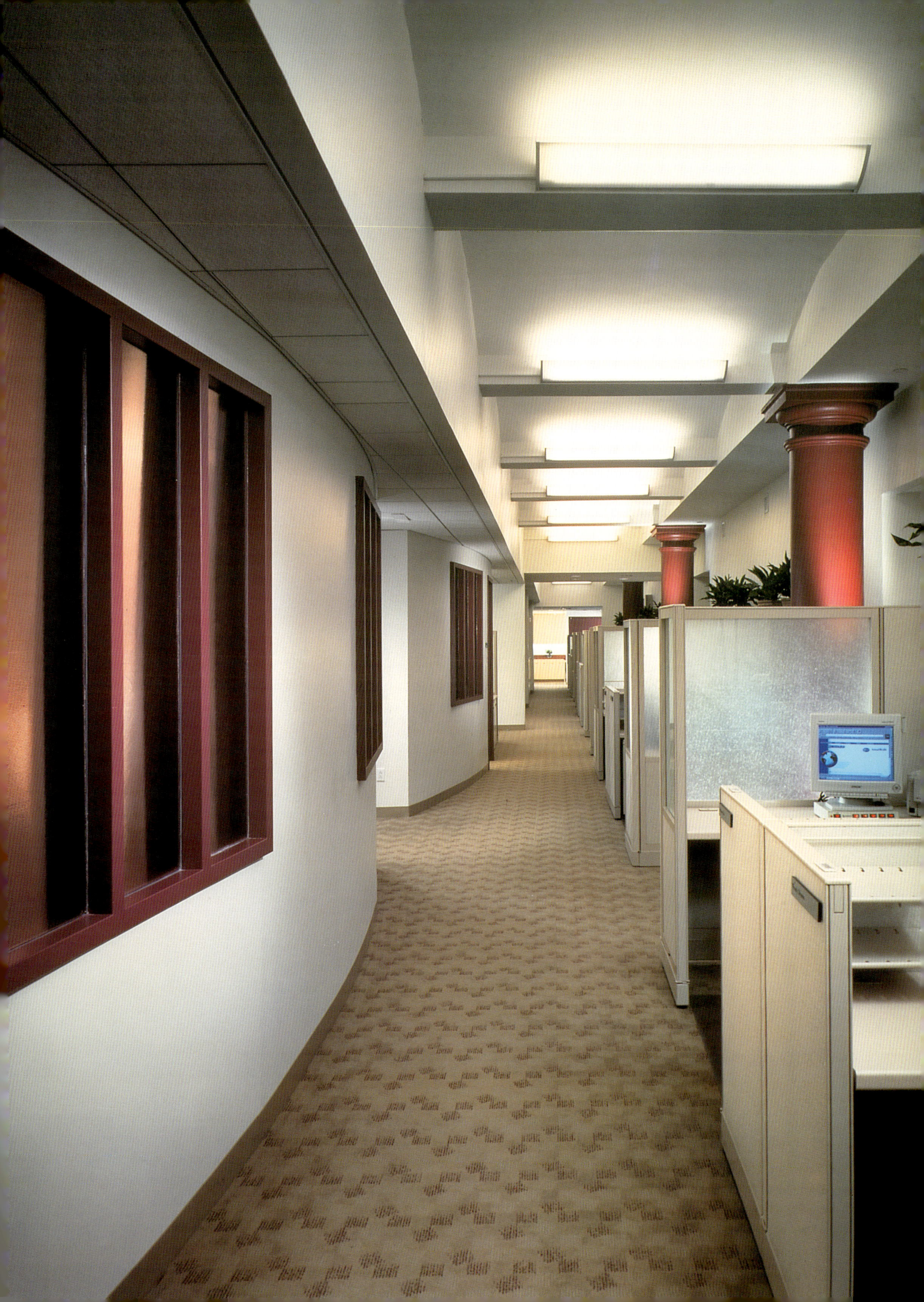

Above: Pfizer's main conference room, seating 20.
Left: Two floor slabs were removed to create the internal stair.

Further preparation for the final design was the presentation for employee review of several different furniture mock-ups. The building's limited number of small windows, combined with a large floor plate, resulted in low light levels away from the perimeter; compensation came with new exposure of exisitng vaulted ceiling planes washed by custom-designed lighting fixtures. Interdepartmental communication was enhanced by removing floor slabs to allow the insertion of a new connecting stair. Proof that the desired flexibility has been achieved came when a department originally slated for move-in was reassigned and another group assigned instead; the change went smoothly, with only a few minor modifications required.

Burt Hill Kosar Rittelmann Associates

Boston
Butler
Moscow
Philadelphia
Pittsburgh
Washington
www.burthill.com

**Burt Hill Kosar
Rittelmann Associates**

**Deloitte & Touche
Consulting Group
Pittsburgh, Pennsylvania**

Above, left: *Perimeter with "touch-down" workstations.*
Above: *Main conference room.*
Left: *Teaming room surrounded by "cockpit" offices.*

This management consulting arm of Deloitte & Touche required a thorough renovation of 45,000 sq. ft. spread over two floors of Pittsburgh's PPG Place. A major requirement was a desirable workplace in which to recruit — and then retain — the industry's top performers. Important, too, was the maximization of productivity for the 310 employees. During programming, the designers learned that 50 percent of those the staff is out of the office 60 percent of the time; they responded, therefore, with some innovative space-sharing ideas, such as "hotellings" with "touch-down" areas throughout the office, not permanently assigned to specific workers, but ready for laptop use. One area dominated by the "touch-downs" is the perimeter window wall, and additional open work spaces are given the prime corner locations. The core contains 17 collaborative team spaces, each containing a partner's office and eight "cockpit" offices clustered around the shared working/meeting area. Principal materials are maple, mahogany, granite, bronze, and leather, and prominent colors are teal, ochre, eggplant, and mahogany.

Above: The Deloitte & Touche reception area with fabric-covered wall.
Photography: Edward Massery.

Burt Hill Kosar Rittelmann Associates

Federal Home Loan Bank
Pittsburgh, Pennsylvania

Right: View into boardroom.
Photography: Scott McDonald © Hedrich Blessing.
Below: An executive office suite.
Photography: Ed Massery.

The Federal Home Loan Bank serves chiefly as a central credit source to housing lenders in Pennsylvania, Delaware, and West Virginia, and it also provides banking, investment, advisory, and safekeeping services to financial institutions. Expectably, its desired image is traditional, conservative, and slightly formal. This effect was achieved within a mid-20th-century office building by employing architectural details, furnishings, color, materials, and accessories that refer to the 18th century. For the topmost floor, where executive offices are located, the designers were able to relocate mechanical systems to the building roof, enabling the creation of 11'-6" ceiling heights in most spaces and an impressive 12'-6" in the boardroom. The color scheme of muted neutrals is accented with rich reds and greens in details such as carpet borders, draperies, and upholstery, and elegant materials include mahogany, marble, brass, and silk. For the multi-floor, 100,000-sq.-ft. installation, Burt Hill Kosar Rittelmann's services included site selection, programming, interior architecture and design, and mechanical, electrical, and fire protection engineering.

Above: Reception area with curving stair.
Photography: Ed Massery.

61

Burt Hill Kosar
Rittelmann Associates

Kvaerner, Inc.
Philadelphia, Pennsylvania

Above: Main reception area beyond a corner of the stair parapet.
Photography: Tom Crane.

Below: Open workstation with private offices beyond.
Right: The private stair.
Right, below: A waiting area.

This 55,000-sq.-ft. installation on two levels of a commercial office building is the United States corporate headquarters for Kvaerner, Inc., a holding company in the fields of shipbuilding, oil and gas, metals, pulp and paper, and engineering and construction. Aside from the creation of an appropriate image — in this case, sleek and contemporary — the greatest challenge for the designers was time schedule, which allowed only 12 weeks from Conception to completion. Burt Hill Kosar Rittelmann completed the design in the first four weeks, allowing eight weeks for the construction process. Details have not been neglected, however, and the facilities, which include private offices, open workstations, reception and waiting areas, and a boardroom, are finished in cool tones of blue and gray in carpets and upholstery, with stainless steel pipe rails and mesh on the stair that connects the two floors. While most wall surfaces are of drywall, golden-toned anigré wood panels have been used in reception areas and boardroom, with the wood also creating a screen on the reception area's window wall.

Burt Hill Kosar Rittelmann Associates

National Public Radio Headquarters
Washington, DC

In the words of William E. Buzenberg, NPR's VP for news administration, "We moved into our well-designed and carefully-crafted new facility on time and on budget, and have thoroughly enjoyed it. We could not be happier or more pleased with Burt Hill's top-notch architects and interior designers." Occupying 152,000 square feet in two six-story structures, this facility houses not only 400 of NPR's employees, but also its main satellite signal distribution and uplink center, responsible for the distribution of NPR programming and the entire public broadcasting satellite network. Involved were the design and construction of acoustically isolated studios, an innovative system of recycling building operations waste, attention to indoor lighting comfort and air quality, emergency generators, transformers, and voltage regulators, and the installation of 3,000 pieces of electronic equipment, over 500,000 audio/broadcast connections, and over a million linear feet of cable, not to mention the more usual offices and workstations. "All Things," it seems, have been "Considered."

Right: One of NPR's studio spaces.
Below: A 1,500-sq.-ft. studio on a concrete isolation slab.
Below, far right: An internal stair rising from the main lobby.
Photography: Maxwell MacKenzie.

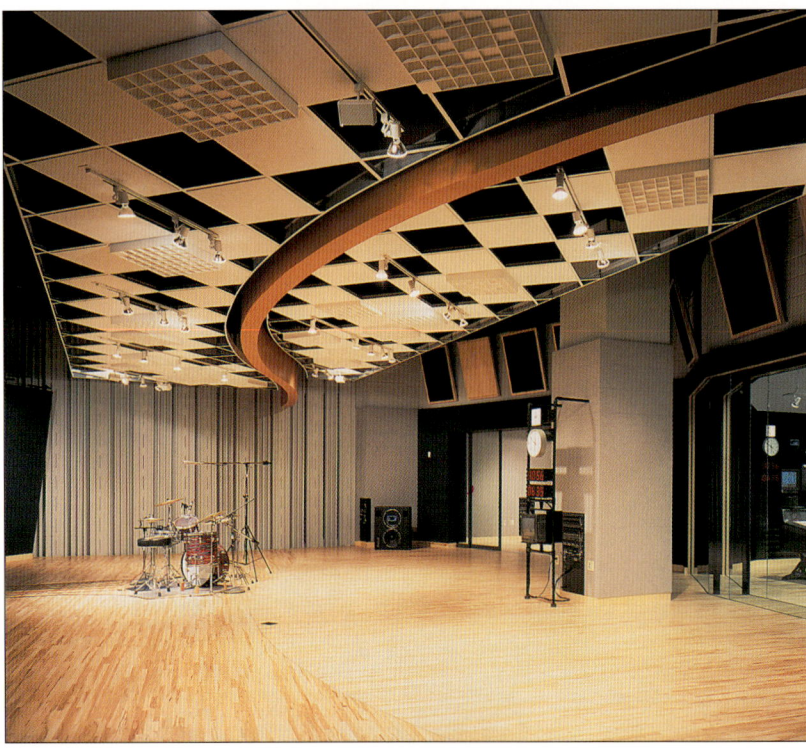

Callison Architecture, Inc.

1420 Fifth Avenue
Suite 2400
Seattle
Washington 98101.2343
206.623.4646
206.623.4625 (Fax)
www.callison.com

Callison Architecture, Inc.

Latham & Watkins
Orange County, California

Right: View of juice bar and multipurpose room.
Below: Corridor adjacent to the window wall.
Photography: Chris Eden.

The law firm of Latham & Watkins occupied the 20th and 21st floors of an Orange County building and recently expanded into an additional 15,000-sq.-ft. partial floor just below. But, according to Nancy Eberhart, Administrator for Latham & Watkins, "When the attorneys first moved to the 19th floor, it wasn't pretty; people were lined up at my door trying to re-negotiate their move." Then Callison Architecture, Inc., was called in for a thorough redesign — but a quick one. On a fast-track basis to accommodate summer interns, the designers devised a new circulation pattern, including corridors along window walls and sequences of unfolding spaces, they designed "inboard" offices varied by faceted fronts and lightened by glazed sliding doors, and in key

Above: Detail of juice bar furniture.
Left: View into typical "inboard" office.
Left, below: Reception area with new interconnecting stair.

locations they introduced touches of some of the fine materials — such as lacewood paneling — found on the older floors. Other materials employed were cherry, painted metal, stainless steel, ribbed glass, and painted gypsum board. Newly chosen colors are soft and rich. And new spaces include a multipurpose room with a generous window area and with a juice bar and open residential-style kitchen adjacent to it. The result? "By the time the summer associates left," Eberhart continues, "attorneys were lined up at my door again; however, this time, they had some very creative reasons as to why they should be moved to the 19th floor. Good design and great furniture have apparently made the 19th floor the 'fun' floor."

Callison Architecture, Inc.

DPR Construction
Newport Beach, California

This 10,000-sq.-ft. headquarters for a young billion-dollar construction firm is only minutes from Newport Beach's oceanside boardwalk and yachting harbor, and Callison Architecture, Inc.'s designers have taken their cues from the character of the location. Calculatedly, their detailing has also allowed DPR builders the opportunity to display their skills. The seaside imagery begins with the office's own "boardwalk" circulation spine, its alternations of natural and striated cork resembling planking. Canted wood and glass walls of offices and conference rooms meet in angles reminiscent of the prows of boats. Custom-designed semi-enclosures for open workstations are likened to "personal harbors." And even the dominant paint color — a faded red — is said to be derived from dinghies on the beach. DPR craftsmanship is evident throughout, in details such as the carved planes of medium-density fiberboard, enlivened by routing and beveling. Facilities provided include a "think tank" for highly focused work sessions, a contractor's digitizer room, conference rooms, a team room, and a multi-purpose room for seminars and training sessions. Callison Architecture, Inc., provided programming, space planning, and interior design services.

Left, above: View of the facility's "boardwalk."
Left: A row of open workstations.
Right: Reception desk.
Photography: Chris Eden.

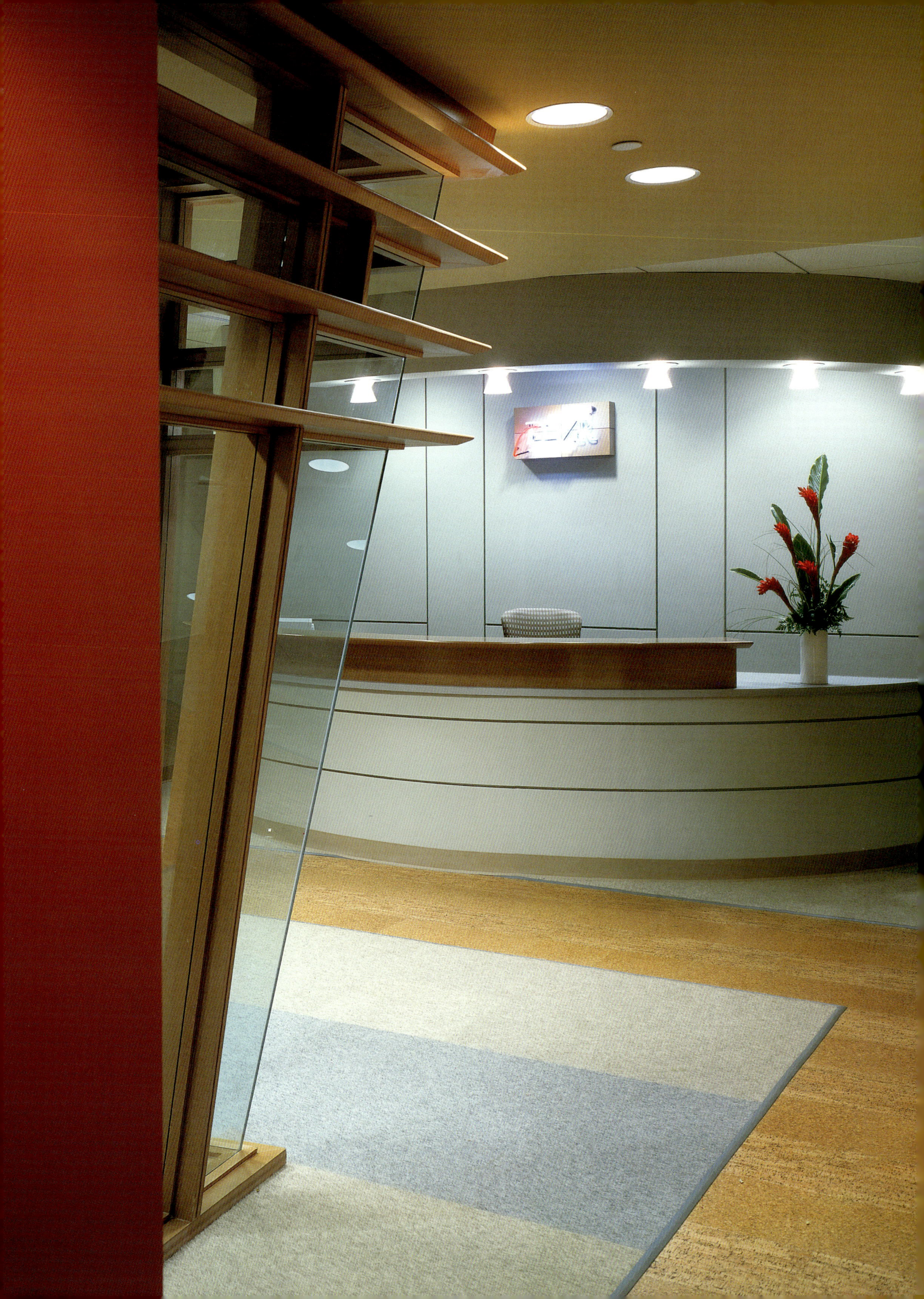

Callison Architecture, Inc.

Nextlink
Bellevue, Washington

Opposite, top of page: Elevator lobby and office entrance.
Left, above: Reception area and view into conference room.
Left: Foyer near main conference room.
Right: The informal "commons" area.
Photography: Chris Eden.

Variety and flexibility are the keynotes of this 37,000-sq.-ft. office designed by Callison Architecture, Inc., for Nextlink, a telecommunications company. Variety appears in the spatial organization, with circulation paths encountering diverse room and wall shapes — linear, curvilinear, oval — throughout the plan. At a more detailed level, it also appears in the front walls of the enclosed offices, composed of three types of glass — clear, fluted, and frosted. Other wall surfaces are varied as well — some upholstered with padded wool, some faced with a custom wallcovering, and others veneered with clear stained maple. Flexibility is apparent in the unusual number of places where Nextlink workers can "plug in" — not only private offices and individual workstations, but also teaming areas furnished with sofas and armchairs, quiet rooms for private or concentrated tasks, a library, and a "commons" area and juice bar for informal, serendipitous meetings. Furniture throughout is flexible as well, designed to increase productivity by providing a wide range of assembly options; it allows for both team activates and a high degree of personal control. For Nextlink, Callison Architecture, Inc., provided space planning, interior design, technical coordination, and the specification of all fixtures, furnishings, and equipment.

Callison Architecture, Inc.

Offices for a High-Tech Company
Seattle, Washington

Left: Private offices with sliding "barn door" fronts.
Right: Screened work area with view of "hoteling" workstations.
Right, below: View into conference room and to break area beyond; the stair is in the foreground.
Photography: Chris Eden.

When a leading high-tech company acquired a Seattle-based company specializing in font and software research and development, Callison Architecture, Inc., was called in for a thorough renovation. The acquired firm had "an informal culture," and there was concern for establishing an esprit de corps for the combined workers (a total of 50) and for retaining the talent. A "hoteling" scheme was developed without permanently assigned workstations, and the resultant reduction in office space allowed the introduction of new communal spaces, wider circulation areas, break areas, a conference room with videoconferencing capabilities, and an interesting sequence of movement. A new internal stair, enclosed in acid-washed glass, links the company's two floors of 15,000 sq. ft. each. Private offices are equipped with sliding "barn doors," a further space saver, and a team work area furnished with lounge chairs is partially wrapped with a circular screen woven from bands of bird's-eye maple, the curved wall outside offices is faced with cork pin-up band for project discussions. Callison reports that the entire job was constructed and furnished for $65 per sq. ft.

CMSS Architects, P.C.

5041 Corporate Woods Drive
Suite 200
Virginia Beach
Virginia 23462

757.222.2010
757.222.2022 (Fax)
staff@cmssarchitects.com

CMSS Architects, P.C.

Media General
Richmond, Virginia

Right: The glass wall behind the reception desk holds a transparent image of the owner's logo.
Below: The company board room.
Photography: Judy Davis, Hoachlander Davis.

Right: View into the entrance rotunda.
Right, below: The executive waiting area.

Honored with an award from the Washington, DC, chapter of the International Interior Design Association, this installation is for a media conglomerate dedicated to collecting and presenting information throughout the Southeast in a variety of formats including newspapers, magazines, and television. The company, Media General, had been housed for the previous quarter century in the headquarters of one of its own subsidiaries, the Richmond Times Dispatch Newspaper Building, a 75-year-old structure in downtown Richmond. Deciding to stay downtown rather than move to a suburban office park, the company also planned to renovate the newspaper building after moving out and to include "swing space" in the new building for Times Dispatch employees, so that they could relocate during the renovation. A flexible plan serving multiple occupants was therefore a necessity. With such flexibility in mind, CMSS Architects designed a building and interiors that total 141,000 sq. ft. on five levels. Its most dramatic feature, just inside the main entrance, is a four-story rotunda floored with marble and granite and rising to a skylighted dome 60 feet overhead. The floor is edged with a compass pattern, symbolizing the gathering of news from the four corners of the earth, and the rotunda is edged with a four-foot-high wainscot of rusticated marble. Within the rotunda is a reception desk built of marble and cherry and backed by a "floating" screen of digitally sandblasted glass, the pattern outlining the company name in trans-

Top of page, left: Stair around the rotunda.
Top of page, right: Coffered ceiling of the rotunda.
Above, left: 4th floor of the atrium space.
Above, right: Typical work station with technology colums brings power from the ceiling.
Right: The rotunda's skylight.

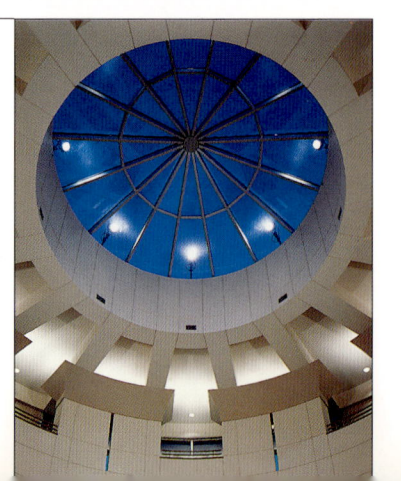

Right: Work station in executive area with technology columns.

parent lettering. Natural light streams into the space during the day, and roof-mounted lights suspended over the skylight illuminate it at night. This space, the designers say, recalls similar spaces in older downtown buildings and expresses the company's corporate culture by opening to surrounding work areas and offering a multiplicity of visual communications among them; visitors, too, are offered generous views into the office areas. Those areas have been designed with less drama but with equal care, using an easily reconfigurable furniture system. The system's partitions of modular panels are varied in height, giving a welcome variety to the open work areas, while the columns were adapted to bring the power and communication supply down to the panels from cable trays located above the finished ceiling plane. Lighting in these areas is largely indirect to provide an even glow and to reduce glare on computer screens. Indirect lighting also prevails in the board room, where cherry paneling opens to reveal a wealth of audio-visual presentation equipment.

77

CMSS Architects, P.C. The Martin Agency
Richmond, Virginia

Right: West Tower lobby.
Left: The "Town Square." (Photo: John Wadsworth, Wadsworth Alliance)
Below, left: An executive area, looking into a conference room.
Below, center: Domed multi-media presentation room.
Opposite page, top: The bridge/gallery.
Opposite page, center: View beneath one of the many connecting stairs
Opposite page, bottom: A teaming area. (Photo: John Wadsworth, Wadsworth Alliance)
Photography: Judy Davis, Hoachlander Davis, except as noted.

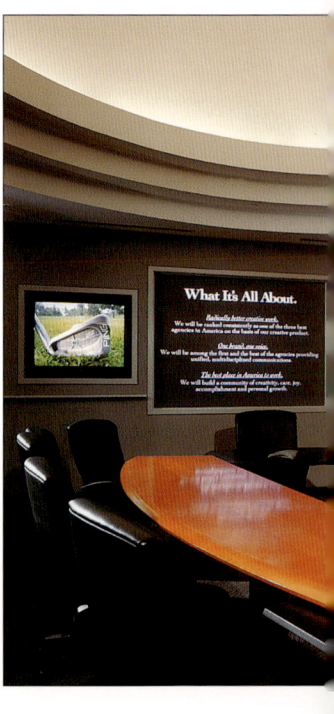

The Martin Agency, a top-ranked national advertising agency with over 300 employees, needed to consolidate their seven offices scattered throughout Richmond into a single facility. They chose a site in Richmond's historic Shockoe District for their new headquarters. The Shocke District, at the center of Richmond's commerce and exchange at the turn of the century, is today characterized by late 19th-century Italianate commercial and warehouse buildings, cobblestone streets, and brick sidewalks. Successful infill into the Shocke District meant tieing the building into the historic neighborhood while juxtaposing a futuristic interior environment. The building's interior transparently blends with Richmond's skyline to bring the urban scale inside. Drawing upon the energy and history of the Shockoe District, a town concept was used. The Martin Agency's town is filled with enterprise areas such as idea factories, support service industries, neighborhoods shops, and galleries. The layout was patterned with an urban context of tying together an eclectic mix of work stations and functions through a network of avenues and boulevards — symbolic of the small streets of the historic area of the City of Richmond. At the building's focal point is "The Town Square," a three story atrium that is the primary place for exchanging information. The Town Square is symbolic of the Shockoe District's role as the centerpiece of Richmond's trade. In addition to being a great meeting place for the employees, The Town Square is also a staging area for company events, festivals, and pitches to potential clients. The Washington DC International Interior Design Association, The National Commercial Builders, and Hampton Roads Chapter of the American Institute of Architects have awarded the building's design. But the ultimate test is the client's satisfaction. John B. Adams, Jr., Chairman and CEO of The Martin Agency stated, "The building has transformational power. The building has transformed us by how it holds us, how it moves us within it, and how it communicates, to us and to the world outside, who we are."

Above: Casual meeting area next to executive office.
Right: A restroom.
Far right: A play of forms under a curved ceiling plane.

DMJM Rottet

3250 Wilshire Boulevard
Los Angeles
California 90010.1599
213.368.2888
213.381.2773 (Fax)

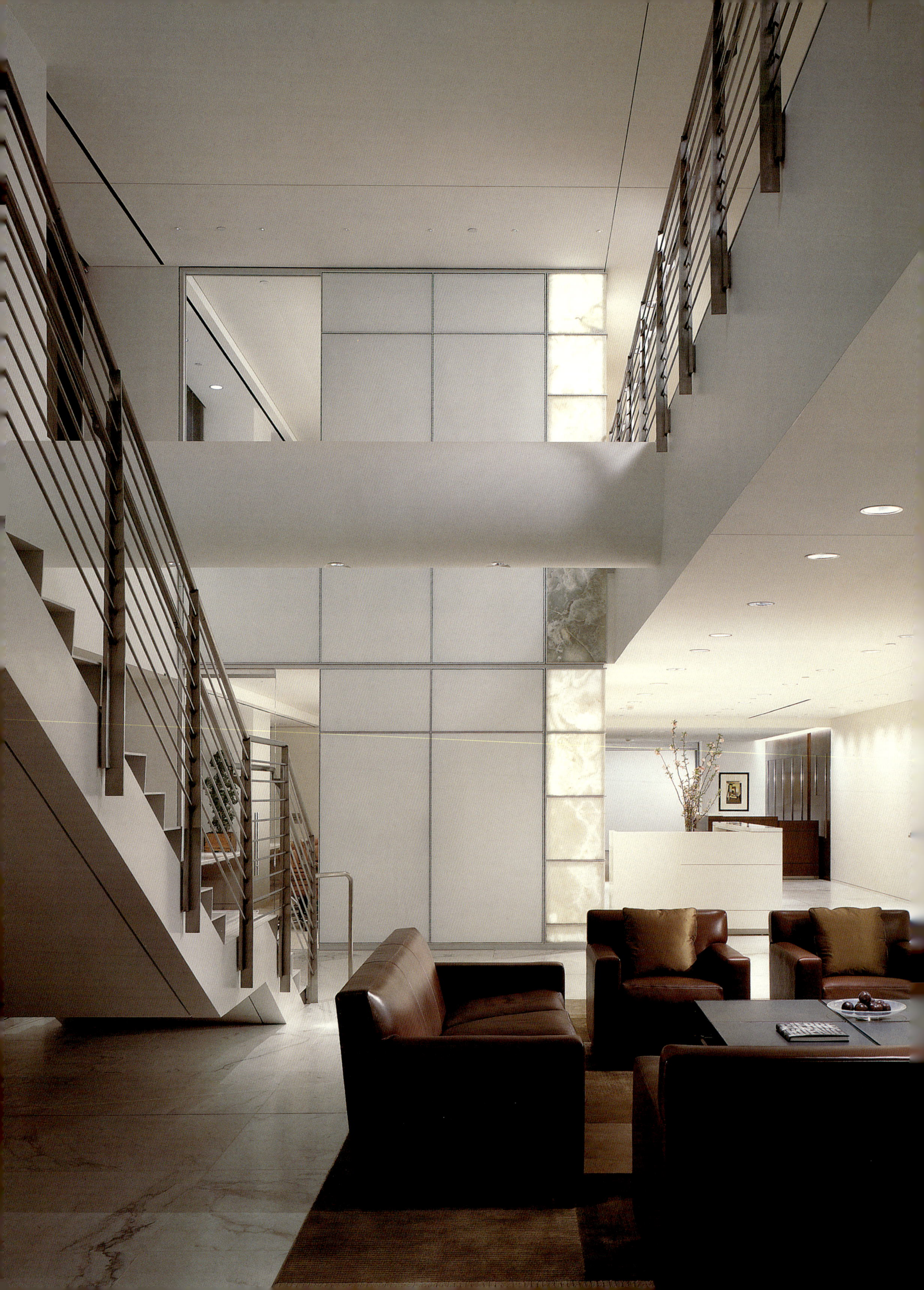

DMJM Rottet

Oaktree Capital Management, LLC
Corporate Headquarters
Los Angeles, California

Oaktree Capital management occupies three floors (27 through 29) totaling 73,400 sq. ft. in the Wells Fargo Center of Los Angeles's Bunker Hill Area. This is the company's world headquarters and the base for most of its investment advisory operations, although it also maintains offices in New York, London, Tokyo, and Singapore. The L.A. space reflects the firm's egalitarian, collaborative culture. Materials are consistent throughout the three floors, and private offices are of two basic sizes, both generous. Workstations have been custom-designed with abundant filing capacity. The two most important communal spaces — a 29th-floor trading room and 27th-floor commissary — have both been planned to facilitate employee interaction, and nine conference rooms are distributed through the space. Guests are accommodated with visitor offices, telephone alcoves, luggage storage rooms, and an after-hours lobby phone. Materials include cherry veneer, opaque, translucent, and transparent glass, steel, aluminum, marble, and onyx, these last two having been selected by principal Lauren Rottet from quarries in Italy. The marble is Calacatta Sponda, known for its white background and subtle veining, and the Italian onyx is known for its whiteness. For the glass office fronts, also, a careful selection has been made: lead-free glass without the green tint caused by lead in normal glass. And technology keeps pace with artistry here: the facility has over 40 miles of voice and data cabling, back-up power sources, and a spacious computer control room.

Opposite page: Double-height reception area with visitor seating. The lobby seating and custom carpet by Edward Fields, along with partner office furnishing and art were selected by the owner's design consultant, Michael Smith.

Top of page: Large conference room has a wall of onyx.
Above: Translucent onyx panels in the reception area.
Left: Administrative workstations opposite glazed office walls.
Photography: Nick Merrick © Hedrich Blessing.

DMJM Rottet

Ernst & Young, LLP
Workplace of the Future
Los Angeles, California

Over the past two years, DMJM Rottet has worked with Ernst & Young to define and implement a new workplace strategy in multiple offices within the greater Los Angeles area and in other cities. The accounting and consulting firm's goals were: to improve service to its clients; to improve the work-vs.-life balance for its employees; to manage growth more effectively; and to reduce workplace costs. To achieve these, two main strategies were devised, a "Design Strategy" and a "Locational Strategy." The second of these recognizes that different geographies require different plans, and six plan types were eventually chosen, the one in Los Angeles being the "Constellation" model with nine different offices, the one seen here being 120,000 sq. ft. The nine branches work together as a flexible system and are non-territorial, with employees allowed access to any office, any day. The aim is to reduce travel time and

Above: Conferencing offices along the perimeter.
Opposite, right: Client briefing and strategy center.
Opposite, above: Main reception area with corridor beyond.
Left: Open workstations and "cockpit" offices.
Photography: Nick Merrick © Hedrich Blessing.

84

increase productivity. Working with the designers on the team organized by Ernst & Young were a contractor, a real estate broker, and other consultants, studying together locations, leases, construction costs, and project schedules, as well as design approaches.

DMJM Rottet

BMC Software, Inc.
Corporate Headquarters
Houston, Texas

Above: "Living Room" spaces on the office floors encourage interaction among employees.
Left: Pivoting doors open the reception lobby to an in-door basketball court.
Below: With the push of a button, accordian-fold walls can transform a large meeting room into smaller spaces.
Opposite, top: Training rooms are separated by small serving kitchens.
Opposite, below, left: Exterior view of "Dot.Com" commissary building
Opposite, below, right: Commissary interior
Photography: Joe Aker, Aker/Zvonkovic

DMJM Rottet teamed with DMJM architects to complete the second phase of BMC Software's 14-acre headquarters campus. The 230,000-sq.-ft. project is comprised of a nine-level office building with a Dealer Briefing Center on the main floor and a fitness center on the lower level, a large café building, retail shops, and extensive site work including herb gardens, recreation areas, and an outdoor amphitheater. The main lobby of the office building overlooks an indoor basketball court outfitted with fold-out stadium seats that convert the court to a company meeting place.

An adjacent commissary building (which the employees call "Dot.Com") is similarly flexible, with banquette seating that folds away to clear the space for special functions. The building's upper floors contain employee offices and "living room" spaces which house kitchen facilities and reprographic functions to promote spontaneous interaction. The Dealer Briefing Center on the main level provides extensive training and conference spaces, with multiple break-out rooms, convenient serving kitchens, state-of-the-art audio/ visual capabilities, and a dedicated banquette facility.

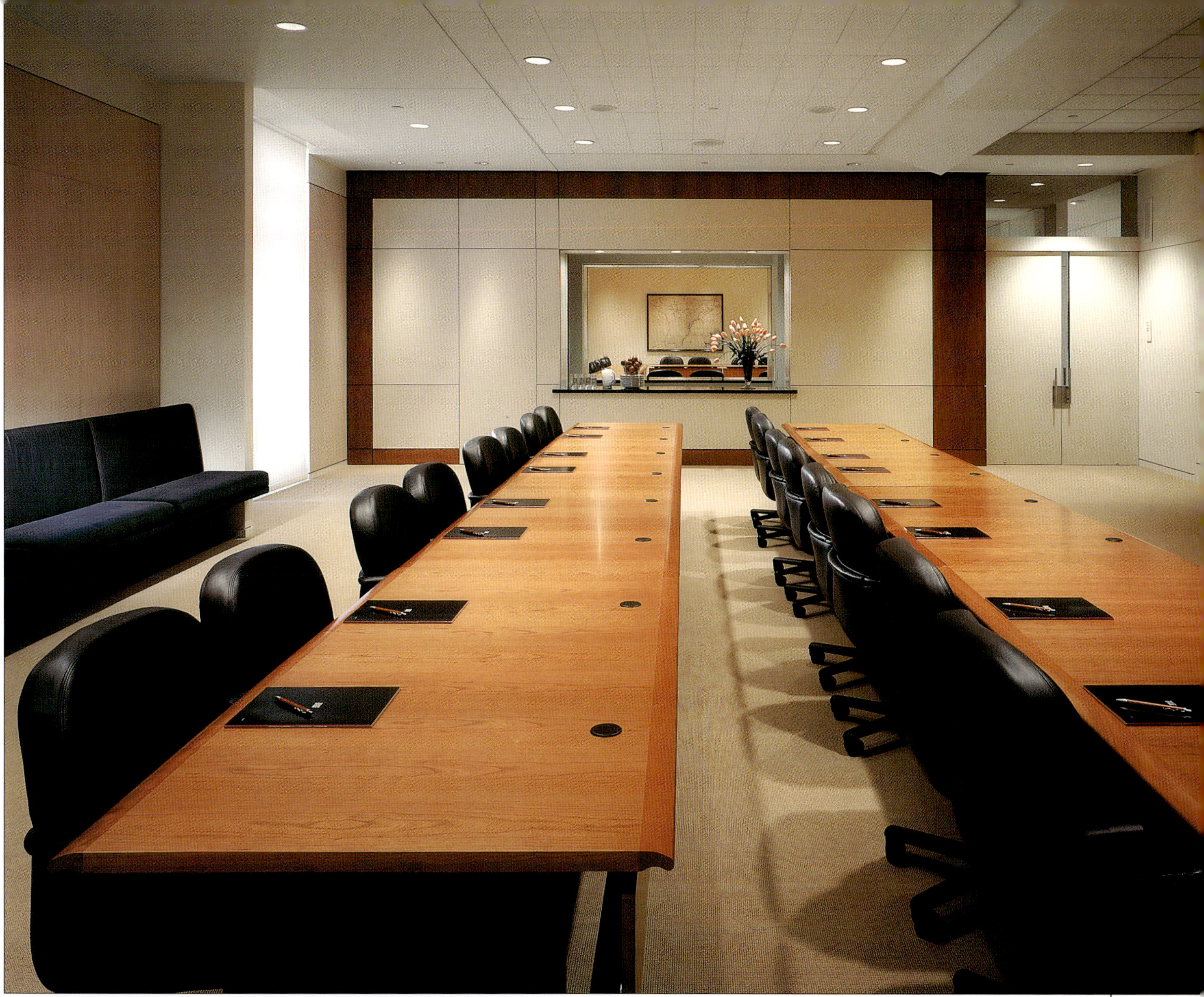

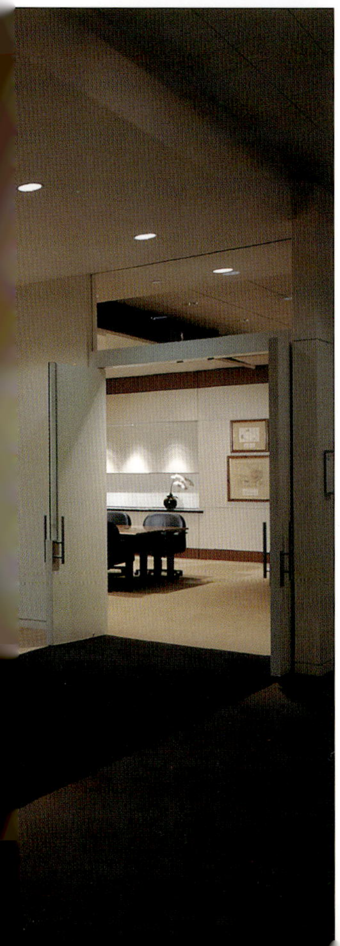

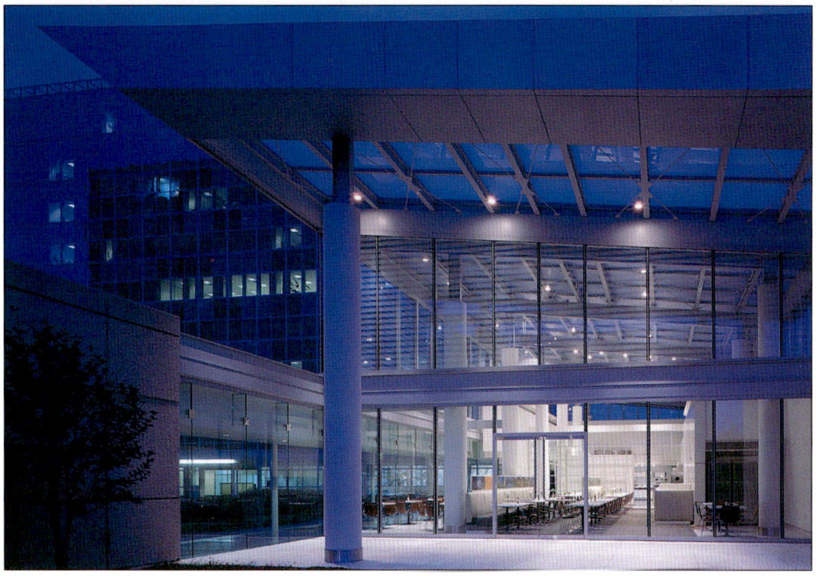

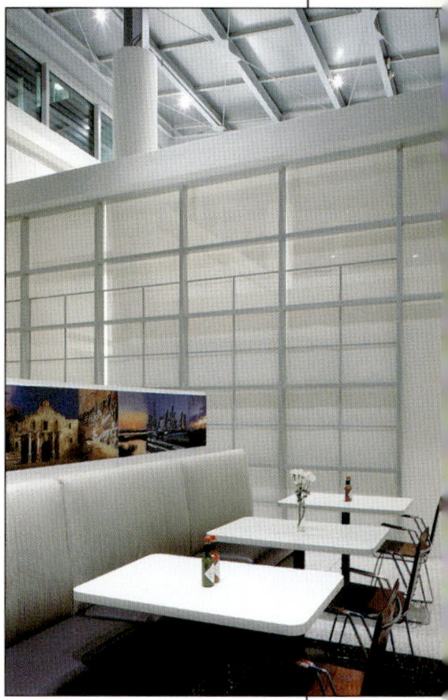

DMJM Rottet

Tokai Bank of California Corporate Offices and Retail Branch
Los Angeles, California

This installation combines a 5,000-sq.-ft. retail banking area with three 22,600-sq.-ft. office floors for a total of 73,000 sq. ft. The client is a hybrid of two organizations, one American and one Japanese, and the design needed to respect both cultural backgrounds and both workplace traditions. The Japanese group favored a modern feeling for its space, and the American group a more conservative one, yet all agreed that there should be consistency throughout. DMJM Rottet's solution includes executive areas that are dominated by traditional private offices, with finishes and furnishings of dark wood and deep tones. For more open areas, cohesion is obtained with carpeting, details, and colors, these last being chiefly steel blue and taupe. Materials repeated throughout include back-painted glass, fire-etched glass, and stretched silk panels as wallcovering.

Top of page: Detail of 7th-floor corridor.
Above: An executive reception area.
Right: The retail branch bank.
Photography: Nick Merrick © Hedrich Blessing.

Felderman + Keatinge Associates

1800 Berkeley Street
Santa Monica
California 90404
310.449.4727
310.449.4729 (Fax)
www.fkadesign.com

Felderman + Keatinge Associates

Interface Americas' Corporate Headquarters "Talimeco"

Right: Library has motorized video conferencing equipment, white board, a restored Wright inspired screen with glass inserts and vintage furniture.
Below: The living room with fireplace and a variety of seating options is being used for video conferencing.
Below, right: A series of customized Knoll workstations.
Photography: Timothy Hursley.

North of Atlanta, in a 30-acre rural setting, this building was designed in the 1970s as a large country house by an architect who is, an admirer of Frank Lloyd Wright. After thorough renovation by Felderman + Keatinge — repairing extensive damage, removing interior partitions, and adding structural reinforcement — it now functions as an executive headquarters for Interface, Americas the largest global manufacturer of commercial carpet. Its 8,500 sq. ft. now accommodate the offices of five of the company's senior executives, their support staff, visiting employees, business partners, and customers. Overnight guest facilities are also provided. But more important than these specific functions, perhaps, is the general character of the facility: small, informal, and removed both physically and psychologically from the bustle and the interruptions of the typical corporate office. This setting has been designed to nurture personal interaction facilitating such activities as videoconferences, brainstorming sessions, and conversations in what the designers call "casual collision areas." The informality, however, is well supported by state of the art technology. Another consideration throughout is the aesthetic allegiance to Wrightian colors, materials, details, and patterns, well researched by the Felderman + Keatinge team. Using such patterns, for example, are the custom carpets they designed that demonstrate the client's manufacturing capabilities.

Top of page: *Exterior view of the former residence.*
Above, right: *One of the guest rooms.*
Detail at left: *Wright-inspired carpet pattern.*
Right: *Knoll currents executive workstations on Interface's carpet designed by Felderman + Keatinge.*

Felderman + Keatinge Associates

Guidance Solutions
Marina del Rey, California

Left, top of page: A door placed high in a wall functions as a clerestory window.
Left: The reception area with a multifaceted desk design by Felderman + Keatinge.
Above: Workstations are detailed with aluminum, Lexan, and medium-density fiberboard.
Photography: David Glomb.

Guidance Solutions is a web development and e-commerce start-up company that, like many such companies, is in a state of rapid growth, evolution, and redefinition. Its staff of 15 employees on the opening day of this new facility had grown to 120 employees 18 months later. Work teams within the office are reconfigured daily. Obviously, flexibility was an imperative. Demanding, too, were time and budget restraints: the entire design/build process was accomplished in only four months and on a budget of $35. per sq. ft. including mechanical and electrical work and furniture. Within the existing 10,000-sq.-ft. bow-truss structure, Felderman + Keatinge created a "kit of parts" vocabulary of elements, including continuous work surfaces with movable dividers between work spaces, allowing expansion and contraction of assigned areas ("fuzzy borders") as needed. The angled and curved surfaces create forced perspectives, and with rich, saturated colors trigger surprise. The result is a town center which fosters community interaction.

Felderman + Keatinge Associates

MTV Networks' West Coast Headquarters
Santa Monica, California

At the intersection of 26th Street and Colorado, an important location in Santa Monica's "entertainment corridor," a previously banal office block has been transformed, outside and in, by Felderman + Keatinge into appropriate quarters for MTV Networks, an organization that helps shape cultures worldwide. This entertainment corporation, which The Wall Street Journal has described as "the arbiter of hip." Nevertheless, the design needed also to relate to Santa Monica's seaside character — an amalgam of beach, bungalows, piers, galleries and artists' lofts — and to reflect as well the fact that MTV Networks is now a mature, global organization with a solid business sense. On a more practical level, the building's 110,000 sq. ft., spread over five floors, had to be made to efficiently serve 450 creative professionals. The tone is established at the entrance with two giant "talking heads" constructed of glass marbles and copper-leafed gesso. A 1957 Airstream trailer nearby begins the sequence of early modern artifacts found in the furnishings used throughout; it can be used for waiting or for small conferences. Other floors have their own personalities, similarly established in their reception areas: the Nickelodeon floor, for example, presents the form of an ocean liner's prow, a form that functions, as many elements here do, as a container for the ever-present television monitors.

Far left: Visitors are greeted by a pair of "talking heads" and by a 1957 Airstream trailer.
Left, above: A waiting area defined by aluminum mesh draperies.
Left, below: Workstations under panels of corrugated fiberglass.
Photography: Toshi Yoshimi.

Above: Downlights are recessed in an overhead surfboard form, above customized workstations.
Above, right: A metal-clad column in a "living room" area.
Right: The Nickelodeon floor's entry is marked by a stylized ocean liner holding television monitors.

95

Further seaside imagery is in the form of surfboard-shaped panels suspended from ceilings; these contain downlights at optimal levels and suggest spatial boundaries among the freewheeling organization. Practical, purely functional workstations also have their place here, too, customized by Felderman & Keatinge. Colors here are not for the timid, and the materials palette is similarly robust, including corrugated fiberglass, corrugated metal, hangings of aluminum mesh, wall panels of overlapping glass, and flooring of custom carpet designs and specially pigmented concrete.

Right: A bright red MTV hallway leads to a pantry with cabinet fronts of multicolored laminate.

Below: Another "living room" with corrugated fiberglass monitor wall, early modern furniture, pigmented concrete floor, and another surfboard form overhead.

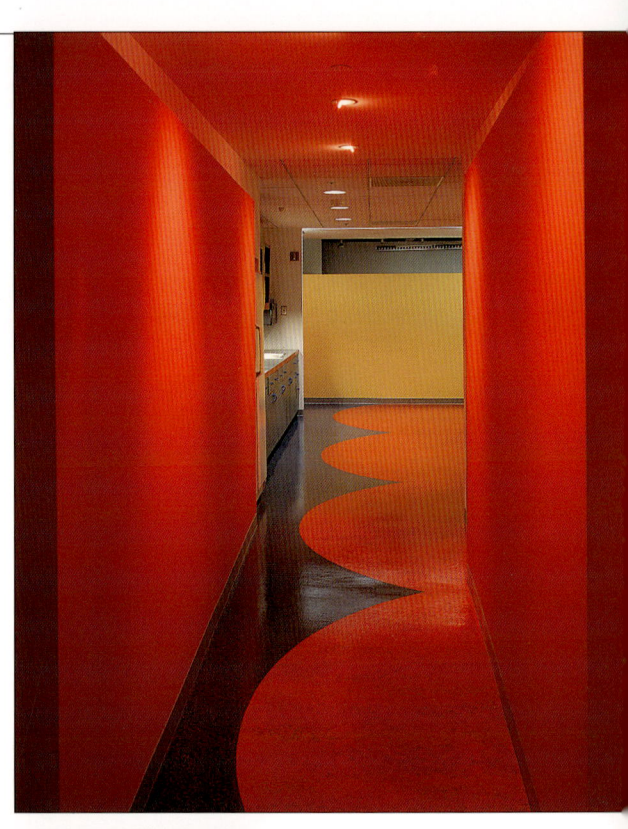

Gary Lee Partners

1743 Merchandise Mart
Chicago
Illinois 60654
312.644.1744
312.644.1745 (Fax)
www.garyleepartners.com

Gary Lee Partners

Gary Lee Partners American College of
Surgeons
Chicago, Illinois

Right: Hallway with a view into the conference room.
Far right: A typical workstation. Photo: Marco Lorenzetti © Hedrich Blessing.
Below: The Regents Room under its vault of steel mesh.
Photography: Christopher Barrett © Hedrich Blessing, except as noted.

After purchasing a 28-story building near Michigan Avenue, the American College of Surgeons sought to consolidate their staff of 250, located in four disparate locations, into 150,000 sf in the new facility. Although functional efficiency was important, the client required a ceremonial space to host conferences for the organization's National Board of Governors and smaller Board of Regents. For these conferences, Gary Lee Partners designed the Regents Room, an 18-ft. high top-floor aerie enjoying a 200-degree panorama of downtown Chicago's skyline. The existing ceiling was raised and replaced with a dramatic doubly curved vaulting of heavy-gauge stainless steel mesh held on anodized aluminum ribs; the stage on which the room is focused is lined with eucalyptus panels. Beyond this special precinct, typical floors are organized with private offices on the ends and flexible work and filing areas in the center. To promote light transmission into the core, the open plan office systems have been given frosted glass panels. An employee lunchroom on the 27th floor, used by executives and staff alike, has wood parquet flooring and fabric-covered wall panels. Other materials recurring throughout the space include wood veneers, back-painted glass, metallic lacquer, custom-designed carpets, stainless steel trim, drywall ceiling bands, and floors of Atlantic green granite. Accent colors of intense blues, purples, and greens complement the warm woods and neutral backgrounds.

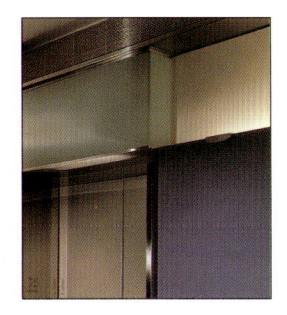

Detail at left: Junction of materials at the head of an elevator door.
Right, above: The director's office. Photo: Marco Lorenzetti © Hedrich Blessing.
Right: Reception area with elevator lobby beyond. Photo: Marco Lorenzetti © Hedrich Blessing.

Gary Lee Partners

Winston & Strawn
New York, New York

A successful relationship with Winston & Strawn's Chicago office led the law firm to request Gary Lee Partners' services for the relocation of their New York office. After Gary Lee Partners' assessment of the available real estate options, Winston & Strawn chose to relocate to the 41st, 42nd, 45th, and west mezzanine of Park Avenue's Met Life Building (formerly Pan Am). Gary Lee Partners took advantage of the large 43,000 sf floor plates while they efficiently addressed the planning issues that arose from the elongated, octagonal building shape. The resultant plan allows for ease of mobility between the law firm's different practice groups. A handsomely detailed internal stair connects the main reception, law library, and conference center located on the 42nd Floor with the secondary reception and conference center on the 41st Floor. Private attorney offices and open support staff workstations are located on all four levels. The materials used throughout the space include paint gypsum board walls, mahogany veneers, custom cut pile carpeting, and Calacatta Machio Oro and Botticino Fiorito marble flooring. Gary Lee Partners also participated in assembling the firm's extensive art collection.

Above: Custom work stations in a support area.
Left: Seating group in the main reception area.
Photography: Marco Lorenzetti © Hedrich Blessing.

Left: Secondary reception area for conference center.
Above, right: Detail of the internal stair.
Right: Main reception area with conference room beyond.

Gary Lee Partners

Madison Dearborn
Partners, Inc.
Chicago, Illinois

Opposite, top: Seating in the reception area.
Left: A partner's office.
Top of page: View from elevator lobby towards reception area.
Above: Custom support staff workstations outside partners' offices.
Photography: Steve Hall © Hedrich Blessing.

Rapid growth forced this venture capital firm to relocate its offices from a tight, dark space on a multi-tenant floor to its own floor within the same building. Now its 38 employees are comfortably housed on a single 23,000 sf floor. The client challenged Gary Lee Partners to create a spacious and sophisticated space reflecting the progressive nature of their business while maintaining a statement of Madison Dearborn Partners' roots in finance. The plan also needed to efficiently organize the space within a highly irregular floor area. Gary Lee Partners' design utilized a series of ceiling bands -drywall alternating with acoustical tile within concealed splines- that provided that basis for the firm's organization. This ceiling bands demark various work areas and emphasize points of entry into the private offices and conference rooms. The alteration of ambient and direct lighting reinforces the concept. Materials used throughout the project include Bottocino marble for the reception room floor, dark emperador marble for the doorway thresholds, and wall panels, door frames, and millwork of pearl movingué, bird's-eye maple, and ebonized mahogany. Areas provided included a reception area, conference center, fitness center, lunchroom, custom workstations, and a large number of private offices. Gary Lee Partners designers performed a wide range of services, beginning with feasibility studies, programming, and space planning, followed by conceptual design and design implementation. The designers were also entrusted with assembling the client's art program, which includes such atypical items as paintings of cast paraffin and bronze Chinese urns.

Right: Corridor outside the Madison Dearborn conference center.
Right, below: One of the center's conference rooms.

Gensler

600 California Street
San Francisco
California 94108
415.433.3700
415.627.3739 (Fax)

Atlanta
Boston
Chicago
Dallas
Denver
Detroit
Hong Kong
Houston
London
Los Angeles
New York
Newport Beach
Parsippany, NJ
San Francisco
Tokyo
Washington, DC

Gensler

Viant
San Francisco, California

Right: Some of the stops along the installation's "Main Street."
Below: Reception area with views into work areas.
Photography: David Wakely.

For the Viant Corporation (formerly known as the Silicon Valley Internet Partners), Gensler has designed offices in San Francisco's renovated Townsend Center. The offices occupy 25,000 sq. ft. of a very large building floor plate and are meant to accommodate a work force of 80 that is expected to grow to 125. The facilities provided include not a single private office. Instead, there are open office spaces, a large divisible conference/training room, a smaller 12-person conference room, six team rooms for six or eight persons each, and a demo lab for product presentations to clients. Support areas include a lunchroom and pantry, copy and mail areas, a computer server room, and a test lab. Important to the client was maximum visibility and interaction, so Gensler responded with a "Main Street" concept, with glass-walled spaces opening to a curved corridor (the "street") traveled by visitors on their way from the reception area to the demo lab and by employees on their way from work areas to the lunchroom. The six team rooms have at least two walls of glass, so that members of one team are in visible contact with members of others. Even some of the ceiling is open, displaying the large supply and return air ducts for the building's atrium. Furnishings are simple, flexible, and — like the installation as a whole — moderately priced.

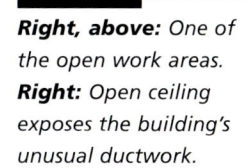

Right, above: One of the open work areas.
Right: Open ceiling exposes the building's unusual ductwork.

Gensler

Viant
Boston, Massachusetts

Above: Reference room promotes sharing of reference materials in a casual atmosphere.
Right: Looking into an open work area.
Photography: Richard Mandelkorn.

108

When Gensler designed the San Francisco offices of Viant, principles and standards were established that were then applied to the same company's quarters in New York and Boston, although each office contains its own references to local culture. The Boston installation, shown here, is planned for an occupancy of 95 and occupies 20,000 sq. ft. Like its San Francisco precedent, it has no private offices, not even for the company president, Bob Gett. The character of an open loft prevails throughout, even though the space is in an older downtown building not at all loft-like. The spaces with walls, such as the client conference rooms and collaborative team meeting rooms, are still open visually, faced with Clestra Hauserman's glass front systems. Also on the straightforward palette of materials are paint, carpet, and rubber bases, and furnishings are totally user-movable for maximum flexibility, suiting the company's rapidly changing team structure. Some ceiling planes are finished, some open to the original rough-finished terracotta vaulting above. Colors are generally muted, but with bright, interesting accents. Viant president Gett says that the resultant space completely supports his company's culture and greatly assists in recruiting and retaining staff.

Top of page: Reception area.
Above, right: One of the team meeting rooms.
Right: The training area projects the message that work can be fun.

Gensler   Caribiner International
           Dearborn, Michigan

Right, above: The reception area.
Right: Commons area bounded by translucent screens.
Below: Corridor to the commons area.

Caribiner International is a public relations and strategic business communications firm specializing in meeting and event planning. For its new 17,000 sq. ft. facility, consolidating two previous ones remote from each other, the firm naturally wanted an environment promoting — and displaying to clients — leading-edge creativity and dynamism. Fortunately, the building to be renovated was not typical office space, but one originally intended for light industry, so that open spaces and high ceilings were both options. Around an original core of toilets and mechanical equipment, Gensler's scheme takes full advantage of these possibilities, and finished ceiling heights have been varied from lows of eight feet to highs of fifteen. Gensler's planning concept creates four "neighborhoods" for individualized work groups — administration, sales, production, and creative — and each of the four is given its own color palette, its own characteristic range of textures and finishes (referred to by Gensler designers as "textural mapping"), and its own organization.

Right: The production "neighborhood" is separated from the commons area by one of the screens.
Photography: Marco Lorenzetti © Hedrich-Blessing.

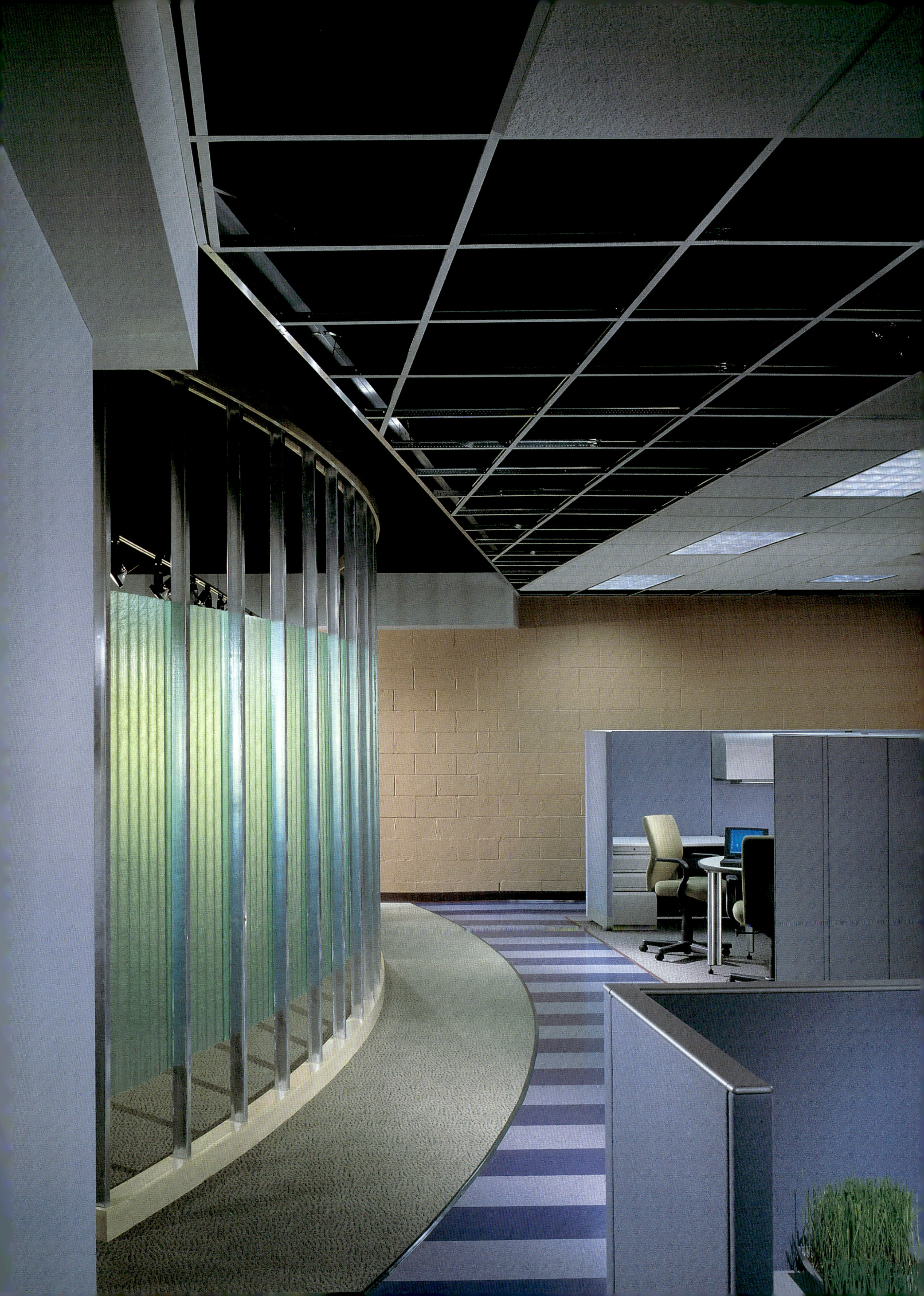

Left: Work areas adjacent to the Caribiner commons area.
Below: View into the main conference room. A cantilevered counter is at the left.

The creative group's neighborhood, for example, is relatively quiet, with private work areas allowing writers to concentrate on their work, while the production neighborhood is more factory-like, a "beehive" of activity with a sense of urgency, and the sales neighborhood has both closed areas for telephone work and open areas for interaction among workers and between workers and clients. Central to these four areas and the heart of the entire office is the commons, an assembly zone for casual staff get-togethers and client entertainment. The commons is separated from the other office space not by walls but by curving translucent screens of corrugated fiberglass; it enjoys the facility's greatest ceiling heights; and it is furnished with comfortable lounge seating. For the design of this installation, Gensler earned a 1999 Honor Award from the Michigan chapter of the American Institute of Architects.

Griswold, Heckel & Kelly Associates, Inc.

55 West Wacker Drive
6th Floor
Chicago
Illinois 60601
312.263.6605
312.263.1228 (Fax)
www.ghk-interiors.com

New York
Boston
Baltimore
Washington, DC
San Jose

Griswold, Heckel & Kelly Associates, Inc.

Allegiance Healthcare Corporation Headquarters
Deerfield, Illinois

Below: Executive offices have glass walls and are located near informal seating areas.
Photography: Jon Miller © Hedrich Blessing.

Griswold, Heckel & Kelly (GHK) renovated two existing buildings for the headquarters of Allegiance Healthcare, a Fortune 500 company in the hospital supply business. In addition, GHK coordinated the space requirements of over 3100 Allegiance employees in the parent company's 1.5 million sq. ft. of campus space, renovating much of it. In the headquarters, shown here, 600 other employees are accommodated in a total of 180,000 sq. ft. But the most carefully studied accommodations, perhaps, are those for the company's visitors and potential clients. A typical customer group coming to the headquarters is from 8 to 25 people, and the customer center is provided with ample seating (in the form of chairs designed by Frank Gehry), convenient coat closets, and an attractive display of beverages and snacks. Nearby is a presentation room, seating 50 in a roundtable setting of concentric rings; it is equipped with video teleconferencing capabilities and sophisticated audio-visual systems, and one wall opens to a private servery that can offer meal and snack service during daylong meetings. For Allegiance employees, there is a separate kitchen and scramble-system servery and a dining area seating 400. Work spaces are a combination of closed executive offices, held back from the exterior walls, and open workstations enjoying outside light. Small lounge seating areas are placed adjacent to the executive offices for informal conversations with the staff and all-important visiting customers. Colors throughout are reinterpreted "earth tones" comprised of touches of violet, ochre, and fawn hues — colors, the designers say, that are found in NASA photographs of the earth and therefore represent the global nature of the client's business. As Jennifer Graham, Allegiance's corporate vice president of communications, says, "Our offices reflect our business, the values embodied in our corporate mission, and the innovative nature of our management practices."

Above: The customer center is provided with food service.
Above, right: Combination of open and closed offices in the general work area.
Right: The 50-seat presentation room.

115

Griswold, Heckel & Kelly Associates, Inc.

**Financial Ideas Exchange
New York, New York**

Financial Ideas Exchange in New York is part of a large multinational consulting firm. This renovated space occupies two floors of 8,000 sq. ft. each and accommodates 55 employees. All construction work was completed in a four-week period over the winter holidays to minimize the interruption of business. Because a complete redesign of the facility is planned for every three years, there was a demand for maximum flexibility and cost-consciousness. Spatial requirements included a conference center, private offices, staff workstations, reception area, and a dining room with a full-service pantry/kitchen. Among these, the most spectacular element is the largest of the conference rooms, a circular arena surrounded by panels of pear wood that open to disclose a 270-degree wrap-around screen for computer animation and virtual reality presentations. In addition, an auditorium houses video conferencing sessions and further demonstrations, and state-of-the-art data technology is employed throughout.

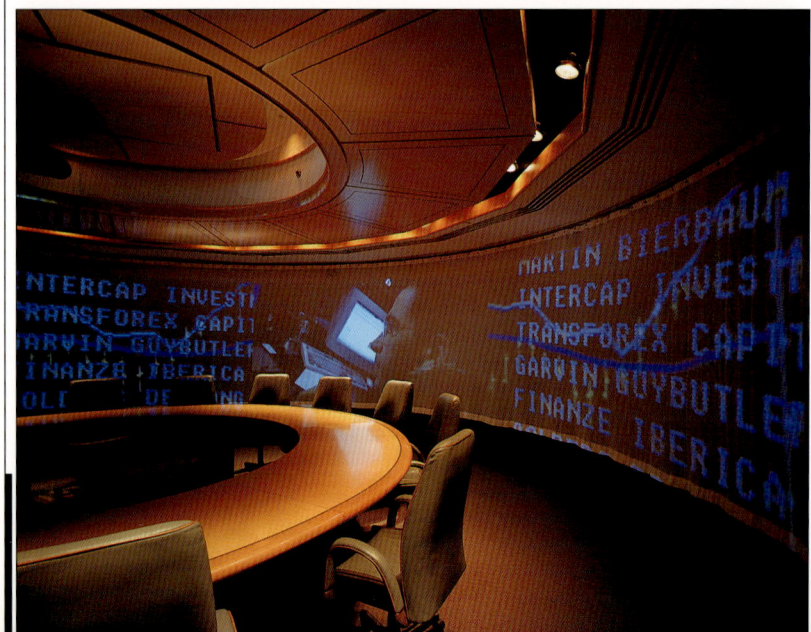

Left: Conference Center One with its perimeter walls closed.
Facing page, left and bottom: Conference Center One with its perimeter walls open for presentation.
Photography: Peter Paige.

Above: Steel doors at the entrance to a small conference room.
Above left: Small presentation room.

Griswold, Heckel & Kelly Associates, Inc.

EarthShell Corporation Headquarters
Baltimore, Maryland

This 8000-sq.-ft. renovation houses EarthShell, a biodegradable food packaging technology company that recently moved its corporate headquarters from Santa Barbara to Baltimore. GHK provided maximum flexibility, both temporally and spatially: A three-phase construction plan was devised to allow partial occupancy while other parts of the headquarters were being readied, and space planning will accommodate as many as 30 workers in job descriptions and department distributions not yet defined. These functional needs were matched in importance by EarthShell's desire for a strong image reflecting its concern for the beauty and value of the natural environment. Although natural materials and allusions to nature occur throughout the installation, the primary supplier of such an image is the feature wall that dominates the trapezoidal reception area. It is built of slate, and the section bearing the company logo is a backdrop for a sheet of gently running water, contributing the sound of a trickling brook. Nearby, a salt-water fish tank is encased in a limestone wall. The entire space was designed with a sensitivity to: "green" issues: The wood species are not endangered, the slate is not fossil-based, and all the furniture manufacturers represented are engaged in programs of environmental protection.

Top of page, left: Corridor and private offices.
Top of page, right: Washroom sink and vanity.
Center: Conference room.
Detail view: Corner of the conference room table.
Right: The reception room's feature wall.
Photography: Ron Solomon.

Griswold, Heckel & Kelly Associates, Inc.

The Gillette Company Headquarters
Boston, Massachusetts

No introduction is needed to this client and its consumer product lines: Gillette, PaperMate, Parker Pen, Waterman Pen, Braun, Oral Care, and Duracell. The headquarters designed by GHK for 1200 of the company's employees is a total of 225,000 sq. ft. on nine floors of 25,000 sq. ft. each. Requirements included private offices, open workstations, conference rooms, training rooms, a board room, a video conferencing center, a company store and a full-service subsidized cafeteria for both breakfast and lunch. Each of the nine floors has an identical reception area, and each of the eight non-executive floors has a copy and information center comprising fax machines, copiers, shredders, bulletin boards, vending machines, and a refrigerator. Care has been given to insure workstation access to perimeter light and views, and — according to Gillette policy — office and work station assignments are based on function, not on paygrade. All 1200 employees were interviewed individually for a review of their furniture options, including a wide choice of ergonomically sound task chairs. On the executive floor, the Board of Directors' suite includes lounge, kitchen, private restrooms, and private offices for visitors' use.

Top, right: *Entrance into the reception area.*
Center, right: *Part of the Board of Directors' suite.*
Right: *Part of the executive floor.*
Photography: *Marco Lorenzetti © Hedrich Blessing.*

Griswold, Heckel & Kelly Associates, Inc.

Polaris Claim Reception Center
Tampa, Florida

As a subsidiary of the St. Paul Companies (formerly USF&G), the Polaris Claim Reception Center is a call center handling nationwide insurance claims. Its 500 employees are housed in 85,000 sq. ft. spread over two floors. A five-phase relocation and construction plan devised by GHK and scheduled over an 18-month period allowed the previous tenant (a rival insurance firm) to move out in stages while Polaris moved in. Another key design consideration was accommodation of the company's 24-hour operation. Twelve-ft.-square work pods, each holding three workers at computerized call stations, are equipped with easily rearranged, lockable storage elements, adjustable desktops and keyboard panels, and adjustable ergonomic chairs, so that all three shifts of workers can be personally suited. In addition to these "triad pods," the Polaris facility includes other open workstations, private offices, training rooms, a fitness center, and a cafeteria with lunchroom. Satisfaction is expressed by John McIlhenny, director of Polaris operations: "The flexibility of the workstations has been put to the test... The ergonomics of the equipment continue to receive rave reviews from our specialists.... I am so exceptionally proud of and impressed by the project."

Top of page: Super sized shared workstations.
Center: The main Polaris reception area.
Left: Mural representing the company's values.
Right: The executive reception area.
Photography: Steve Hall © Hedrich Blessing.

The Hillier Group

500 Alexander Park CN 23
Princeton
New Jersey 08543.0023
609.452.8888
609.452.8332 (Fax)
www.hillier.com

Philadelphia
New York
Washington
Scranton
Dallas
Kansas City
Newark
London

The Hillier Group

Intech Corporation
Philadelphia, Pennsylvania

The Intech construction company began as a partnership of two friends and classmates in an industrial neighborhood of Philadelphia. Now grown into a credible competitor among the region's established construction firms, it celebrated its tenth anniversary with a move into 20,000 sq. ft. of downtown space. The chosen location, once occupied by heavy machinery, offered both advantages — such as 18-ft. ceiling heights — and disadvantages — such as the almost total lack of views and daylight. Three-ft.-diameter concrete columns with mushroom capitals dominated the volume. The Hillier Group's response was to house the more than 50 Intech employees in quarters where lighting and colors simulate the experience of daylight, and where interposed shapes and planes modulate and humanize the spatial

Right: *In a windowless area, artificial daylight above private offices.*
Below: *An open work area.*
Photography: *Tom Crane.*

expanse. Both the client and the design team also felt it appropriate that the design display the virtues of construction materials and methods. Accommodated within this constructionist assemblage are open work areas, glass-doored individual offices, a reception area, conference room, library, lunch room, fitness center, mail room, and other support elements. Prominent materials include exposed steel framing, painted drywall, back-painted glass, "art glass," French limestone, Burlington stone, carpet, vinyl composite tile, acoustical ceiling tile, and — lending a pleasing warmth to the more industrial materials — natural maple. The installation design has earned The Hillier Group a Bronze Medal from the New Jersey chapter of the American Institute of Architects.

Above: Main corridor, with private offices beyond.
Right, above: Gallery wall at left, leading to conference room.
Right: Corridor between reception area and offices.

The Hillier Group

PNC Bank
Regional Headquarters
Philadelphia, Pennsylvania

Right: The private banking receptionist's custom-designed desk.
Below: Seating area, with view into the boardroom.
Photography: Tom Crane.

For the PNC Bank's regional headquarters, The Hillier Group has renovated 15 floors in an existing Philadelphia high-rise. At 23,000 usable sq. ft. per floor, the total area is 350,000 sq. ft., and between 1,700 and 2,000 PNC employees can be accommodated here. Facilities designed include private offices, executive suites, private dining and conference rooms, and reception and work spaces for PNC's various divisions — private banking, corporate banking, retail banking, retail brokerage, and trust. Finding the most appropriate design idiom was complicated by recent multiple mergers, combining various corporate cultures, and by the fact that local users of the building expressed some tastes different from those of the bank's corporate headquarters in Pittsburgh. A satisfactory solution for all was found in a contemporary/transitional style with traditional furniture and accents. Planning of floor layouts is similarly traditional, with private offices on the perimeter, open workspaces on the interior, and support functions at the ends of each floor. Millwork is chiefly of light to medium woods, with anigré most prominent, flooring is a combination of travertine and carpet, and other materials include lacquer panels, back-painted glass, and stainless steel detailing. Key to the total success is the contribution of The Hillier Group's Graphic Design Studio, a coherent program of signage based on the use of sandblasted glass and stainless steel hardware.

Above, right: Corridor in private banking connecting meeting rooms.
Right: Lounge area and executive dining/conference room.

The Hillier Group

Merrill Lynch
New York, New York

Above: *The main boardroom.*
Photography: *James D'Addio.*

The Hillier Group has been involved with numerous interior design projects for Merrill Lynch, an obviously satisfied repeat client. The installation shown here is for the offices of Merrill Lynch's general counsel at 222 Broadway in Manhattan. It covers four complete floors for a total of 75,000 sq. ft. and is designed to house 400 employees. For this space, The Hillier Group developed office and furniture standards and provided space planning, design, construction documentation, and construction administration services. Requirements included a reception area, private offices, open work areas, a range of conference rooms (small, medium, and large) clustered around the reception area, a 75-person board room with audio-visual and video conferencing equipment, an interconnecting stairway, and the necessary support areas clustered near the building's interior core. For the open work areas, the designers used standard furniture systems to develop two workstation configurations of different size. The library has been divided into feature niches throughout the space, rather than located in one large room. Stainless steel has been used for portals and column enclosures in the reception area, and office fronts have been composed of translucent frosted glass in wood frames. Throughout, the look is tailored and warm.

Right, top of page: Conference room and reception area.
Right, center: View into one of the conference rooms.
Right: Another conference room.

Left: *A view from the elevator lobby into the Merrill Lynch reception area.*
Below: *A group of open workstations.*

HKS Inc.

1919 McKinney Avenue
Dallas
Texas 75201.1753
214.969.5599
214.969.3397 (Fax)
www.hskinc.com

HKS Inc.

HKS Inc.

Fina Oil and Chemical Company
Plano, Texas

Right: Semi-private office areas of the executive suite.
Below: Chairman's office is also semi-private.
Photography: Chas McGrath.

HKS has designed a campus totaling 270,000 sq. ft. for Fina Oil and Chemical, which is a large petroleum company. The facility accommodates 600 of Fina's employees. The building includes four stories at 29,500 sq. ft. per floor and another five stories at 25,000 sq. ft. per floor. Linking the buildings is a glass and granite atrium space circular in plan, which serves as an entry point for both employees and visitors. This space is also a dramatic venue for special events. The highly visible atrium floor is of Texas cream-colored limestone with radiating lines of black granite and accents of Yellow Veneziano granite from Brazil; at the center, an abstracted version of Fina's shield logo is set flush with the floor. Elevator banks adjoin the atrium, their walls faced with stained Makore wood paneling, and the space above and beyond is devoted almost exclusively to open plan office areas, supplemented by shared coffee, copy, file, and conference areas. Also provided are a credit union, a training center, and an employee fitness center with locker rooms. A 250-seat dining room doubles as a meeting space with audio/visual capabilities. For all this, HKS performed a full range of services — architecture, interior design, and graphic design.

Right: Atrium is faced with wood and granite.
Below: Team-based workstation groups in the gas trading area.

131

HKS Inc.

HKS Corporate Headquarters
Dallas, Texas

Proverbially, the shoemaker's children go barefoot, but the proverb has no application here, for HKS has designed for itself exemplary quarters. They occupy 112,000 sq. ft. in what was once an architectural woodwork and store fixture manufacturing plant, abandoned for 15 years; its three connected structures are now one. The move demonstrates the commitment of HKS to remaining in downtown Dallas, the firm's home for the last 40 of its 60 years, and is serving as a catalyst for new development in the area. The existing brick and concrete structural elements of the 74-year-old building have been cleaned but left exposed, as is newly installed ductwork. New mechanical, electrical, lighting, and data systems have also been added and left visible. The 400 employees of HKS's Dallas office now enjoy three large floors of open office design, with partitions kept low (48 in.) to maintain visual openness; this open space is broken into interdisciplinary teams (architecture, interior design, engineering, and graphics) devoted to specific building type specialties; closed office spaces are few and modest. The open character is enhanced by an outdoor courtyard area for breaks and informal conferences. Also provided are a multi-purpose room, conference centers, vending centers, an employee commons, and in-house printing facilities. Complementing the existing building shell are new elements of terrazzo, glass, metal, wood, sheetrock, red tile, brick, and carpet, and the color palette throughout is of neutrals with black and metallic accents. The result? Since moving, HKS reports a noticeable increase in communications among longtime employees and a positive response from new ones.

Top left: An informal conversation area adjacent to a conference room.
Left: In the general office area, exposed structure and ducts retain the building's original industrial character.
Photography: Steven Vaughan.

Left: Reception desk is equipped with switchboard and security monitoring systems.
Below, left: Open stairs promote communication among levels.
Below: A visitor waiting area is adjacent to the reception space.

133

HKS Inc.   Citibank Tampa Center
            Tampa, Florida

Right: Amenities building two-story rotunda are used for informal dining, meeting and event gatherings.
Below: One of the teaming areas located within open plan areas.
Photography: Dan Forer.

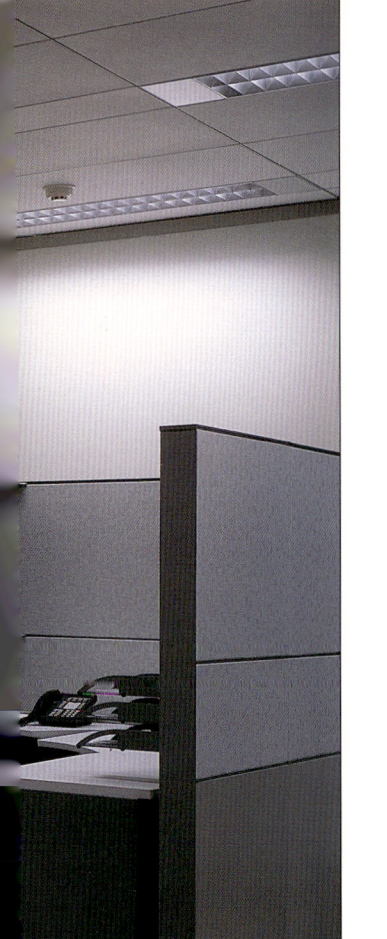

Above, left: *First-floor corridor connecting the dining, medical, banking, and fitness facilities.*
Above: *Varying panel heights and demountable office partitions provide maximum flexibility.*

For the 2,500 financial workers of the Tampa branch of Citicorp Realty Services, HKS envisioned a cluster of four three-story office buildings plus a single two-story amenities building, the total square footage coming to 672,500. Pairs of office buildings are linked with three-story entry elements, and adjacent are exterior covered walkways and two parking facilities accommodating a total of 3,000 cars. The cluster itself needed to serve as an exemplary real estate solution, both flexible and cost-effective. To allow future changes in use, each building was designed with stand-alone mechanical and electrical systems with double redundancy for technologically intense operations. Internally, floor plates are large (42,000 sq. ft. each) and equipped with raised floors for power supply.

Workstation partitions in a variety of heights combined with full-height movable walls allow a multitude of layout reconfigurations. The amenities building serving these office blocks includes a fitness center with free weights, aerobics, and fitness training, a clinic, a day-care facility, a sundries shop, an ATM banking center, and training/conference facilities for both on- and off-campus employees. A double-height dining area, seating 700, has a curved window wall complete with black-out shades so that the room can double as an audio-visual presentation center.

Throughout, the principal materials are carpet, vinyl wallcoverings and painted surfaces, limestone, and wood veneer, and both primary and secondary colors are used as accents against neutral backgrounds. The entire Citicorp campus has been designed to be barrier-free.

Above: One of Citicorp's employee break area and coffee bar within the building core.
Right: Dining space connects to patio and can also be used for presentations.

IA, Interior Architects Inc.

350 California Street
Suite 1500
San Francisco
California 94104
415.434.3305
415.434.0330 (Fax)

Boston
Chicago
Costa Mesa
Dallas
Denver
Ft. Lauderdale
Hong Kong
London
Los Angeles
Miami
Minneapolis
New York
Silicon Valley
Washington, DC

IA, Interior Architects Inc.

PG&E Energy Services
San Francisco, California

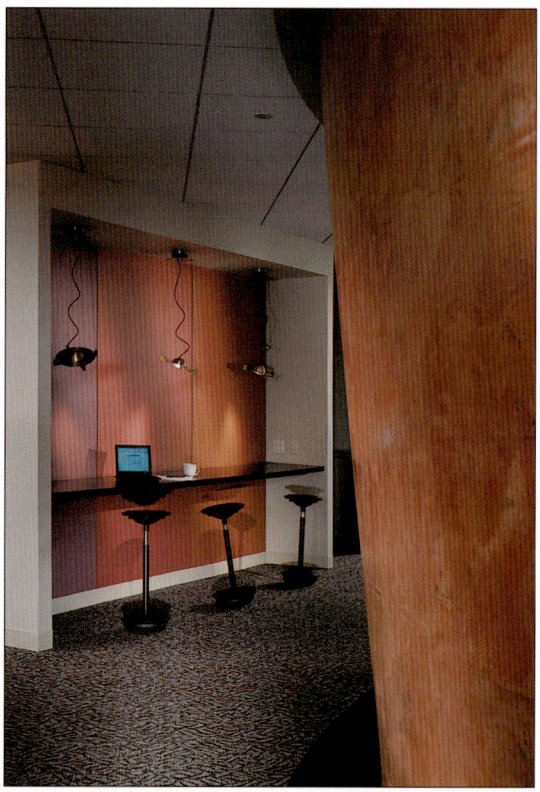

138

Opposite page:
Top left: Lounge seating area with conference room beyond.
Top right: Perching stools at one of the conference bars.
Bottom left: Reception desk.
Center right: Corridor with seating group.
Bottom right: Open workstation with curved wall beyond.

This page:
The reception area's double-height waterfall.
Photography:
Beatriz Coll.

To accommodate the world headquarters of this new company formed by PG&E (Pacific Gas and Electric), IA provided 80,000 sq. ft. of office space on four and a half floors, and did so on a fast-track schedule and within a construction budget of $50 a sq. ft. Some key components of the facility are a Customer Conference Center adjacent to the main reception area, a cluster of offices for guests or "hoteling" staff members, open team project areas, and impromptu meeting areas called Conference Bars. These last are furnished with perching stools and are strategically located next to coffee areas to encourage chance meetings. The main conference and teleconferencing room has individual microphones and a 100-inch flat-screen display monitor. The most visually striking element, however, and an apt metaphor for power generation, is a two-story-high waterfall in the main reception area. The wall of this feature is made of textured laminated glass, backed by an array of computer-programmed fiber-optic lighting that provides a wide range of effects symbolizing dynamic energy. Both the water and the surrounding air are kept clean by electronically charged ions in the water that attract dirt molecules and carry them to a filtering system.

IA, Interior Architects Inc.

The Prime Group Inc.
Chicago, Illinois

Left: View from elevator lobby into reception area.
Bottom, left: The colonnaded corridor from executive offices to main conference room.
Photography: Howard Kaplan.

The Prime Group, a diversified real estate investment holding company, acquired the 22,000 sq. ft. 42nd floor of a Chicago tower in which its subsidiaries already occupied the 39th floor. IA was hired to plan and design the new space so that it communicated the client's identity and allowed for great flexibility in office configuration. The reception area, with a functioning stock ticker over the receptionist's desk, takes its aesthetic cue from a 16th-century oil painting of classical ruins purchased in Italy by a company executive. The art also inspired a painted circular ceiling cove and, linking the main conference room with the executive offices, an arcaded passageway lined with Roman Doric columns. IA's Chicago office did programming to assess the client's space needs, determined adjacencies, created the design and construction documents, and oversaw the construction.

Right: View into a private office.
Far right: View into conference room.
Below: The reception and visitor waiting area.

141

IA, Interior Architects Inc.

Offices of
IA, Interior Architects Inc.
Washington, DC

Right, above: The custom-designed reception desk.
Right: Workstations under the suspended tensile structure.
Photography: Eric Taylor.

Right: Looking into the semi-enclosed meeting alcove.
Right, below: Detail of the level changes.

IA's Washington, DC office occupies a historic freestanding brick building in the Georgetown area, fronting on the Chesapeake and Ohio Canal. Planning was complicated by existing variances in floor level, an unalterable exterior, and the need to provide for handicapped accessibility within the building. Ramps and stairs lead up from the reception and studio areas to the main conference room, principals' offices, and galley kitchen. A smaller, semi-enclosed conference area, directly behind the reception area, is available for brief meetings with vendors and other visitors. Beneath the ceiling plane, left exposed to maximize height, a sail like tensile structure, backlit from above, defines the boundary between studio and support areas. Workstation partitions are low to foster team interaction, concrete columns are bare, and colors are bright yellow, green and purple against white walls with touches of natural wood.

IA, Interior Architects Inc. **Asian Headquarters
for an international financial institution
Hong Kong**

IA has designed all of the regional offices in the Asia Pacific region for this major international financial institution. An example is the 30,000 sq. ft. executive floor of the company's Asia headquarters from where it conducts its operations in Taipei, Manila, Singapore, Seoul, Bangkok, and other locations. The floor was planned to accommodate private offices, administration areas, a videoconferencing room, and other conference rooms, as well as the reception/waiting space seen above. Adjoining the executive floor are other business units of the firm, including equity trading, research, investment banking, information technology, finance, and operations. These units occupy several additional floors, bringing the total area to 120,000 sq. ft. Throughout, IA has provided a blend of ancient Asian and modem elements in a light and balanced environment.

Above: The reception and waiting area of the Asian headquarters facility.
Computer image: Shiro Aw of IA.

Juan Montoya Design Corporation

330 East 59 Street
2nd Floor
New York
New York 10022
212.421.2400
212.421.6240 (Fax)

Juan Montoya Design Corporation

Universal Studios Offices
Universal City, California

Above, far left, and left: Three views of an executive corner office. The cherry and cane armchairs are designed by Juan Montoya.
Right: Custom bookcase unit with an electronic lift television.
Photography: Tuca Reines.

Right: General office space with open workstations.
Below: Montoya-designed reception desk with bronze detailing.

The previous executive offices of Universal Studios, occupying these same 19,000-sq.-ft. quarters on three floors, were paneled in "knotty pine" and crowded with a collection of English baroque antique furniture. A new group of managers, however, noting that Universal was "not in the antiques business," called on the Juan Montoya Design Corporation for a more appropriate image. The space needed sophistication, it needed a more welcoming quality than it previously had had, and it needed to reflect a degree of forward thinking. Functionally, the space needed to house a staff of 75 plus visitors, and they required a reception and waiting area, a number of private executive office suites, open workstation areas, a 14-seat teleconferencing room. kitchens, baths, and support spaces. And all had to be accomplished on a "fast-track" schedule of eight months from concept to move-in. The solution devised by the Montoya office, with Shaler Ladd III credited as Project Director, is an extraordinary amalgam of old and new, primitive and refined, historic and futuristic. One available resource, of which the Montoya team has taken full advantage, was Universal's own archives of irreplaceable vintage movie posters and memorabilia; a selection of these, handsomely framed and carefully positioned, leaves no doubt about what business Universal is in.

Right: *From Universal's archives, an original "Phantom of the Opera" poster; the planter is from the Philippines, the bench from Blackman Cruz.*

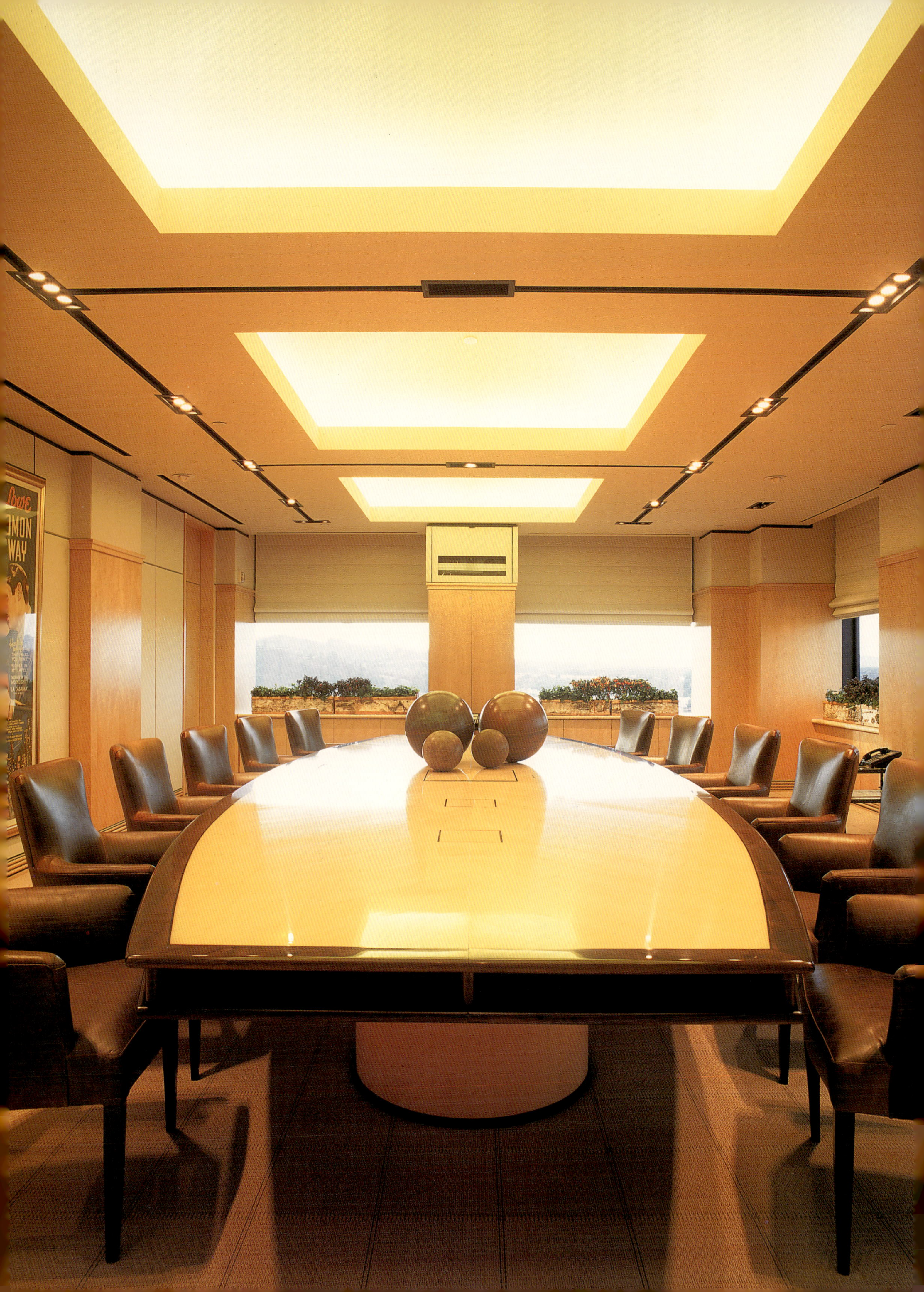

Hints of the future come in subtly concealed technology, such as the central panel of the teleconferencing table that rises to reveal projectors and electronic equipment, in the ceilings that integrate lighting and HVAC supply and return into modular patterns, and in the lighting itself, some of which uses fiber optics. These effects are softened and warmed by the use of wood, with maple and cherry the most prominent; base details are of cherry and ebonized mahogany, the executive bath is paneled in sycamore, a low table is carved from coconut wood by the Igorot people of the Philippines, and a Russian bureau plat, circa 1800, is of mahogany. Metals include wrought-iron stair balusters and door hardware, and the reception desk is detailed with hand-cast bronze fluting. Seating is covered in fabrics, leathers, and blonde caning.

Left: Teleconferencing room with custom-designed table.
Above, far right: Executive private bathroom.
Detail at right: Custom door lever in iron.
Right: Guest bath with marble mosaic wainscoting.
Far right: Detail of custom cherry and ebonized wood base.

A wealth of characterful decorative accessories includes 19th-century Japanese figures, stone urns, planters carved from tree trunks, needleweave baskets from the Philippines, and an end table created from an 18th-century European safe. Cohesion prevails, however, partly due to a color palette that is neutral and calming, and entirely due to the skills of the Juan Montoya Design Corporation.

Above: *Private interior stair with wrought-iron railing climbs beside a wall of cleft limestone.*

Keiser Associates, Inc.

410 Park Avenue South
New York
New York 10016
212.213.4500
212.213.6623 (Fax)

Keiser Associates, Inc.

Paul, Weiss, Rifkind, Wharton & Garrison
New York, New York

Right: One of the private partner offices.
Below: View of reception area from elevator lobby.
Photography: Peter Paige.

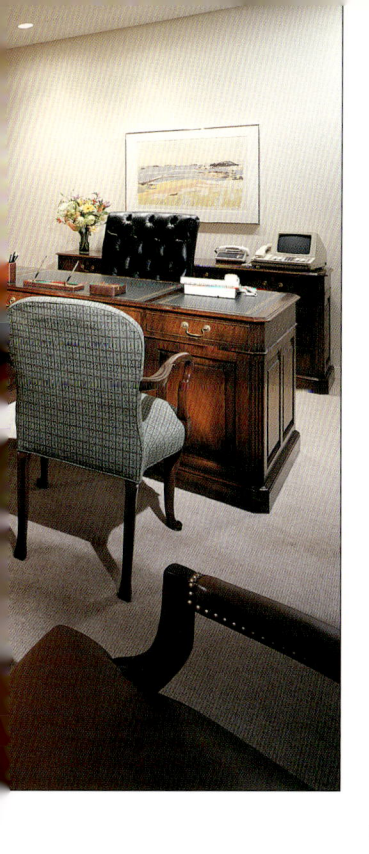

Paul, Weiss, Rifkind, Wharton & Garrison (or, for short, Paul Weiss) is one of New York's largest law firms. It commissioned Keiser Associates to design 300,000 sq. ft. of space on 11 floors with an additional support area in a Sixth Avenue tower. Needed were reception rooms, private offices, conference rooms, a computer room, word processing areas, a cafeteria, and accommodation of a 13,000-sq.-ft. legal library. Also requested was an interconnecting stair visible throughout all floors. The second-floor support area, accessible by escalator from street level, was designed to contain the word processing, accounting, and office services departments; from there, an elevator stops at all other Paul Weiss floors. On those floors, partner offices are exactly double the size of associate offices, providing flexibility in changing the ratio of uses. Shared finishes throughout include impressive amounts of black granite flooring and mahogany veneer cabinetry, and colors are dominated by neutral tones enlivened by bright upholstery fabrics. Keiser Associates was responsible for a full range of services — building selection, programming, design, construction documents, furniture selection, construction supervision, and, move-in coordination.

Right: The circulation desk for the firm's extensive library.
Below, left: Conference rooms double as dining rooms.
Below, right: Internal stair connects all floors.

Keiser Associates, Inc.

White & Case, LLP
Los Angeles, California
and New York, New York

Two Keiser Associates designs for the same client are shown together here. At upper right is the reception area for an installation in New York; other views are of its Los Angeles counterpart. The New York office houses 313 attorneys and a 300-member support staff in 151,000 sq. ft. spread over ten floors. The smaller Los Angeles office accommodates 80 attorneys and a support staff of 125 on four equal floors of 25,000 sq. ft. each. There are functional and spatial differences also: The New York layout gives the top floor (the 41st) to the law firm's conference center, one of the first of its kind to have full food service; all attorneys' offices are on lower floors, with a reception room on every third level, connected by stairs to levels above and below; adjacent to each reception room are guest toilets and an additional conference room. The Los Angeles layout, within an oval-plan I. M. Pei tower, the city's tallest, utilizes broad exit circulation paths — which incorporate secretarial stations, workspaces, and parts of the library — for a general sense of spatial flow. Finally, there are differences of character as well: more contemporary in Los Angeles, more traditional in New York. In all, an interesting demonstration of design fine-tuned to specific local conditions.

Above, left: Reception area, Los Angeles, seen from the 12-ft. corridor.
Above, right: Reception room, New York. Photograph: Peter Paige.
Right: Secretarial workstations within the 12-ft. corridor, Los Angeles.
Far right: Associate's office, Los Angeles.
Photography: Nick Springett, except as noted.

157

Keiser Associates, Inc.

Morgan, Lewis & Bockius, LLP
New York, New York

Above: The conference center control desk is backed by copiers, faxes, printers, and data lines for computer use.
Right: The reception room adjacent to the conference complex.
Photography: Max Hilaire.

Right: The reconfigurable table in the large conference room can seat up to 32.
Below, right: The custom secretarial bays enjoy direct, indirect, and pendant lighting.

This Manhattan law firm occupies 209,000 sq. ft. on eight and a third floors of a Park Avenue tower. In addition to the usual planning challenges, the building (101 Park) presented some of its own: an irregularly shaped floorplate with multiple angled corners. Within this multisided boundary, the client required a generous reception area, attorney offices, support spaces, and — perhaps most critical of all — a conference center. The center's numerous conference rooms required flexible seating capacities and a central control desk equipped to function as a working environment during conference sessions. Large conference rooms are divisible into smaller ones, and all conference rooms are equipped for food service from the center's service pantry. Principal materials are carpet, fabric-wrapped panels, and wood paneling and moldings of dark cherry. Colors are primarily neutrals with a few saturated accents. Keiser Associates' services for Morgan, Lewis & Bockius included all planning, design development, construction and FFE Documentation and project management.

159

Keiser Associates, Inc.

A Financial Institution
New York, New York

Although not named here, this Manhattan financial office is far from anonymous in character. Accommoda-ting 190 employees on one 44,000-sq.-ft. floor, the facility includes a reception room, private offices, open workstations, pantries, and the like, but the heart of the matter is a self-contained video conference center that is a model of its kind. At the central table and surrounding galleries are 40 seats, all wired for PC, fax, and telephone; both front and rear screen projection are available; and most presentations are made with a laptop and Power Point. Because the room is adjacent to a 3rd floor window wall overlooking Park Avenue, special acoustical shutters have been designed to block traffic noise, and dimmers create a variety of lighting scenes. Important adjuncts to the room are toilets, food service gallery, warming pantry, telephone area, and break room. Within the desired context of traditional furnishings, the conference center is a technological showcase, encompassing the company's motto: "Times change, values endure."

Above, right: This reception room also serves for conference breaks and various entertaining functions.
Right: Video/conference room seating 40.
Below, left: Telephone area for conference participants.
Below, right: Open office area.
Photography: Max Hilaire.

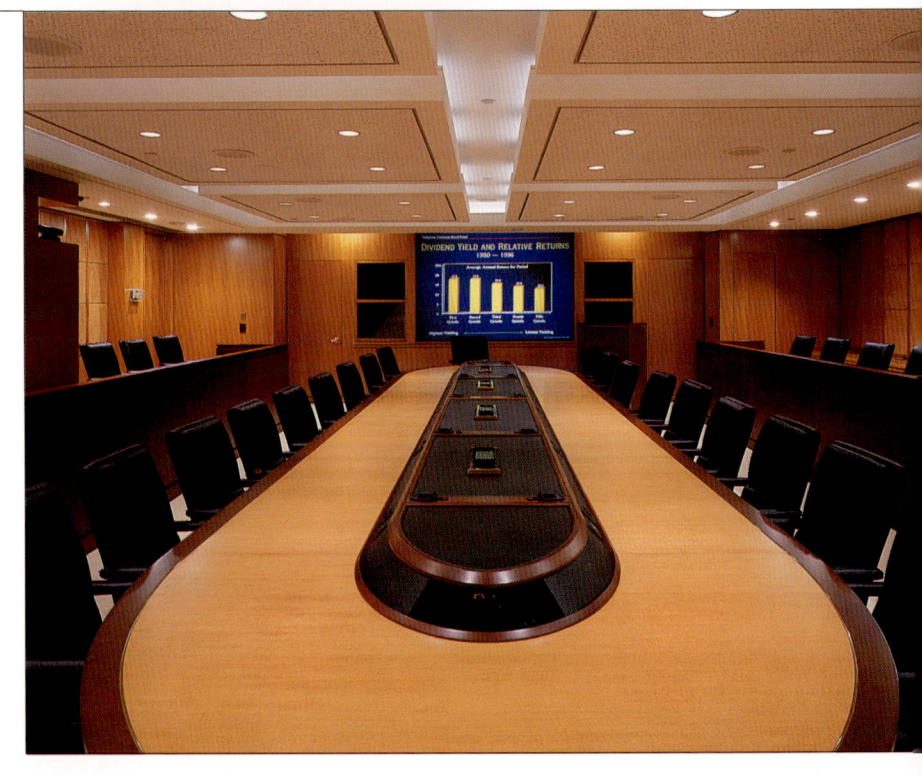

Kling Lindquist

2301 Chestnut Street
Philadelphia
Pennsylvania 19103
215.569.2900
215.569.5963 (Fax)
www.tklp.com

Kling Lindquist

Kling Lindquist

Deloitte & Touche LLP
Philadelphia, Pennsylvania

Right: A universal "hoteling" office.
Below: Common area with secretarial station.
Photography: Tom Crane.

Deloitte & Touche, one of the country's largest corporate accounting firms, has been experiencing a national change in its work culture. It has been experimenting with the concept of "hoteling" work areas shared by numbers of employees. In its 84,000-sq.-ft. Philadelphia offices, 28,000 sq. ft. divided among three floors were set aside for applying the concept to two of the firm's consulting groups. The design process began with a "hoteling" feasibility study comprising focus groups and interviews to determine daily work routines and analyze support requirements. These led in turn to the provision of identically sized perimeter offices, cockpit offices, team areas, conference rooms, and informal drop-in areas, all encouraging employee interaction. These general support functions are supplemented with an employee service center, an in-house travel agent, and a full-time concierge, whose duties include scheduling the occupancy of the "hoteled" offices and distributing files and personal items to those offices prior to the arrival of the occupants. Remarkably, this thorough renovation occurred in a two-phase construction process during which the offices continued to be occupied.

Above, right: An "interaction hub."
Right: One of the team areas.

Kling Lindquist

GE Capital Mortgage Services Inc.
Cherry Hill, New Jersey

Left: View of the main lobby.
Left, below: The information display in another part of the lobby.
Left, bottom of page: Display "kiosks" near the elevator lobby.

The new CEO of this mortgage financing firm directed Kling Lindquist to create a dignified, contemporary environment to reflect her vision of the firm's culture. Within this directive, an existing first-floor lobby had to be divided to create independent lobby areas for two major building tenants, and an information display system had to be developed to eliminate disparate graphic clutter. The redesigned public spaces occupy about 3,500 sq. ft. The designers' solution opposes two new freestanding arc-shaped wall elements to an existing circular ceiling feature. These wall elements are constucted of English sycamore, their curves emphasized by darker bands of American cherry, and their concave sides shelter and define the two waiting areas without fully enclosing them. For the ancillary elevator lobbies, rows of similarly detailed display "kiosks" create separate exhibition zones; they incorporate full-height tackable surfaces to accommodate company posters and notices within limited areas. The largely monochromatic palette, deriving visual interest from textural variety, includes Breccia Travera marble, Roman travertine, Grey Buff limestone, broadloom carpeting, and both painted and fabric-covered wall surfaces. The installation has earned a 1999 Award for Corporate Interiors from the Pennsylvania East chapter of the American Society of Interior Designers.

Above Visitor seating in the main lobby.
Right: The lobby's sweeping walls.
Photography: Jeffrey Totaro of Tom Crane Photography.

Kling Lindquist

Reliance Insurance Co.
Philadelphia, Pennsylvania

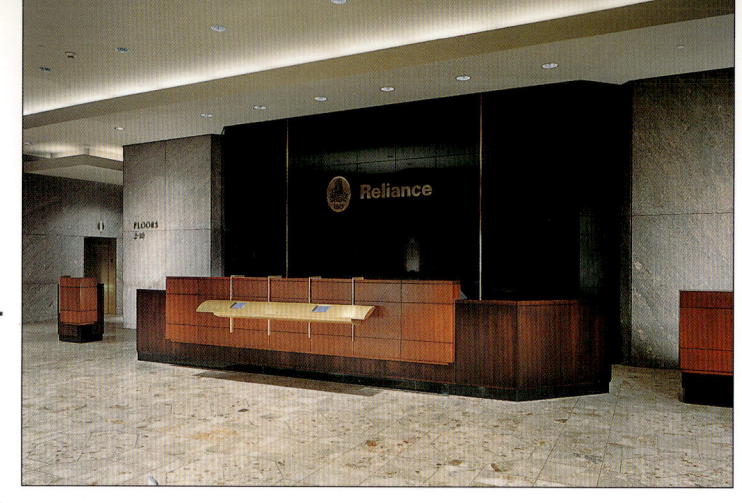

Reliance, a nationally known insurance company, wanted to maintain its strong — but understated — presence in the heart of Philadelphia. It bought a prominently located 21-story, 440,000-sq.-ft. building constructed in 1970 and asked Kling Lindquist to undertake a comprehensive renovation. This entailed a new building lobby, renovation of all elevator lobbies and core elements including restrooms, a cafeteria and servery, a private dining room, fitness center, training center, conference rooms, data center, executive suite, extensive office areas, and support areas. In all, 1,200 Reliance employees are accommodated in the newly designed quarters. Kling Lindquist's services began with space planning, included interior architecture and engineering, and extended to details such as the design of custom lighting fixtures and elevator call lanterns. Because the building's floor-to-floor dimension of 11'-1" was

Top of page: Main building lobby.
Above: Main elevator lobby.
Left: Executive floor conference room.
Photography: Tom Crane.

small by current standards, careful above-the-ceiling planning was required to coordinate new power supplies, a new sprinkler system, and new exhaust ducts while still keeping ceiling heights at their maximum. In some places, an open grid ceiling system with black masking above suggests a taller height than actually exists. Suiting the client's image, furnishings throughout are traditional or transitional in character, color schemes are conservative, and the materials palette includes wood, porcelain panels, ceramic tiles, carpet tiles, granite, bronze, and brass.

Top of page: Executive floor elevator lobby.
Above: Executive floor reception area.
Right: An executive floor corridor.

Above: Reliance Insurance's cafeteria dining space.
Right: The servery for the cafeteria.
Right, below: Exercise equipment in part of the employee fitness center.

Lehman-Smith+McLeish PLLC

1150 Eighteenth Street, NW
Suite 350
Washington, DC 20036
202.263.7400
202.263.7404 (Fax)

Lehman-Smith+McLeish PLLC

Dechert Price & Rhoads
Washington, DC

Right: Breakout seating area with conference room beyond.
Below: Reception area with lounge seating and pearwood desk.
Photography: Jon Miller © Hedrich Blessing

The client, a Washington law firm, sought the help of Lehman-Smith+McLeish in moving their firm into smaller — and therefore necessarily more efficient — offices. The new quarters occupy a total of 47,000 sq. ft. spread over three floors and accommodate 120 employees. Under the new plan attorneys are allotted 620 sq. ft. To maximize the usability of the space, corridors have been kept at minimal width; they are enlivened, however, by serving as galleries for the client's expanded art collection. Support services have been clustered in the centers of the floors, as have conference rooms, leaving the perimeter for office use. Glass sidelights in these offices allow light penetration to corridors and secretarial stations. Creating a dramatic first impression, the reception area and other public spaces have been given Calcutta white marble floors and wall cladding.

Within the marble floors, a custom carpet is inset, defining a waiting area furnished with leather lounge furniture. The wall behind the reception desk is faced with pearwood. In other parts of the office, the materials of the reception room reappear, but only as accents, creating unity while respecting the client's budget restrictions. Other prominent materials used throughout are etched glass, high-gloss lacquer, and trim of polished stainless steel, and the color palette has been limited to black and white with accents of bright red. The light finishes and the minimal details contribute to a pervasive sense of space, despite the planning limitations.

Above, right: Employee café features a panelized aluminum wall.
Right: Expandable conference room with custom conference table.

171

Lehman-Smith+McLeish PLLC

Howrey & Simon
Menlo Park, California

With existing offices in Washington and Los Angeles, both already designed by Lehman-Smith+McLeish (LSM), the Howrey & Simon law firm wanted to expand its practice and improve service to its West coast client base. It leased a two-floor, 40,000 sq. ft. space in Silicon Valley's Stanford Research Institute at Menlo Park, but the lease was short-term, leading to a desire to minimize capital expenditures on the building. At the same time, the firm wanted the same high level of finish and detail LSM had provided in its earlier quarters. The designers satisfied the demands for both independence from the building shell and quality appearance by designing — in conjunction with a national furniture manufacturer, Steelcase Wood — a furniture system based on interchangeable components. Elements of the system, in different configurations, serve the requirements of all the office's 90 employees, including legal secretaries, clerks, legal assistants, associates, and partners. The system's flexibility also supports reconfigurations for the firm's cross-teaming work processes and insures adaptability to a more permanent setting in the future. In addition to the furniture system, LSM has employed French limestone pavers, pearwood, fluted glass, high-gloss lacquer, and stainless steel. A stair connecting the two levels is graced with a double-height panel of book-matched St. Laurent marble.

Above: Courtyard view.
Below, left: Breakout seating area, with conference room beyond.
Below, center: Group of open office spaces.
Below, right: An attorney office.
Right: Reception area stair.
Photography:
Jon Miller © Hedrich Blessing

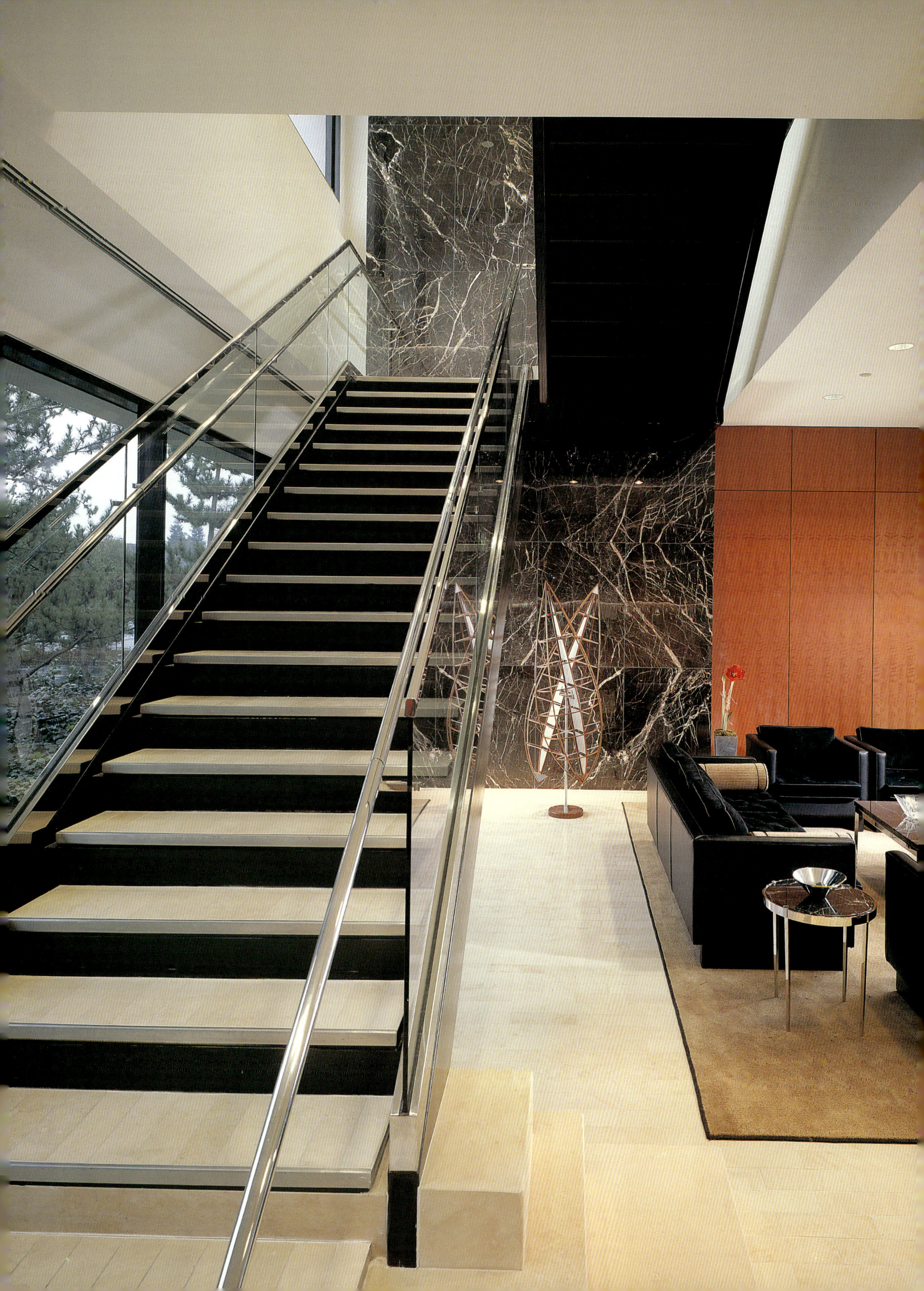

Lehman-Smith+McLeish PLLC

General Dynamics
Falls Church, Virginia

General Dynamics, a leading defense contractor, had kept its executive offices until recently in St. Louis, even though its corporate headquarters and its chief client base — the federal government and specifically the Pentagon — had long been in Washington. Consolidating in completely reconfigured quarters in suburban Washington, the corporation now occupies three administrative levels and one executive level housing a total of 120 employees in 65,000 sq. ft. The reconfiguration was in accordance with a long-term plan developed by Lehman-Smith+McLeish (LSM), who also provided programming, space planning, workplace analysis, and comprehensive interior design services. Executing these last-mentioned services, LSM employed a simple modern aesthetic to suggest the client's progressive nature. Complementing this aesthetic, LSM incorporated a significant contemporary art and graphics program that centers on information about the client's history and is emphasized by the installation's lighting design. More comprehensive is

Above: Chairman's office with custom desk design and lounge seating area.
Right: Reception area with leather seating group.
Photography: Jon Miller © Hedrich Blessing

Left: Private dining area with view into circulation corridor.
Right: Boardroom table has integrated audiovisual technology.

a prominently placed "history wall" graphically depicting highlights of General Dynamics's past accomplishments. Its current accomplishments and technological expertise are alluded to in seamlessly equipped conference rooms and in the boardroom with its state-of-the-art digital and audio-visual equipment. A training center is similarly well equipped. Support areas and amenities include an executive dining facility with a private dining room. Colors throughout are neutral, and a materials palette of high quality includes Macassar ebony wood panels, high-gloss lacquer, French limestone pavers, textured glass screens and sidelights, and — adding a final bright fillip — stainless steel trim.

Right: The "history wall" illustrates the accomplishments of General Dynamics.
Below: The training room with posters from the company's past.

Little & Associates Architects

5815 Westpark Drive
Charlotte
North Carolina 28217
704.525.6350
704.561.8700 (Fax)

4309 Emperor Boulevard
Suite 220
Durham
North Carolina 27703
704.525.6350
704.561.8700 (Fax)

Sequoia Plaza
2120 Washington Boulevard
Suite 360
Arlington
Virginia 22204
703.486.4501
703.486.4502 (Fax)

One Penn Square West
Suite 1801
30 South 15th Street
Philadelphia
Pennsylvania 19102
215.832.1101
215.832.1102 (Fax)

One Summit Plaza
5727 South Lewis Street
Suite 300
Tulsa
Oklahoma 74105
918.293.2000
918.293.2002 (Fax)

129 Bonifant Road
Silver Spring
Maryland 20905
301.879.3261
301.879.3262 (Fax)

Little & Associates Architects

BB&T Center for Little & Company
Charlotte, North Carolina

The BB&T Center in downtown Charlotte is a mid-day destination for center city office workers and tourists and a major link between two adjacent buildings with similar public spaces. BB&T's heavily trafficked corridor provides space for retail establishments, restaurants, and professional services. Little & Associates was asked by BB&T's owners, Little & Company, to completely redesign 24,000 sq. ft. of its public spaces, but to do so without interruption of public access. Work was therefore done in several phases, and care was taken to minimize disturbance to existing tenants. New flooring surfaces are chiefly of travertine with accents of noce and black slate. Walls are of maple veneer with metal detailing and regularly spaced reveals, and they meet the floor with a slate base and travertine wain-

Above: Corridor with bas-relief panels on right.
Right: Elevator lobby with custom wall and ceiling light fixtures.
Photography: Tim Buchman.

scot. The focal point of the space at a circulation intersection is a bowed accent wall of travertine that is the background for a series of terra cotta panels sculptured in low relief; they tell the story of the building's owners and their enterprises. Custom-designed lighting fixtures — ceiling-mounted pendants and wall-mounted sconces — incorporate abstractions of the building logo. Ceiling planes have been artfully shaped, some in convex forms, others concave, to add variety to the pedestrian experience, and way-finding graphics provide orientation for center city visitors.

Right, above: Travertine and slate flooring in corridor.
Right: Curved, perforated metal ceiling treatment in corridor.

Little & Associates Architects

First Union Corporation Customer Information Center
Charlotte, North Carolina

Below: The corporate fitness facility.
Bottom of page, left: 75-seat conference room with tiered seating.
Bottom of page, right: Auditorium can seat 575.
Photography: Stan Capps.

First Union is a leading bank holding company, and its 2.1-million-sq.-ft. Customer Information Center is one of the nation's largest single office buildings, second only to the Pentagon. In a suburban Charlotte location, it houses almost 10,000 employees of First Union's operations divisions. As architect of record, Little & Associates managed the entire project, provided all base building architecture and the interior design for all public spaces.

Because of the large number of employees on site, First Union was able to offer an unusual array of amenities within these spaces. Among these are one of the largest daycare centers in the country, a complete retail mall, and a branded vendor food court. A full-service fitness center has a floating oak aerobics floor and offers free weights and an array of exercise machines. A small, tiered auditorium accommodates 75 with electronic voting and teleconferencing capabilities, and a larger 575-seat auditorium serves as meeting space for employee groups, visitors, stockholders, and other audiences. In all cases, design attention has been extended by Little & Associates to all visible surfaces, including a variety of dramatically expressive ceiling treatments and the incorporation of appropriate lighting.

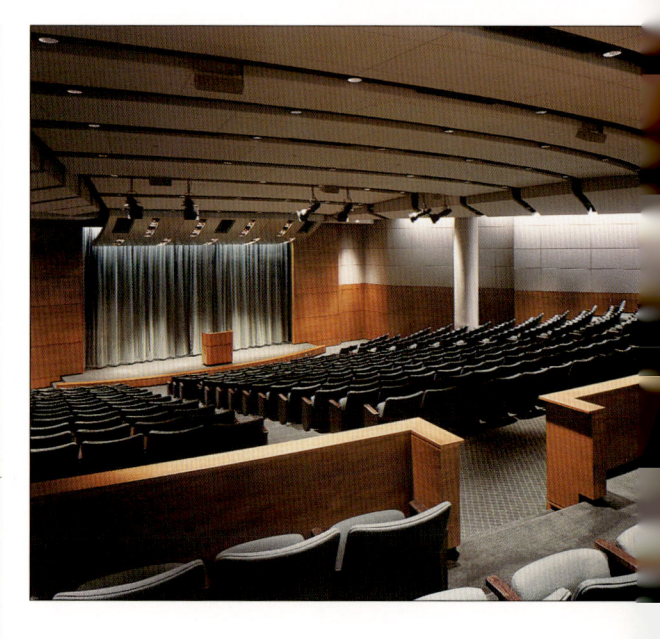

Above: Reception desk for the fitness center.
Right: Food court is one of two main dining facilities.

Little & Associates Architects

**McDevitt Street Bovis
Corporate Headquarters
Charlotte, North Carolina**

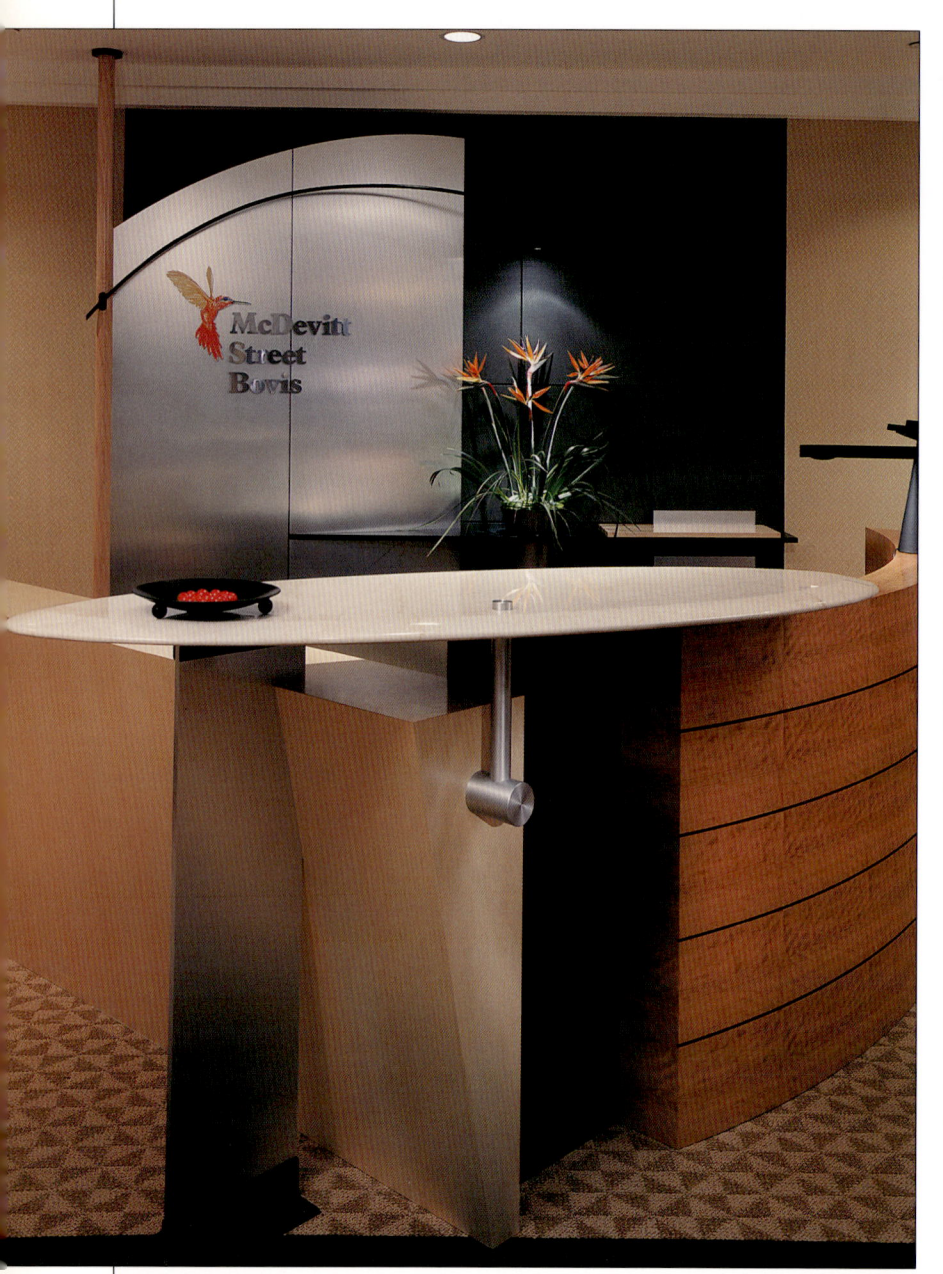

Above: *Pendant fixture over conference table.*
Left: *Reception desk.*
Below, left: *Individual open workstations.*
Below: *Stair with main conference room beyond.*

182

Right: Curved steel stair with seating area for visitors in the first floor lobby.
Photography: Tim Buchman.

Charlotte-based McDevitt Street Bovis is a construction firm of international scope and reputation. Little & Associates recently completed its 42,000 sq.-ft. corporate headquarters. Client and designers alike wanted the facility to emphasize the intrinsic artistry within the common building materials that are the mainstay of construction, and this philosophy has been pursued throughout, particularly in the design of the lobby, reception areas, conference rooms, and other public spaces. A variety of rich woods, suggesting the range of McDevitt Street Bovis's materials vocabulary, is juxtaposed with brushed steel, aluminum, marble, and glass, all this deliberately designed to dominate a more recessive neutral backdrop of cream carpeting and pale wall surfaces. Furnishings, too, are understated. Most dramatic of all the elements in this composition is a freestanding curved stair executed in brushed steel; the central focus of the main lobby, the stair is a testimony to the client's daring, skill, engineering knowledge, and meticulous attention to detail. This corporate headquarters, therefore, serves eloquently as an advertisement without words.

Little & Associates Architects

**Bank of America
Executive Offices
Interstate Johnson Lane Tower
Charlotte, North Carolina**

Left: Bank of America's executive "brainstorming room."
Left, below: Main corridor among executive offices.
Photography: Stan Capps.

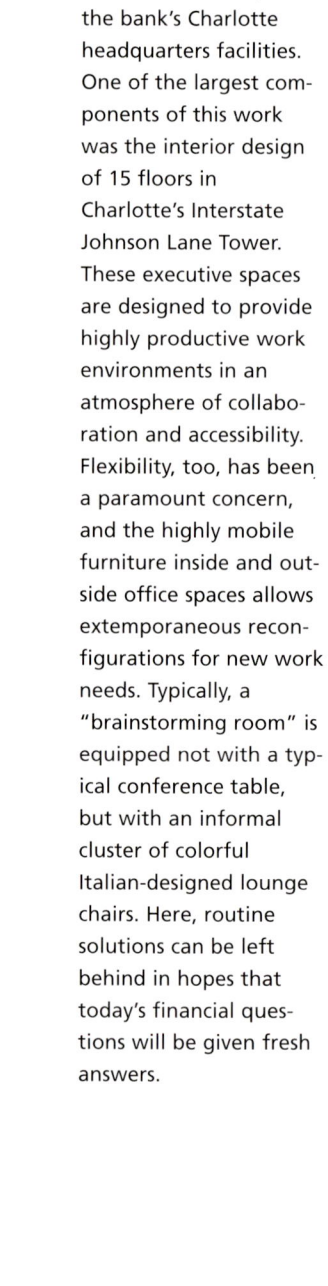

Little & Associates Architects and the Bank of America's real estate partner, The Trammell Crow Company, have together provided build-out services for more than 3.6 million sq. ft. in the bank's Charlotte headquarters facilities. One of the largest components of this work was the interior design of 15 floors in Charlotte's Interstate Johnson Lane Tower. These executive spaces are designed to provide highly productive work environments in an atmosphere of collaboration and accessibility. Flexibility, too, has been a paramount concern, and the highly mobile furniture inside and outside office spaces allows extemporaneous reconfigurations for new work needs. Typically, a "brainstorming room" is equipped not with a typical conference table, but with an informal cluster of colorful Italian-designed lounge chairs. Here, routine solutions can be left behind in hopes that today's financial questions will be given fresh answers.

Looney Ricks Kiss

88 Union Avenue
Suite 900
Memphis
Tennessee 38103
901.521.1440
901.525.2760 (Fax)

Memphis
Nashville
Princeton

Looney Ricks Kiss

Looney Ricks Kiss

CB Richard Ellis
Memphis, Tennessee

Right: Entrance to the reception area.
Below: Corner of main conference room, with reception area beyond.
Photography: Scott McDonald © Hedrich Blessing.

Having outgrown office space that Looney Ricks Kiss (LRK) had designed for them six years earlier, CB Richard Ellis (formerly known as CB Commercial/Interstate Realty Corporation) again retained the firm for a full scope of architecture and design services — including graphic design — for their new offices. These occupy 7,700 sq. ft. in a new Memphis building, and they accommodate two dozen employees. A long lease was signed, so the client wanted an interior design that would serve for years without becoming dated, and a requested change from the previous design was for fewer private offices, more open workstation areas. Glass walls for the offices, the boardroom, and the "living room" conference space (using the Blumcraft glazing system) lend an open feeling and allow daylight to penetrate spaces far from the window wall. Veneers of harewood and mahogany have been used throughout the installation, including the boardroom table custom designed by LRK. Other materials include Absolute black granite and leather upholstery, and the general color scheme is light and neutral. The installation won for LRK the Gold Award in the 1998 architectural corporate design program of the American Society of Interior Designers, Tennessee chapter.

Top of page, right: Open office area with private offices at right.
Right: Private office with custom furniture.

Looney Ricks Kiss

FedEx
World Technology Center
Collierville, Tennessee

The FedEx World Technology Center is the new home of the overnight-delivery giant's Information Technology Division. Previously, the division's employees had been spread among several physically separate sites. FedEx wanted a consolidation that would provide a collaborative environment for Internet computing development and that would be an asset in the recruitment and retention of the best and brightest "knowledge workers." The campus is being developed in two phases. Phase I, seen here, consists of a three-story central services (or "core") building and four identical two-story office buildings, the five

Far left: Typical building lobby.
Left: Central building lobby.
Below, left: Employee dining room.
Below: Training room break-out workspaces.
Bottom of page: View towards the coffee bar and "Express Room."

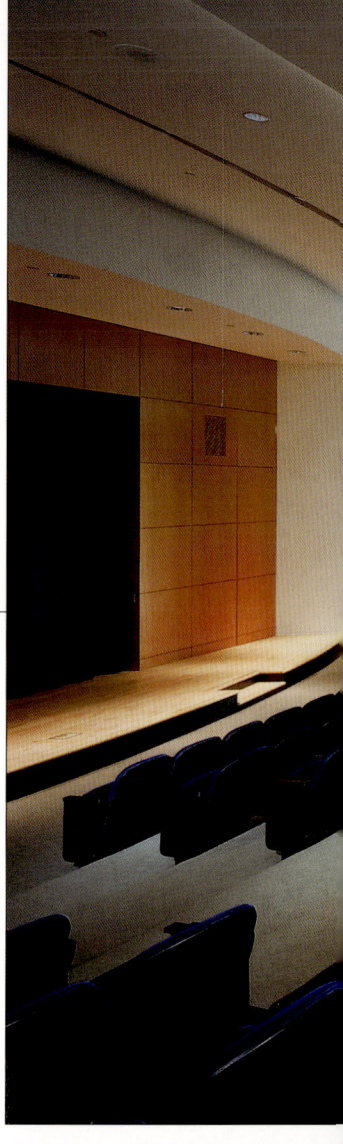

188

Above: Training auditorium.
Right: The "Express Room."
Photography: Jon Miller © Hedrich Blessing.

units totaling over half a million sq. ft. Phase II will consist of four more two-story office buildings totaling an additional 400,000 sq. ft. Altogether, 3,000 FedEx employees will be accommodated. The core building of Phase I includes a reception area, a full-service cafeteria with both indoor and outdoor dining, a 300-seat auditorium, a sundry/gift shop, a credit association, a print shop, a training center, a copy center, computer labs, and an Information Technology resource room, as well as private offices. Each office building contains work space, of course, and also an "Express Room" for impromptu meetings, equipped with a large whiteboard for noting ideas in a teamwork environment. Lounges adjacent to the conference rooms have multiple computer terminals for easy e-mail checks. The entire campus, in fact, is interactive, with employees free to use their laptops wherever they feel comfortable.

189

Looney Ricks Kiss

AutoZone Corporate Headquarters
Memphis, Tennessee

Right: View of lobby from parking connector.
Far right: Three-story lobby.
Below: Typical private office.
Photography: Marco Lorenzetti © Hedrich-Blessing.

Top of page: part of the eight-story stair.
Above: View from private office towards open workstations.
Above, right: Circulation spine with gallery alcoves at right and a conference room at the end.

This 270,000-sq.-ft. corporate headquarters for the nation's largest auto parts retailer has been a multiple award winner for LRK. Honors include a Merit Award from the Gulf States region of the American Institute of Architects, an Award of Honor in New Construction from the Memphis chapter of the AIA, and a Competition Award from the Tennessee chapter of the American Society of Interior Designers. As these varied awards suggest, LRK performed a full range of services here, including the architecture of a new building, its space planning, and its interior design. The site, in the historic cotton district of downtown Memphis, is on the bluffs of the Mississippi River, but it contained an unsightly garage and required construction with seismically resistant foundations. The LRK solution was an eight-story building on seismic base isolation; its exterior walls have been faced with limestone-colored precast concrete and have been given appropriate fenestration patterns to harmonize with the historic structures nearby. A generous glass wall takes advantage of the spectacular river views, as does a 10,000-sq.-ft. terrace atop the structure. Inside, the three-floor-high main lobby is dominated by a monumental stair connecting to the parking garage, now renovated to match the new structure. This lobby space, with the river as its backdrop, provides the client-mandated single point of entry and security control. Elsewhere, an equally monumental stair connects all eight floors of office space, facilitating interdepartmental communication.

191

Left: The AutoZone Corporate Headquarters boardroom.
Below: Part of the employee dining room.

On typical floors, a standardized central core holds conference rooms and support services, with private offices along exterior walls. A main corridor runs from one end of the building to the other, terminating with the river view, which is thereby shared by all employees in their travels through the building. The elevator core and service centers for copying and coffee are located off this chief corridor, and alcoves along it serve as prominent gallery space for AutoZone's corporate art collection. Despite the building's spatial drama, its materials palette has been kept simple and inexpensive: terrazzo, carpet, metal, glass, beech veneer doors, and painted gypsum board. And colors reflect those of the AutoZone corporate logo: red, orange, black, and gray.

LPA, Inc.

1/848 Sky Park Circle
Irvine
California 92614
949.261.1001
949.260.1190 (Fax)

LPA, Inc.

FileNET
Regional Headquarters
Kirkland, Washington

For FileNET, a computer software corporation, LPA, Inc., has designed four 22,000 sq. ft. floors totaling 90,000 sq. ft. in a new building in Kirkland, Washington. The facility accommodates approximately 250 employees and their visitors, and includes a reception area, private offices, training rooms, an audiovisual presentation room, a data center, and breakrooms. These breakrooms double as game rooms and snack bars, where staff members can grab a soda, play a game of pinball, and share ideas. For the office space, the client wanted closed, private offices for most of the staff, yet the overall character desired was "open and airy, with lots of daylight." Offices with solid walls were therefore located near the centers of the floors, with views outward towards the shared perimeter window walls. Offices were also organized into neighborhoods, and the neighborhoods were alternated with the breakrooms and other spaces for chance meetings and conversations. Many of these, equipped with whiteboards, laptops, and stool seating, encourage on-the-spot collaboration. Woods throughout are maple and cherry, and other materials include glass, limestone, loop pile carpet, and brushed stainless steel.

Above: Interconnecting stair at the breakroom.
Above, left: Reception and visitor waiting area.
Left: Staff breakroom.

Above: Corporate image and identity in the reception area.
Right: Client presentations and new product demonstrations are made with multi-media technology.
Photography: Robert Pisano.

LPA, Inc.

Mission Imports
Laguna Niguel, California

Right: New car delivery area and customer lounge.
Far right: The pre-owned automobile showroom.
Below: Some of the 60 service bays.
Below, right: The main showroom space.
Photography: Adrian Velicescu.

196

Mission Imports is a large Mercedes-Benz dealership in the oceanfront town of Laguna Niguel. LPA, Inc., was asked to provide the company with a wide range of design services including site planning, architecture, landscaping, interior architecture, and signage/graphic design. The total square footage is 90,000, composed of a 10,000-sq.-ft. new car showroom, a 6,000-sq.-ft. pre-owned car showroom, sales and administration offices, parts storage, an accessory sales area, and 60 service bays, these last all built to Mercedes-Benz's own exacting standards. The chosen site is a dramatic linear stretch of land along the Interstate 5 freeway, offering roadside exposure but necessitating design care in making the building and its automobiles visible to fast-moving traffic. The LPA solution is crisp, sleek, and simple, providing a refined but neutral backdrop for the automobiles. Dramatic custom lighting fixtures were also designed to highlight the sparkling finishes of the cars, and a projection system was built-in to display changing images on the showroom walls. The design was a 1997 Merit Award winner and a 1999 Honor Award winner from the Orange County Chapter of the American Institute of Architects.

LPA, Inc.

EPT Landscape Architects
San Juan Capistrano, California

Right: Reception area designed around the existing bank vault door.
Below: Conference room on mezzanine level.
Below, right: Circulation spine.
Photography: Scott Rothwall.

Designed by LPA, Inc., in collaboration with the client and with John Chipman, AIA, this design studio for EPT Landscape Architects is a thorough renovation of a vacated branch bank building. Thorough, that is, except for the unmovable bank vault and its monumental door. The vault space itself was converted to restrooms, entered from another side, and the door was retained and polished as an effective "conversation piece" for the reception and visitor waiting area. A mezzanine level above the vault was converted to conference room use, its concrete walls cleaned by sandblasting and then stained and sealed, and a new stair was built along the exposed brick wall for better access. The rest of the space was long and narrow with very few windows, so care had to be taken to maximize exposure to the precious element of daylight. The staff of 16 is organized into teams in open work spaces along a central corridor, and other facilities include private offices, workstations for support staff, a reference library, and a print room. The total area is 3900 sq. ft.

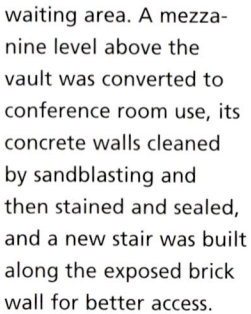

LPA, Inc.

Paramount Park K-8 School
Paramount, California

Above: Bold colors and forms in the auditorium.
Above, right: The administration office.
Below: Science lab desks face a teaching wall.
Photography: Adrian Velicescu.

Built for 20 percent less than its budget and on a 16-month schedule, Paramount Park is a school for over 800 students from the kindergarten level through the 8th grade. It occupies a total of 45,300 sq. ft., and, in addition to classrooms, it contains science labs, art labs, a computer lab, a library, administrative offices, and a large auditorium/multipurpose room. These facilities have been clustered in a series of separate "villages" connected by an arcade and centered on courtyards designed as "outdoor rooms." Kids meet here on a less formal basis than in the classrooms, but planning keeps these areas safe and secure. Interior spaces are animated with bold colors and geometrics, and finishes throughout are appropriately durable and cost effective — sealed colored concrete, loop pile carpeting, vinyl composition tile, and vinyl wallcoverings. Deep-cell parabolic light fixtures in classrooms and office areas minimize glare. The client was the Paramount Unified School District, and services for it by LPA, Inc., included programming, space planning, architecture, landscape design, and interior design.

LPA, Inc.

Playmates Toys, Inc. Corporate Headquarters
Costa Mesa, California

Playmates is a toy company, but it is a serious business. The proper image for its 27,000 sq. ft. corporate headquarters, therefore, was considered by LPA, Inc., to be professional, not childlike. Yet there is nothing dour or excessively formal in these two floors of open work areas and private offices. Interaction, the designers say, is the key to their concept development, expressed in floor patterns that make a transition to wall elements and continue to ceiling planes. Granite planes continue from one space into the next, subtly relevant to the interactions of children with toys and to the cooperation of employees in creating toys. The materials thus manipulated include foot-square granite tiles, carpet, plaster, durable wallcoverings, and paneling of cherry veneer. The offices accommodate 100 Playmates employees and their visitors.

Above: Curved wall in an open work area.
Above, right: The reception area.
Right: The boardroom adjacent to the reception area.
Photography: Jim Brady.

Mancini•Duffy

Two World Trade Center
Suite 2110
New York
New York 10048
212.938.1260
212.938.1267 (Fax)
info@manciniduffy.com

Mancini•Duffy

ITG Inc.
New York, New York

Right: Elevator lobby, looking towards reception area.
Below: The board room with teleconferencing capability.

The investment management firm of ITG Inc. needed to relocate its Manhattan quarters to an office building offering 17 watts per sq. ft. of power (rather than the standard 9 watts). The chosen building had the problem of low beams, however, and the need to raise the floors to accommodate necessary wiring compounded the problem of low ceiling heights. Creative solutions were called for. One of these, in the 60-person trading room, was an arching form, its low points covering the beams and its higher parts serving as reflectors for ambient lighting. The use of low dividing partitions (48 inches high) also contributes to an impression of spaciousness, as do the glass fronts on the private offices. The overall visual effect is of warm neutral colors and natural tones. Light panel fabrics contrast with black workstation elements, and other prominent materials are natural maple and stainless steel. At the completion of the project, ITG Vice President Susan L. Nelson wrote to Mancini•Duffy project designer Ilene Bernstein, "The office is beautiful; everyone is very pleased to be in such a lovely space. More importantly, the legwork we did up front with the program ensured that the space works effectively for the people who come in to do their jobs everyday. And that is probably the biggest accomplishment - to design space that is as attractive as it is functional." The design has won an Award of Honor from the Fourth Annual Design Awards Program of the Society of American Registered Architects, New York Council.

Right: *Glass-walled private offices and corridor.*
Photography: Peter Paige.

Mancini•Duffy

Investment Firm
New York, New York

Above: Elevator lobby.
Left: Foyer, looking towards typical doorway with glass transom and sidelight.
Left, below: Secretarial corridor enjoys a variety of lighting effects.

For this New York investment firm, Mancini•Duffy performed a comprehensive range of services, including programming, the development of space use standards, design development, construction documentation, and field and contract administration. The installation houses 32 employees in a single-floor area of 20,000 sq. ft. atop a Park Avenue highrise, the space having been chosen in part because of its generous ceiling height.

A major design determinant was the accommodation of the client's collection of antiques, building models, and large-scale Beaux Arts drawings. In addition to height, contributions to this accommodation were a color scheme of rich tones and patterns and a materials palette including Australian lacewood, English bluestone, and Neoclad, a glass wall surfacing more often used for exterior walls but offering an attractive reflective sheen in the elevator lobby. The owner's collection was further enhanced by the lighting (with Susan Brady acting as lighting consultant), including display spotlights picking out key objects and carefully calculated general light levels. The four corners of the floor plate have been given to the boardroom and three conference rooms, allowing the best views to be shared by the staff. Two reception areas were created, one for the executive office area and another for the boardroom and private dining room. The design has earned an Honorable Mention from the Fourth Annual Design Awards Program of the Society of American Registered Architects, New York Council.

Above: Administrative assistant's area, with views into a conference room and a private office.
Photography: Durston Saylor.

Mancini•Duffy

ING Barings LLC
New York, New York

For this 400,000-sq.-ft. facility on nine floors and a mezzanine of a New York building, Mancini•Duffy began work with the merger of ING, a Dutch diversified financial company, and Barings, a British investment company; in the course of the project, the scope expanded when the company acquired the international investment bank Furman Selz. One obvious goal, therefore, was to recognize but unify the three different corporate cultures within a single workplace. Accommodating approximately 1200 employees, including 465 on the trading floor, the facility includes reception areas, a multipurpose meeting room, eight conference

Above: The 465-person trading floor. Its custom lighting armatures provide uplighting into ceiling coffers.
Right: The executive reception area, with its luminous glass ceiling and partitions of textured glass and anigre
Photography: Peter Paige.

rooms, three teleconferencing rooms, three conference/dining rooms, five client dining rooms, an employee cafeteria, a full kitchen, and a training room. Office areas have an open-plan concept and, for flexibility, a universal workstation size, and the trading floor uses innovative flat screen technology.

Above: The clubroom's ceiling features theatrical fabric stretched on wire frames and lit from behind.
Right: In the elevator lobby, unique lighting solutions include call lanterns incorporated into the elevator door architecture.

Mancini•Duffy

Mitsui Trust & Banking Co., Ltd.
New York, New York

Left: *The elevator lobby with its lighting canopy and walls of back-painted glass.*
Left, below: *Conference room wall with shoji-like glazing effect.*
Photography:
Peter Paige.

For 150 employees of this international banking company, Mancini•Duffy has redesigned a full floor and another partial floor in a Manhattan building, totaling 50,000 sq. ft. A broad scope of design services was provided, beginning with assistance in site selection and extending to graphics and signage. In fact, Mitsui's own existing corporate logo, a symbol with a hatch of interlocking lines, served as the key to many of the interior's design motifs — not only other graphic devices but also flooring patterns and banded wall treatments. Because the client was moving here from fairly lavish quarters, there was a desire for the new space to have similar visual interest, yet there was a demand that such interest be realized economically; recognizing these budget concerns, Mancini•Duffy put design emphasis on the more public spaces and made every possible effort to re-use and integrate the client's existing furniture. Even so, some impressive effects have been achieved. The walls of the twin conference rooms, for example, are treated with panels of glass with an integral film, transmitting light but providing privacy and recalling the look of traditional Japanese shoji screens. The glass walls of the elevator lobby have been back-painted a pale green for another striking effect. Other colors are primarily neutrals, with accent walls of vivid plum. In addition to the lobby and conference rooms, there are private offices, general office spaces with open workstations, and a small conference room. Typical of the thoughtful planning throughout is the fact that the waiting area is behind the reception desk, giving visiting clients an impressive window view.

Mitchell Associates

One Avenue of the Arts
Wilmington
Delaware 19801
302.594.9400
302.656.7926 (Fax)
mitchell@mitchellai.com

Mitchell Associates

Kahunaville
Carousel Center
Syracuse, New York

Above: *Animatronic talking totem pole like wood carvings flank the restaurant entrance.*
Left: *Faux greenery abounds, as over this thatch-sheltered booth.*
Photography:
Ron Trinca

Left: Tropical nature theme extends to wall surfaces, tabletops, seating.
Below: Dancing waters are choreographed for 20 different tunes.
Bottom of page: A night sky is visible overhead.

For this client, a firm aptly named Adventure Dining, Mitchell Associates was asked to transform an oddly-shaped 27,000-sq.-ft. space in a Syracuse mall into a 450-seat restaurant and masquerading as a tropical paradise. In addition to the restaurant a bar, there is a 10,000-sq.-ft. arcade/midway/ game room area, and, of course, a kitchen. This Kahunaville has 250 employees or — a term coined by Disney — "cast members." For this is assuredly a theatrical environment, and its stars are not only its food — pastas, steaks, wraps, fish, and specialty drinks — but also its special effects — animatronic turtles, an animatronic octopus, palm trees, waterfalls, fountains, and talking tiki statues. Materials employed in creating this jungle fantasy are both real (such as kahuna rock and recycled barn siding) and make-believe (epoxy flooring, fiberglass castings, and glass fiber reinforced concrete). Two measures of the design's success are that it has received a "1999 Hot Concepts" Award from Nations Restaurants, and that Mitchell Associates has been retained to duplicate Kahunaville in Youngstown, Ohio, Buffalo, NY, Grandville, MI, and Holyoke, MA, and Adventure Dining owner David Z. Tuttleman is said to be actively looking for new locations.

211

Mitchell Associates

First USA Bank
Three Christina Center
Wilmington, Delaware

Above: A sculptured eagle, the bank's logo, marks the main entrance.
Left: The reception and visitor waiting area.
Left, below: The lobby offers facilities for check-in, information, or for filling out employment applications.
Photography: Barry Halkin.

The most obvious indication of client satisfaction in this case is the surest one of all: repeat business. For First USA Bank, formerly Mbank USA, Mitchell Associates has designed all the installations in Delaware, as well as at additional sites in Pennsylvania, Maryland, Indiana, and Florida. Of all these, this headquarters in Wilmington is the largest. It is a 14-floor building, with floor sizes ranging from 18,000 to 23,000 sq. ft, and with a total area of slightly more than 270,000 sq. ft., 90 percent of which is currently occupied by the bank. Facilities here include a main lobby with computerized visitor check-in desks, a customer service center, executive offices, administrative space, conference rooms, an employee cafeteria, a fitness center, and the bank's various operating departments. For their design, Mitchell Associates has performed a full range of services, beginning with programming and space planning, including budget specifications and construction documentation, graphic design, and supervision of an art program, and ending with coordination of a phased move-in. For all their First USA projects, Mitchell Associates has also performed the valuable services of developing a widely applicable standards program and, for every floor at every site, updated maintenance of comparative data in digital format. These services allow the swift fulfillment of the client's present needs and the accurate prediction of future ones.

Top of page: The corporate fitness center.
Above: An area for corporate conferencing and networking.
Left: Elevator lobby and entrance to the Partnership Marketing area.
Right: The multi-media and audiovisual room.

213

Mitchell Associates

The Eugene du Pont Preventive Medicine and Rehabilitation Institute
Wilmington, Delaware

This health care facility occupies a four-floor, 35,000-sq.-ft. building a few miles north of Wilmington that was once the residence of Eugene du Pont. It had been empty for decades until Mitchell Associates transformed its interior for its new uses, focusing on "wellness" and dedicated to encouraging patients to adopt healthier lifestyles. Specifically, the institute includes a main lobby, spaces for conferences and seminars, a series of rooms for individual examinations and doctor/patient consultations, administrative offices, a gift shop (selling educational books, CDs of soothing music, and health-conscious foods — *no candy*), a wood-paneled library (more educational books, plus computers for self-directed research on the web), a residential-style demonstration kitchen (where patients are taught to make healthy meals), a dining room (where sample meals can be served), a well-equipped fitness room, showers, and changing rooms furnished with wooden lockers. For more contemplative moments, there is a Yoga/meditation room, and outside there are walking paths among the gardens. It was of utmost importance to the client that the environment be a patient centered design. The design process was begun in April of 1996, and construction was completed in June of 1997, only 14 months later. And work continues: The most popular program of the institute, for Cardiac Rehabilitation, has already been expanded twice.

Left, below: The institute's main entrance.
Left, bottom of page: A patient examination room.
Below: The demonstration kitchen.
Photography: Barry Halkin.

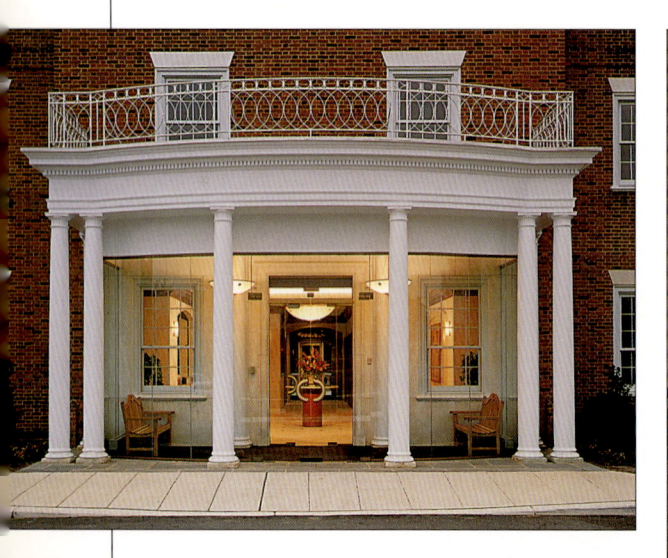

Top of page: Main lobby and reception area.
Right, above: The institute's dining area.
Right: The third floor exercise facility.

Mitchell Associates

First USA Bank
Pennsylvania Railroad Building
Wilmington, Delaware

Mitchell Associates' design for First USA Bank's Wilmington headquarters building has been shown on a previous spread. The installation seen here is one of several branches in the same city, this one housing two of First USA's fastest growing business groups, a total of 175 staff members. They are accommodated in renovated space on six levels of 7,500 sq. ft. each, a total of 45,000 sq. ft., and throughout the design's emphasis is on openness and flexibility. Closed office space is anathema here, in fact, open plan workstations have been used almost exclusively, resulting in great economies in the use of the limited space available. Multi-purpose rooms function well for presentations, for large or small meetings, for informal team chats, or even for employee breaks. And the "Mega-Byte" café, accommodates a number of different functions such as dining, informal meetings, and small presentations.

Top of page: General work area.
Above: Multi-functional room can accommodate team meetings, presentations, or breaks.
Right, above: The main reception area.
Right: The "Mega-Byte" café.
Photography: Barry Halkin.

Mojo•Stumer
Associates, P.C.

55 Bryant Avenue
Roslyn
New York 11576
516.625.3344
516.625.3418 (Fax)

Mojo•Stumer Associates, P.C.

Omni Building
Garden City, New York

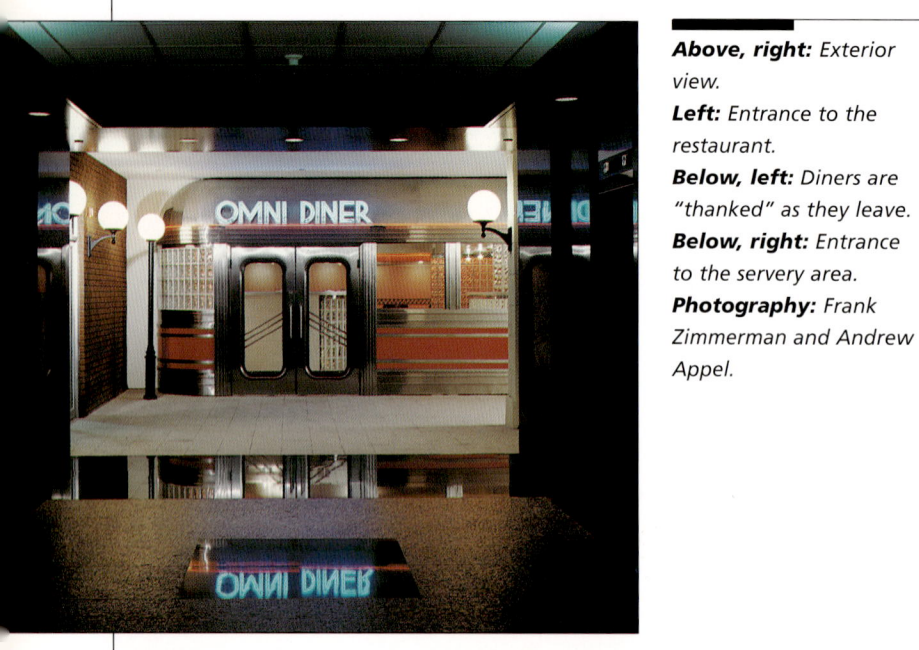

Above, right: Exterior view.
Left: Entrance to the restaurant.
Below, left: Diners are "thanked" as they leave.
Below, right: Entrance to the servery area.
Photography: Frank Zimmerman and Andrew Appel.

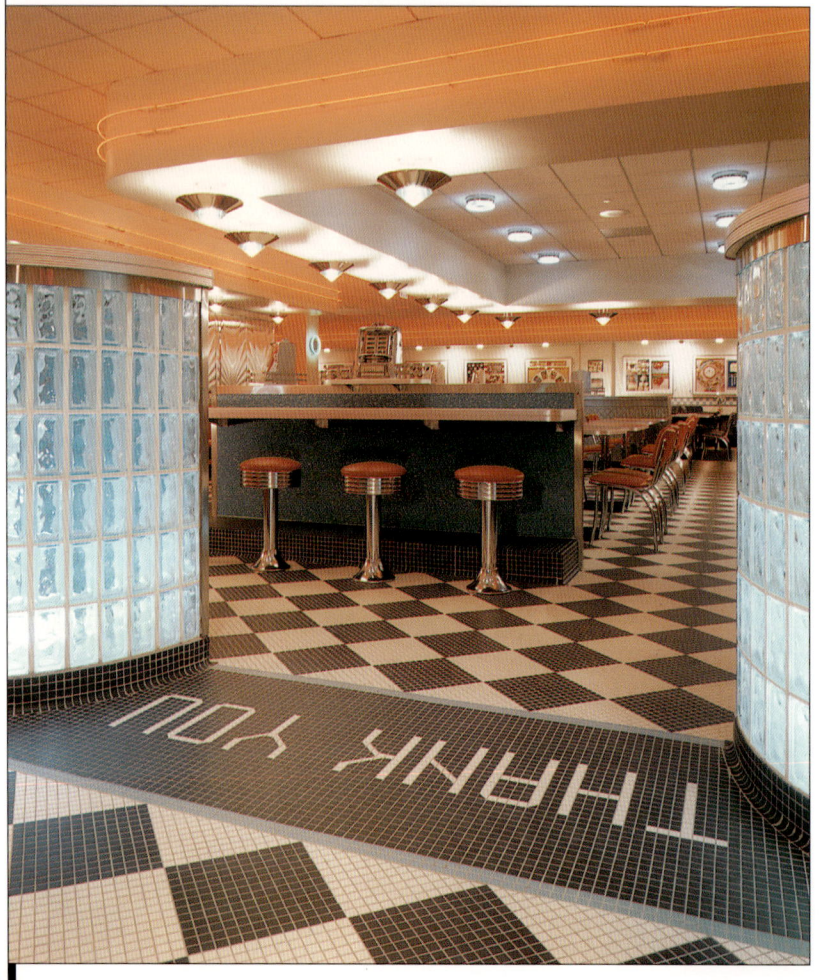

Right: Booth and counter seating in the restaurant.
Below, left: The fitness area with pool beyond.
Below, right: Glass-walled teleconferencing center.

For the development company Reckson Associates, Mojo•Stumer developed this new 650,000 sq. ft. office building in Garden City, Long Island, NY, providing both the architecture of the base building and interiors for a number of interior facilities. These included a cafeteria/lunchroom intended to attract both executives and their support staffs. A theme of a 1950s-style diner was adopted and carried through from the sheet-metal and glass block entrance façade to the counters, stools, lighting fixtures and neon strips, and surfaces and details throughout.

The result, the designers say, is a "total success," attracting not only all levels of workers within the building, but also those from other buildings nearby. Other facilities provided were a lobby/reception area, a well-equipped fitness center visually open to an adjacent indoor pool, and a number of meeting rooms. These last include a teleconferencing center that, in contrast to the playful "retro" character of the lunchroom, demanded a serious corporate feeling expressive of the technology it offers. The design of the whole has earned Mojo•Stumer an award from the Long Island chapter of the American Institute of Architects.

219

Mojo•Stumer Associates, P.C.

Motor Parkway
Corporate Center
Hauppauge, New York

For this new 220,000-sq.-ft. office building on Long Island, Mojo•Stumer provided not only the architecture, the interior design of all the public spaces, and the graphic design; the firm also acted as artists, providing the three-dimensional mural that animates the triple-height lobby space around which the building is centered. At first glance, the mural is composed of purely abstract geometry, but on closer inspection it is seen to be derived from the building's own floor plan and site plan, as well as from the underlying structural elements. The result, reportedly, was "very well received." Beneath the mural, a glass-walled dining area overlooks the lobby space, and other features within it are balcony parapets and a freestanding stair that are examples of virtuoso treatment of pipe rails. The developer was the Racanelli organization, and the design brought Mojo•Stumer another in a series of design awards from the Long Island American Institute of Architects chapter.

Above: Exterior view at entrance portal.
Left: Lobby wall with mural designed by Mojo(Stumer.
Photography: Andrew Appel.

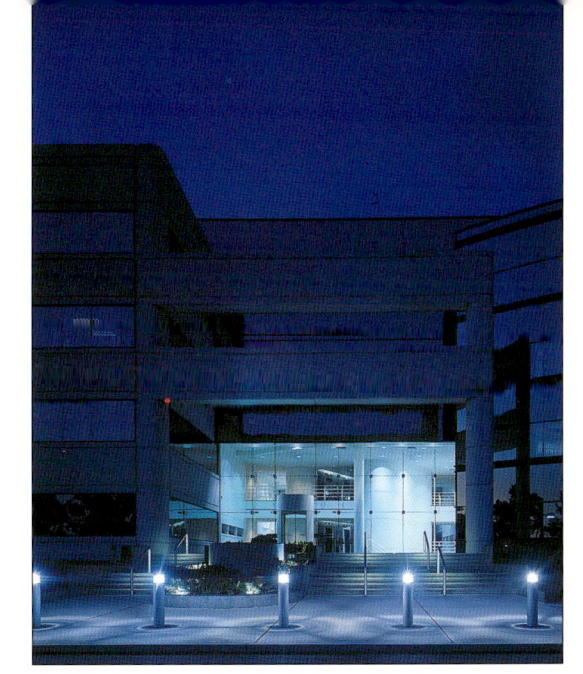

Above, left: Evening view of the exterior.
Above: The lobby stair.
Left: View through elevator lobby towards the building entrance.

221

Mojo•Stumer Associates, P.C.

G.G.K. Satellite Offices
Garden City, New York

The client for this installation is a successful accounting firm with its corporate headquarters in New York and with offices throughout the country. What was needed was a 10,000-sq.-ft. satellite office serving the firm's clients on Long Island. The space chosen was within Mojo•Stumer's own Omni building, shown on a previous spread. Despite the branch's relatively small size, it was important to present an impressive corporate image and a reflection of the parent firm's size and success, as well as a feeling of responsibility and security. The space planning puts the conference room near the reception area, limiting most visitors' penetration into the space and their awareness of the office's size. The materials palette is rich with a generous use of wood paneling and cabinetry, custom doors employ two types of patterned glass, and there is a sparkle of metal trim throughout. Colors, in addition to the wood tones, are warm, rich neutrals.

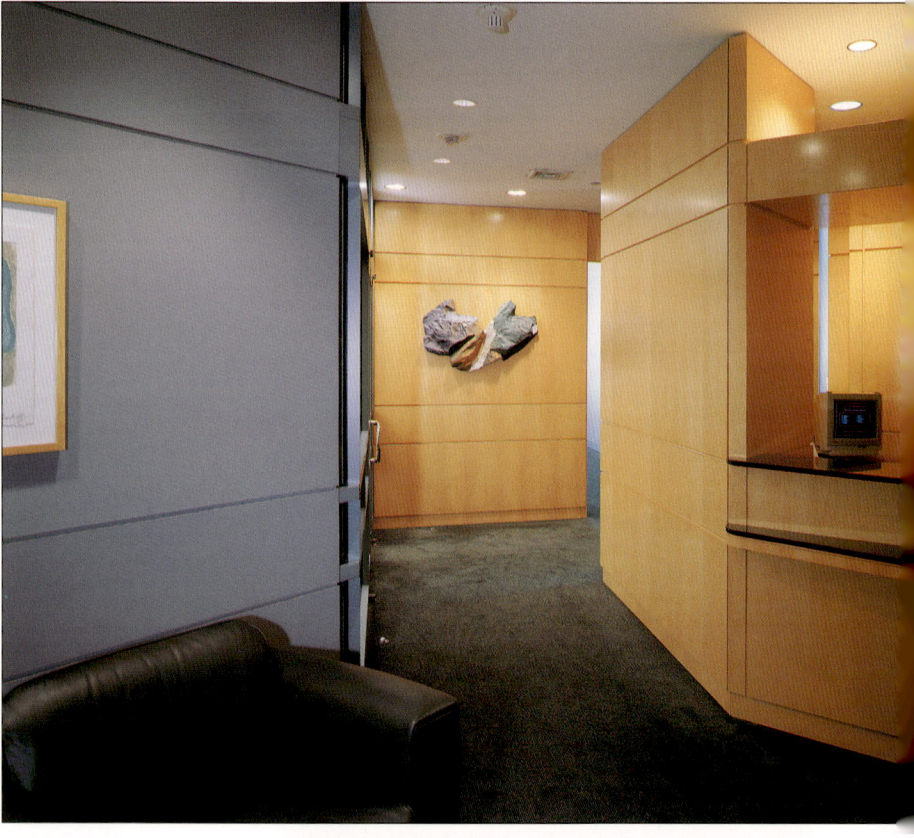

Above, left: *View into a conference room.*
Above: *A corner of the reception area.*
Right: *Corridor with wall-mounted artwork.*
Opposite page: *Detail view of reception desk.*
Photography: *Mark Samu.*

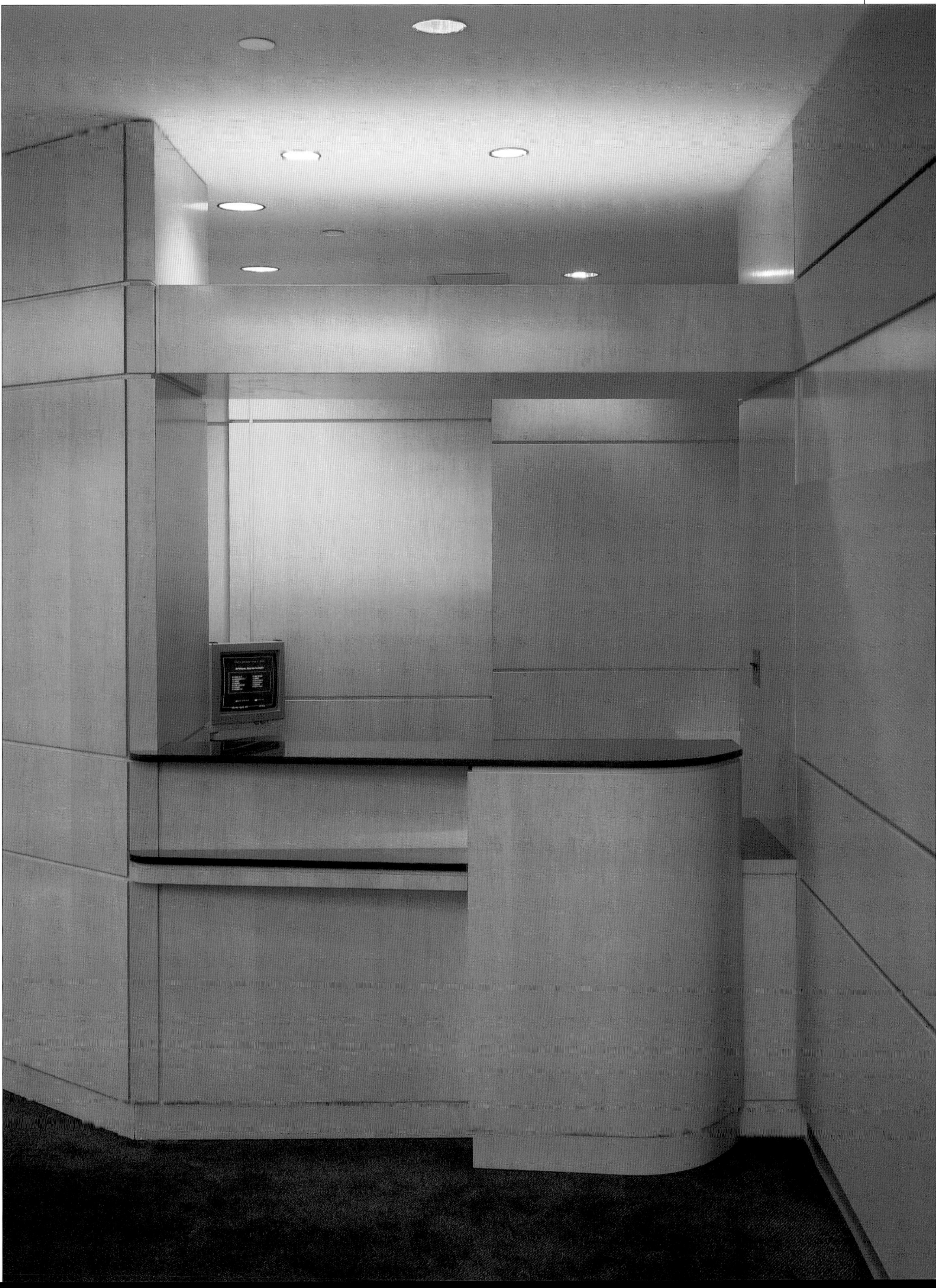

Mojo•Stumer Associates, P.C. Hewlett-Packard
Paramus, New Jersey

Electronics giant Hewlett-Packard asked Mojo•Stumer to turn a sow's ear — in the form of a 380,000-sq.-ft. New Jersey factory building previously used for the manufacture of computer printer parts — into something more like a silk purse. The upgraded facility was to house corporate offices and was to be made to appear appropriately dignified and welcoming for its new role. The designers added a new entrance façade, a new lobby and reception area within it, and a new glazed corridor leading from the lobby to the office space beyond. This corridor is generous in scale, flooded with light, and its axis terminates at a feature wall of natural wood that marks a change of direction in the visitor's approach. Sow's ear no more, the building has been given a completely new and much more winning personality.

Above, left: New entrance façade.
Above: Glazed circulation space within the new addition.
Photography: Mark Samu.

Montroy Andersen Design Group, Inc.

432 Park Avenue South
10th Floor
New York
New York 10016
212.481.5900
212.481.7481 (Fax)
www.madgi.com

**Montroy Andersen
Design Group, Inc.**

Wilmington Trust, Inc.
New York, New York

Above: Conference room with wall of African slate.
Photography: Phillip Ennis.

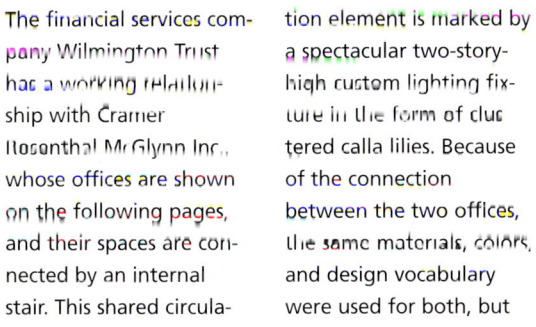

The financial services company Wilmington Trust has a working relationship with Cramer Rosenthal McGlynn Inc., whose offices are shown on the following pages, and their spaces are connected by an internal stair. This shared circulation element is marked by a spectacular two-story-high custom lighting fixture in the form of clustered calla lilies. Because of the connection between the two offices, the same materials, colors, and design vocabulary were used for both, but with distinctions that give each its own personality. African slate, for example, used for CRM as flooring, appears in the Wilmington Trust space as wall surfacing in the reception area and conference room. And, in place of CRM's tilted wall planes of cherry-framed glass, Wilmington Trust's corridors have been given custom angular light standards of cherry. The facility provides offices and support areas for 15 employees, it covers 7500 sq. ft., and its cost was $85. per sq. ft.

Top of page: Entrance view of reception area.
Above, left: Custom light standards in corridor.
Above: The "calla lily" light fixture in the stair.

227

Montroy Andersen Design Group, Inc.

> Cramer Rosenthal McGlynn Inc.
> New York, New York

Right, above: Reception area with a conference room beyond.
Right: Tilted panels lining the corridor.

Cramer Rosenthal McGlynn Inc. is a financial services company for which Montroy Andersen designed this 22,000 sq. ft. corporate headquarters. It occupies a single floor of a Madison Avenue building in Manhattan and accommodates 70 employees in its layout of corporate offices, reception and waiting areas, conference rooms, telecommunications room, and securities trading room. An unusual client request was that the installation have "the feel of the outdoors." To this end, the designers have assembled a materials palette both professional and natural, including slate, maple, and cherry. A panel of slate flooring is inset in front of the reception desk, setting the tone at the entrance. Tilted walls of cherry-framed glass, both clear and frosted, enliven the corridors and the edges of open work areas. For a dash of more urbane finishes, the conference and trading areas are detailed with custom-designed lighting fixtures of stainless steel and copper mesh. Services performed include interior architectural design and the selection of furniture and finishes, and Montroy Andersen brought the job in for $90. per square foot.

Above: An area of open workstations

Photography: Paul Warchol.

Montroy Andersen Design Group, Inc.

Federation Employment and Guidance Service, Inc.
New York, New York

This major new facility brings together previously scattered Manhattan operations of the Federation Employment and Guidance Service, Inc., to create the largest health-related and human services center in the United States. This facility was designed as a building within a building. Complete with its own building lobby and new street address, the facility is on six floors varying in size from 10,000 sq. ft. to 50,000 sq. ft. The facility totals 180,000 sq. ft. It houses 2,000 staff members and large numbers of visitors who come for the company's employment training, day treatment, education, and youth services. Nine different programs are administered here, each with its own functional and spatial requirements. Some of these necessarily share a floor, and a design challenge was to keep an open flow of space while giving each department a sense of territory. In addition to workspaces, requirements included classrooms, workshops, nursing stations, kitchens, dining areas, conference centers, a gym, a computer center, and a warehouse area. Costs were kept to $70. per sq. ft., finishes are appropriately durable, and the colors and materials have been chosen to be bright, dramatic, and psychologically uplifting.

Left, top: Reception and waiting area.
Left, center: Open plan workstations.
Left: A kitchen and lunchroom.
Photography: Bernstein Associates.

Montroy Andersen Design Group, Inc.

Fragrance Resources
New York, New York

Left: View of the communal space from the entrance.
Below: The same space, viewed from the conference table.
Photography: Paul Warchol.

The fragrance company Fragrance Resources asked Montroy Andersen for renovation of 4,400 sq. ft. of Manhattan space for a dozen employees. In addition to offices and conference space, a perfume lab was required. Most striking of the accommodations is the large (700 sq. ft.) communal room at the entrance, combining the receptionist's desk, lounge chairs for waiting visitors, and an open conference area where wares are openly presented. Custom built niches display the company products. The placement of the art was strategically located in conjunction with design elements. Cost was $85. per sq. ft.

Montroy Andersen Design Group, Inc.

Sciens Worldwide
New York, New York

Above: Reception and visitor waiting area.
Left: Conference room with executive office beyond.
Photography: Phillip Ennis.

Sciens Worldwide is an advertising company, and for its Madison Avenue offices in New York Montroy Andersen has designed a total of 50,000 sq. ft., divided equally on four rather small floors. Chief design problems were circulation and group identification. Within a generally open loft environment, the designers have grouped support spaces with centrally located copy/file/fax rooms to put most of the 170-person staff in close proximity to office equipment and client files. The look throughout is stylized but informal, with open-grid ceiling assemblies, unusual lighting fixture designs, and eclectic furniture. Carpet, drywall, and paint are the chief materials, and costs were held to $55. per sq. ft.

Oliver Design Group

One Park Plaza
Cleveland
Ohio 44114
216.696.7300
216.696.5834 (Fax)
www.odgarch.com

Oliver Design Group

Wayne Dalton Corporation
World Headquarters
Mt. Hope, Ohio

The location is a 10-acre site in a picturesque rural agricultural area noted for its Amish population, and the client is a manufacturer of wood and steel garage doors. Design criteria included: the representation of the client's commitment to the community and to its values; the representation of the client's commitment to research and modern technology; and the use of an untested new insulated steel sandwich panel as exterior skin for the purpose of helping the client enter the metal panel market. The resultant composition is clearly modern, but has been divided into several distinct components to relate to the nearby clusters of vernacular farm buildings, also white in color. The main entrance is a cylindrical form with sections removed to reveal the dramatic three-floor-high, 60-ft.-diameter atrium that serves both as reception/waiting area and as the building's chief circulation hub, crossed by clear-span bridges on the upper levels. Specifics of the building composition, however, have been designed from the inside out, beginning with workstation standards based on the specific tasks and equipment they must accommodate. These standards, in turn, determined the structural bay spacings. Enclosed offices and conference rooms are clustered at the ends of the floors, leaving open plan areas between with generous exposure to daylight and views. Inside as out, white is the basic color, warmed by a custom carpet blending gray, peach, honey, and rust hues, while jewel-toned accepts in seating fabrics add depth to the visual experience.

Top of Page: Exterior mass is broken into three elements.
Right: The cylindrical entrance element.
Below: Shaded glazing on the exterior opens the entry rotunda to pastoral views of the agricultural countryside.
Photography: Dan Cunningham.

Right: The president's office.
Left: Boardroom with panoramic views.

235

Oliver Design Group

M. A. Hanna Co.
World Headquarters
Cleveland, Ohio

Above: Entrance lobby with ceiling fixture of stainless steel and sycamore.
Left: Video-teleconferencing room.
Right: Custom millwork for administrative and support staff work areas.
Bottom, left: Seating area for visitors is shielded from office traffic.
Photography: Dan Cunningham.

Moving into the 36th and 37th floors of Cleveland's BP America building, the client — a Fortune 200 company — asked Oliver Design Group for a new image suiting its new role. Previously a traditional U.S. iron ore mining and shipping company, it had become a world-wide manufacturer and distributor of synthetic chemical/polymer products. The space offered dramatic views but was "building standard" with drywall partitions and fluorescent lighting, so that complete demolition and redesign was needed to reach the client's goals. The custom ceiling fixture in the elevator lobby, faced with English sycamore fiddleback veneer, may be likened to a ship's hull from the company's former fleet, but all else bespeaks an involvement with current technology. State-of-the-art data and video equipment connect the office with its dozen domestic and foreign businesses to improve communications and decrease executive travel. Managers and directors are all provided 13'-6" by 14'-8" offices with well planned work surfaces and 48" conferencing tables, and the same high standards of custom millwork extend to the support staff workstations. These also share daylight from the perimeter through panels of clear and translucent ribbon glass. Also prominent in the materials palette are panels of ceramic crystallized glass. These hard surfaces are softened visually and acoustically with fabric-wrapped tackboards, nylon upholstery, and nylon carpet. Martin "Skip" Walker, the client's CEO, said that the new interiors express our culture and values with quality without being ostentatious.

Below: Typical perimeter office with large work areas and a round table for small meetings.
Bottom of page, left: Spiral stair stands free of glazed wall surfaces.
Bottom of page, right: Office of an executive vice-president. On the far wall, a row of paper management slots for work in progress.

Oliver Design Group

**Deloitte & Touche
Consulting Group
Cleveland, Ohio**

Right: Reception area with conference room beyond; at left is the "hoteling" check-in computer.
Below: A row of glazed conference rooms along left side open to a corridor flanked by a phone counter.
Photography: Dan Cunningham.

Right: A corner consultant "neighborhood" offers a variety of work environments
Below, right: Internal corridor with modulated ceiling and a "focal point" terminus.

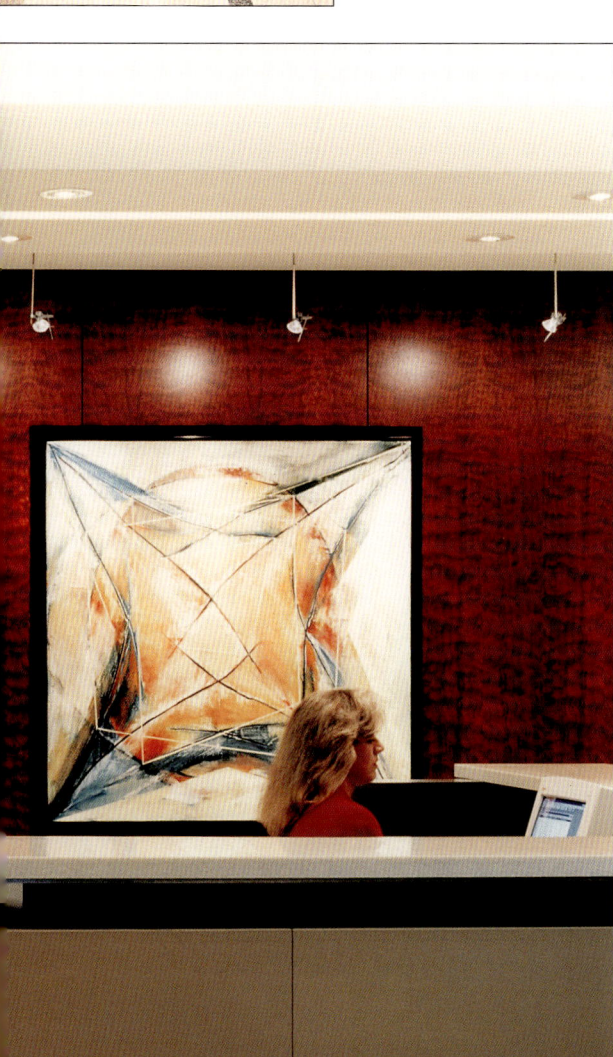

The figures speak for themselves, and quite impressively: Comparing this installation with the client's previous quarters, the area per employee has been reduced from 207 to 153 sq. ft., the occupancy cost per employee has been reduced by 27%, and the revenue per sq. ft. has been increased dramatically. Yet functional efficiency, graded by the client at "C" level before the move, has become "A," flexibility has gone from "B" to "A," and overall user satisfaction has gone from "C" to "A." The client, of course, is a prominent management consulting firm, and the location was a single 24,000-sq.-ft. floor in a Cleveland high-rise. The remarkable results came from a close examination of the "hoteling" installations being used by the client in other locations and by the development of a new model that successfully resolves the dichotomy of the employees' own view of their work processes as "informal" with their desire to project an image their clients would perceive as "formal." This has been accomplished with a calculated variety of work environments; in corner work "neighborhoods," for example, there is a choice of open tables along the full-height glass wall, conventional open-plan workstations, and enclosed stations manufactured by Steelcase and called Personal Harbors. All these options have full connectivity to communications networks, and they are supplemented by "front porch" areas with short term filing, printer output, paper storage, and other types of support. Oliver Design Group says that the project "establishes a new standard for non-traditional office design."

239

Oliver Design Group

First National Bank
Akron, Ohio

This lobby and banking area share the ground floor of a 1931 multi-tenant office building, and the last renovation here occurred in 1969. Aims of the redesign were not only to update the appearance, but to provide a bank that would reflect new merchandizing strategies with fewer tellers and more representatives of lateral product and marketing services. Also important was an improvement in circulation, so that visitors to the upper floors could move freely even when the branch bank was closed. The separation between bank and lobby is effected with custom gates of stainless steel and brass, and the traffic patterns are reinforced by the patterns of the terrazzo and tile flooring. The tellers' stations are new assemblages of marbles and anigré wood, but the check writing desks of ornamental brass have been restored from the original installation.

Above: The main banking hall is a dramatic double-height space.
Above, right: Beyond the tellers' stations, the domed pavilion houses an elevator to the vault below.
Right: Exterior with the new canopy.
Photography: Dan Cunningham.

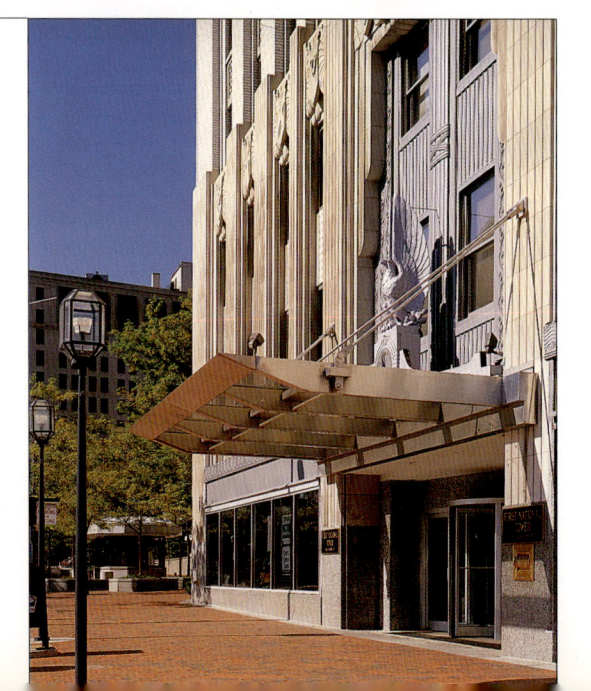

O'Donnell Wicklund Pigozzi and Peterson Architects Incorporated (OWP&P)

111 West Washington Street
Suite 2100
Chicago
Illinois 60602.2714
312.332.9600
312.332.9601 (Fax)
www.owpp.com

OWP&P

BT Office Products International
Deerfield, Illinois

The client is an international office furniture dealer, and these new quarters consolidate its U.S. headquarters and its regional accounting office. They occupy two and a half floors of a speculative office building for a total of 62,000 sq. ft. In previous locations, the company's offices had been traditionally hierarchical, but here a more informal, more interactive environment was wanted. Fortunately the space was almost column-free, and ceiling heights were a generous 12 ft. Each of the three floors has its own reception area and each a mixture of private offices and open workstations. The chief reception area has been given a distinctive elliptical shape, its curving walls faced with custom panels of maple. These panels also line the corridor to the boardroom, and the boardroom itself, which can seat 35, has tackable wall surfaces, white boards, a cabinet of teleconferencing equipment, and a wall of sandblasted glass. Employee amenities include a lunchroom with floor-to-ceiling windows overlooking a landscaped pond. Colors throughout are soft earth tones, with purple walls indicating shared facilities for copying, coats, and coffee.

Above: Maple panels line the elliptical reception area.
Left: Curved corridor leads to the boardroom.
Photography: Christopher Barrett © Hedrich Blessing.

Right: Boardroom cabinets hold A-V equipment.
Below: Break-out area privides teaming space.

243

OWP&P

CNA Cafeteria
Chicago, Illinois

Above: View of the facility from the rotunda.
Right, top of page: A reflective mobile over the escalator.
Right, center: Some of the varied seating arrangements.
Right: Space is modulated by varying ceiling heights.
Opposite: A water feature at the entrance.
Photography: Christopher Barrett © Hedrich Blessing.

244

Many of the 6,000 employees of the CNA Insurance Companies had recently had to adjust to reductions in personal work spaces and in numbers of private offices and conference rooms. With this new 40,000-sq.-ft. cafeteria, CNA wanted to "give back" to them an enjoyable and useful amenity. The entrance to the cafeteria is through a generously scaled rotunda, animated by the sights and sounds of a fountain, pool, and water feature. Inside, the cafeteria can comfortably seat 750 in a single shift, but its large size has been broken into relatively intimate areas by means of etched glass dividers. The full-service facility allows food to be prepared on site, rather than simply being prepared elsewhere and brought in for display. But lunch and coffee breaks are not the only activities here: The entire space is wired like a high-tech conference room, with laptop hookups available throughout the seating areas, and the space is open 24 hours a day, encouraging a variety of meetings and conferences. An extensive art collection adds a finishing fillip.

245

OWP&P

USG Conference and Training Center
Schiller Park, Illinois

Above: Lounge seating in a quiet alcove.
Right, above: Undulating Diamond Flex panels and a Curvatura ceiling system demonstrate USG products.
Right: Intriguing plays of planes and curves.
Photography: Steve Hall © Hedrich Blessing.

The USG Corporation, formerly known as U. S. Gypsum, is, of course, a leading manufacturer of drywall and ceiling building products. This 15,000-sq.-ft. training center designed by OWP&P is used by USG staff from all over the country. It includes a cafeteria seating 46, a café, and a large variety of rooms for sales meetings, training sessions, and conferences: a 42-seat conference room, three conference rooms each accommodating 12 plus an instructor, a video conferencing room, and four break-out rooms. In addition, quiet alcoves hold pairs of comfortable chairs with tablet arms, where visitors can share notes with a colleague or plug in to check their e-mail. A secondary set of functions that the complex serves is to demonstrate some of USG's products; built-out conical shapes that wrap exposed columns, for example, show some of the potential uses of plaster, and an undulating ceiling plane of aluminum slats demonstrates the versatility of the metal ceiling product line. USG Sheetrock brand drywall is present too, painted in colorful stripes and checkerboards, and all these material displays are designed to be easily changed, allowing the client to continue showcasing the newest product lines.

OWP&P

American Airlines Flagship Lounge
Chicago, Illinois

At Chicago's O'Hare Airport, this 4,000-sq.-ft. renovation houses American Airlines' Flagship Lounge for its international first-class passengers. About 85 passengers can be accommodated here at a single time. The facilities include seating areas, self-service food and beverage counters, and a "skipper's desk" for ticketing and other customer service activities. Numerous telephone jacks and electrical outlets are placed throughout, and a separate, more private alcove offers eight computer docking stations. The large space is made more intimate with the placement of screens designed of wood and art glass, and seating areas are further defined by suspended ceiling canopies of anodized brass and aluminum mesh. Panels of acoustical tile above these canopies dampen sound. Seating areas are carpeted, but main circulation paths are floored with polished granite. Other materials sustain an appropriate level of luxury; they include stainless steel, granite counter tops, American sycamore cabinetwork, columns wrapped in zebrawood, all highlighted with incandescent lighting. Background colors are neutral and calm, but there are bright accents in the artwork and in the seating fabrics.

Above, left: Glass and wood dividers create intimate seating areas.
Above: Main circulation path is floored with granite.
Right: The "skipper's desk" for customer services.
Photography: Christopher Barrett © Hedrich Blessing.

OWP&P

Allstate F Lobby
Northbrook, Illinois

Until OWP&P's recent redesign, this 4,000-sq.-ft. lobby — the main entrance to the Allstate insurance company's executive offices on its corporate headquarters campus — had remained unchanged for more than 20 years. Updating was overdue. The client wanted durable furniture and finishes capable of lasting another 20 years and able to endure the direct sunlight that floods the double-height space. A key design decision was the choice of Dark Emperador marble, carefully selected in Italy for the desired veining patterns, as a finish for some of the 25-ft.-high walls. Contrasting with this rich brown marble is the ivory-colored travertine selected for other vertical surfaces and for elevator cabs. Brass and stainless steel hardware and handrails add sparkle and an element of human scale. Furniture of rich cherry and makore woods, although traditional, was chosen for its distinctive silhouettes.

Above: A ceiling-high plane of marble is a dramatic backdrop for a seating group.
Right: View towards the elevator bank.
Photography: Christopher Barrett © Hedrich Blessing.

Quantrell Mullins & Associates Inc.

999 Peachtree Street, NE

Suite 1710

Atlanta

Georgia 30309

404.874.6048

404.874.2026 (Fax)

Quantrell Mullins & Associates Inc.

Prudential Bank & Trust
Atlanta, Georgia

Right: Part of the Kryptonite Café.
Below: Entrance and reception area.
Photography: Brian Robbins.

Quantrell Mullins was involved from the early planning stages in the relocation of Prudential Bank & Trust's corporate headquarters. After preparing detailed building evaluation and comparison studies for the client, the decision was made to move to 220,000 sq. ft. of space spread over 10 floors of a Class A building in Atlanta. Quantrell Mullins provided a full range of services from budget and schedule development through construction administration. The project incorporated a variety of facilities and functions, including executive offices, general offices, a conference center, spaces for employee breaks and leisure activities, and a calling center. This last requirement, often buried in "back office" locations, was

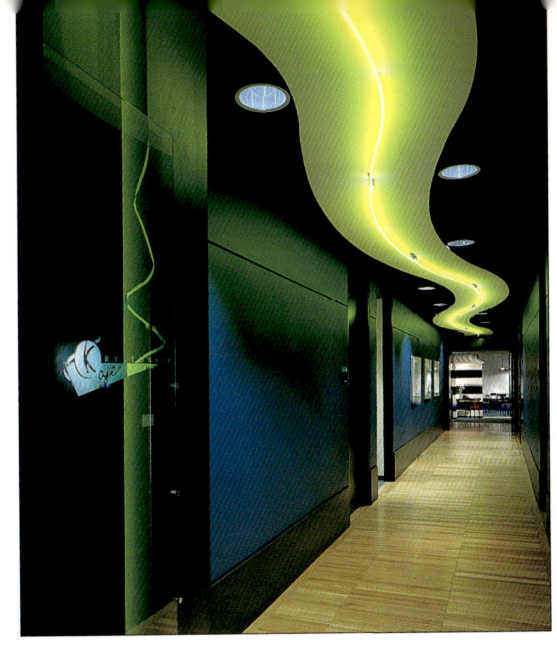

Far left: Meandering neon strip leads to the café entrance.
Left: Display niche in corridor.
Below, left: Open office area for the calling center.
Below, right: Another part of the Kryptonite café.

given prominent placement. Although the space allotment in the calling center was limited to only 109 sq. ft. per person, functional and aesthetic levels were kept on par with neighboring areas. Throughout, partitioning was kept low to encourage worker interaction, and traditional layouts with full-height partitions were used only for the management and executive offices, boardroom and conference rooms. The generously proportioned first floor reception area acts as a control point for all visitors and staff. Two conference rooms, which are accessible to visitors without disturbing other operations, the computer switch room, and Management Information Systems are also located on the first floor. On upper floors, conference rooms are similarly convenient, placed on either side of the elevator lobbies. Team rooms, storage areas, library areas and lounges are also grouped near the building core, leaving the perimeter of the odd-shaped floorplate free for workstations. For these general office areas, colors were selected to complement the bank's existing systems furniture which was re-used. The materials palette is dominated by highly lacquered panels of sapele wood from West Africa, painted gypsum board, glass and carpet. The exuberant Kryptonite Cafe, an escapist retreat with appropriately unconventional decor, enlivens the entire installation.

251

Quantrell Mullins & Associates Inc.

**Lancaster Group Worldwide Inc.
New York, New York**

Quantrell Mullins was selected as the U.S. Liaison for the relocation of Lancaster Group Worldwide's headquarters to New York City after working with Lancaster's parent company, a fragrance and cosmetics conglomerate, on their international headquarters in Germany and facilities in Paris, Montreal and Milan. The New York installation houses 140 employees on three floors, two of them joined by a private stair and the third serving the firm's advertising and public relations personnel. In addition to functional efficiency, the client, accustomed to strict German mandates for natural light exposure, wanted—and got—similar exposure here, through both worker proximity to windows and generous amounts of interior glazing. Decorative motifs throughout, such as repeated wavy lines, are taken from the company logo. Desks and workstations are either custom designed or customized, and lighting blends daylight, low voltage downlights and ambient torcheres. Client satisfaction is attested not only by repeat commissions but also by word of mouth from CEO Peter Harf "Quantrell Mullins & Associates was the integral force behind the organization, management, planning and design of our corporate headquarters relocation. Their creativity, professionalism and sensitivity to our needs set them apart."

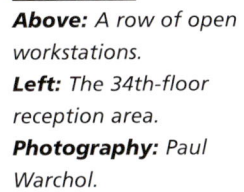

Above: A row of open workstations.
Left: The 34th-floor reception area.
Photography: Paul Warchol.

Above: Boardroom on 33rd floor.
Below: Private office suite on a corner of the 34th floor.

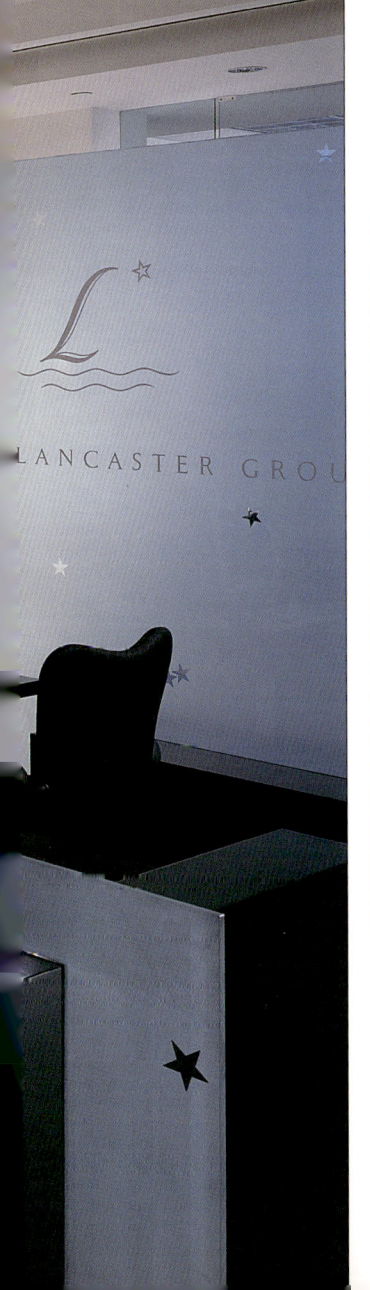

Quantrell Mullins & Associates Inc.

Halstead Industries, Inc.
Greensboro, North Carolina

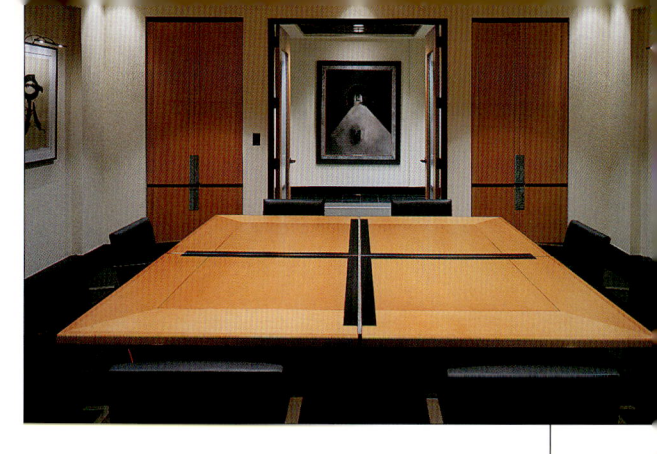

Top, far left: Reception area and stair.
Top, left: A private office.
Left: The office of the CEO.
Top, right: A small conference room.
Right: Large conference room with audio-visual equipment.
Photography: Brian Gassel.

Halstead Industries, a Greensboro-based manufacturing company, serves clients in Asia and around the world. Thus, while a multi-cultural design vocabulary was required, local ties and a strong corporate identity were important as well. As an unusual part of its services, Quantrell Mullins was given the task of designing a corporate logo and adapting it for different applications, including office signage, company letterhead and collateral, and even graphics for the corporate airplane. More conventional work included master planning, the inventory and analysis of existing furnishings, an equipment and furnishings migration plan, the design and specification of interior systems and custom furnishings, an art program, project management and coordination of the eventual move-in. A sculptural internal stair is a key design element that links the reception area and adjacent conference center to the executive suite on the floor above. In addition to the CEO's office, this suite houses the company's library, a conference room, refreshment center and administrative support area. General office space is located on two lower floors and was designed with a significantly different budget, yet with equal demands for up-to-the-minute technology and communications.

255

Throughout the four-floor, 53,000 sq. ft. installation, the principal materials are honey-stained maple, painted gypsum board, granite, copper, stainless steel and glass. The warmth of the maple is complemented with a color palette of eggplant, black and cream. The detailing of custom furniture, doors and lighting fixtures particularly emphasizes elements of copper, one of Halstead's metal products and the heart of the art program is a series of innovative, signature photographs taken in the company's metals manufacturing plant.

Top, left: Lighting fixture in elevator lobby.
Top, right: Bottom of private stair.
Above, left: Bird's-eye view of stair.
Above: Stair railing detail.

Ridgway Associates
Planning & Design

414 Boyd Street
Los Angeles
Callifornia 90013
213.620.0550
213.620.1964 (Fax)
www.ridgwaydesign.com
pridgway@ridgway.com

1007 Ocean Avenue
Suite 301
Santa Monica
California 90403
310.458.4423
310.581.9243 (Fax)

**Ridgway Associates
Planning & Design**

Focus Media
Santa Monica, California

Focus Media is a privately held entertainment related company that trades in radio and television advertising time. Because of tremendous California growth, the company has moved to new 50,000-sq.-ft quarters in the MGM Plaza complex in Santa Monica, CA. Left behind were its obsolete systems, furnishings, and equipment. Focus Media's image was updated with both facilities and fine art and 20th Century antiques. The new location including a well equipped training facility dividable by a concealed partition, and banks of built-in television monitors airing recent promotions representing clientele throughout, used for viewing commercials currently on the air. The art program combines a collection of authentic 20th Century French sculpture of Diana, the Roman goddess of the forest and the moon, and a collection of local contemporary photographs by California artist Suzanne Sutcliffe. Sutcliffe's chief subject is—appropriately—communications, including rooftop microwave dishes and radio wave beacons photographed in New York. Media buyers and media assistants, equal in number, are pair together, the buyers in

Top of page: *The main entrance.*
Above and left: *Soft conference area in an executive office.*
Photography: *Toshi Yoshimi.*

glass-walled offices finished in natural maple. The owner's suite includes an office for his executive administrative assistant, a workstation for his executive receptionist, and private bathing area, serving area with kitchen, bar, and gym. Here finishes combine aniare wood, maple wood, veneer, bronze flecked granite and crystal clear glass.

Above: *Lunchroom adjacent to the garden.*
Above, right: *Media buyer area.*
Right: *Video monitors in the reception area. Vintage radios and televisions are featured here including the famous "tube on top" television.*
Below, right: *Executive desk and credenza.*

259

Ridgway Associates Planning & Design

Think New Ideas
Hollywood, California

For Think New Ideas, a dynamic young computer-based graphics and Internet advertising firm and a division of the Omnicom Advertising Group, Ridgway designed a 15,000 square foot headquarters on the Sunset Strip in Hollywood, California after the ad agency decided to abandon their warehouse space in Culver City. The space is on the top floor of a retail mall environment overlooking the famous "Laugh Factory," and the challenge was to create high-energy office space for the rapidly growing agency's 80 employees. To do so, the floor was transformed into an open plan office space with some of the familiar warehouse character, with the existing structure and a new mechanical system, both left exposed. Concrete floors have been sealed and polished, and carpet covers them only in private office areas. The majority of space is open and filled with Herman Miller's EthoSpace workstations, their panel heights graduated and staggered to promote a sense of openness and worker views.

Right, top of page: Audio-visual boardroom.
Right, center: Work environment for the "creatives."
Right, bottom of page: Display area in boardroom.
Below: Seating group in reception area.
Opposite page: The receptionist's desk.
Photography: Toshi Yoshimi.

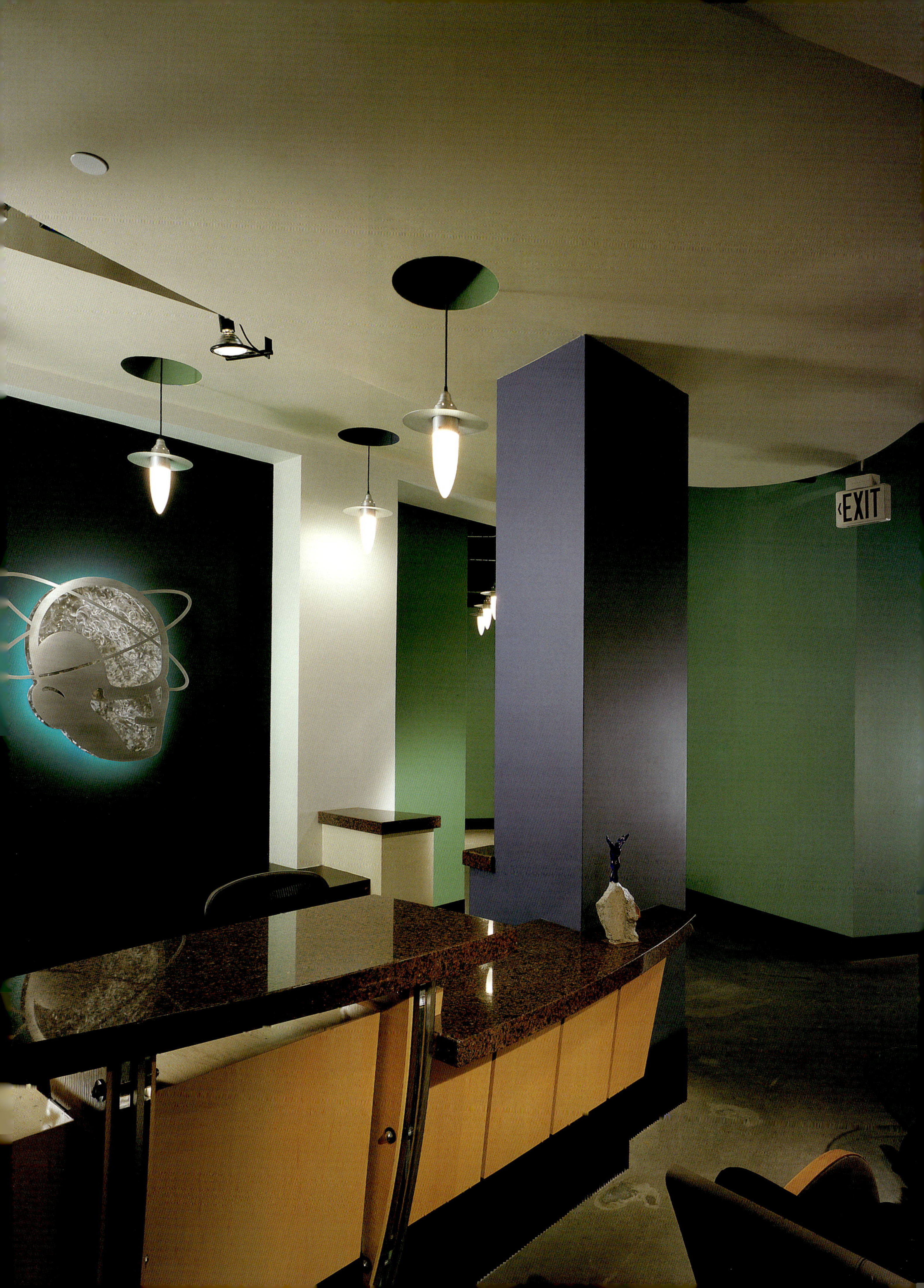
EXIT

**Ridgway Associates
Planning & Design**

Allianz Insurance Company
Los Angeles, California

Top left: Reception area.
Above: Entry corridor.
Top right: Corporate dining room.
Left: Entrance and reception desk.
Right, below: Reception desk.
Right, bottom of page: President's office.

Warner Brothers is a neighbor. Disney is down the street. And Hollywood is just over the hill. This media-rich location is the context for the chief U.S. offices of Allianz Insurance, an international organization based in Germany but with 700 affiliate companies in 68 countries, including the recently acquired AGF insurance group from France. The 40,000-sq.-ft. Burbank office design by Ridgway Associates accommodates 400 Allianz employees and reflects both the cosmopolitan character of the company and the artistic interests of its CEO, Dr. Wolgang Schlink, a collector of fine art, folk art, and photography. The art photographer Suzanne Sutcliffe was commissioned to produce appropriate works for the interiors, and they make a strong first impression in the reception area, where images repeat the Warner Brothers tower that the visitor has just seen outside. Also impressive here are a rhythmically shaped ceiling cove and flooring inlaid with a sweep of stainless steel and black granite. The two-person reception desk is a composition of glass, marble, and anigré veneer. In the staff lounge area, Sutcliffe's subject matter is a series of classic drive-in diners that are familiar L.A. landmarks. For other locations, Sutcliffe has photographed palm trees, those other Southern California icons. Throughout, the simplest of materials — drywall and paint — have been beveled and shaped to suggest movement and a continuity of space.

263

Ridgway Associates Planning & Design

DavisElen Advertising
Los Angeles, California

For DavisElen, an advertising agency formerly known as Davis Ball & Colombatto, Ridgway Associates has designed almost 40,000 sq. ft. of office space on two floors of a downtown Los Angeles "Class A" high-rise. Reconstituted particle board known as OSB board was attached to common chain link fence pipe which was wire brushed to achieve a distressed surface finish. Laminated work surfaces were assembled inside to support state of the art computer generated graphics all networked to strategically placed television monitors for client viewing in private rooms. An adult sandbox was assembled in the creative area using black and white sand with suspended construction plum-bobs which daily create circular patterns naturally since the high-rise moves with wind and earth movement. Black and white carpet runs through the sandbox on an imaginary line with carpet meeting sand separated with stainless steel dividers.

Right, top of page: The elevator lobby.
Right, center: Staff recreation area.
Right, bottom of page: Audio-visual boardroom.
Below: A lounge area and a group of custom workstations.
Photography: Toshi Yoshimi.

RMW Architecture + Design

160 Pine Street
San Francisco
California 94111
415.781.9800
415.788.5216 (Fax)

RMW Architecture + Design

RMW Architecture + Design

KPMG
Mountain View, California

Below: Presentation room table with for laptops connections
Bottom of page, left: Steel-ceilinged ante area for presentation rooms.
Bottom of page, right: An interior private office.
Opposite: Reception area seen from the street.
Photography: Steve Hall © Hedrich-Blessing

The project shown here is not the first designed by RMW Architecture + Design for the "Big Five" accounting firm KPMG, nor, due to its success, will it be the last: Eight more projects for the same client are currently underway. This one is located in Silicon Valley's Mountain View, about 50 miles south of San Francisco, and occupies a new four-floor speculative office building with a total area of 136,000 sq. ft. Before the completion of construction, RMW's input brought about a number of design changes in windows, stairs, elevators, structural bracing, and more. Within this modified shell, RMW's design calls for the ground floor to be devoted to public reception, semi-public functions such as presentations and meetings, support elements such as a computer room, graphics lab, technology lab, and employee amenities such as espresso bar, lounge area, learning center, and exercise room. Many of these spaces flow together seamlessly, the double-height reception area with its wall of book-matched anigré opens to a central rotunda where visitors are directed to their destinations by a touch-screen monitor; this in turn opens to an espresso bar used by staff and visitors alike; and beyond that, enjoying views from its corner location, is a comfortably furnished lounge with TV monitors supplying the day's financial (and other) news. The rotunda also leads directly to a ante area serving participants in any or all of seven clustered presentation rooms, the largest of which has leather-upholstered seats focused on rear-projection screens that, the designers say "put IMAX's to shame." The three higher floors are devoted to work

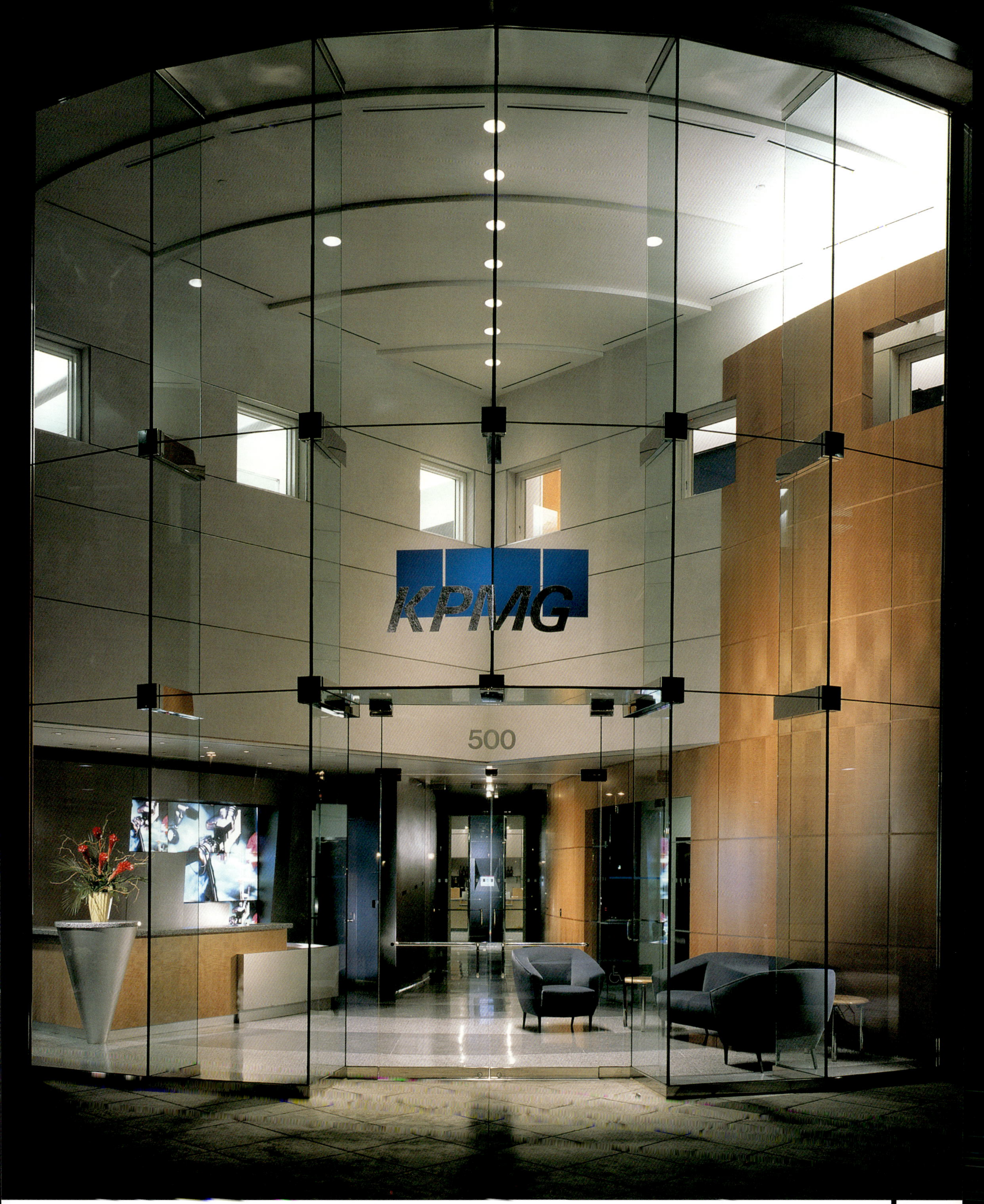
KPMG
500

Right: In rotunda, a touch-screen directory is built into column.
Below, left: Espresso bar.
Below, right: Corridor among work areas.

spaces for 900 KPMG employees. Most of these, however, work outside the office much of the time, so a "hoteling" concept was adopted, making offices and work stations available for limited times to those who "check in." Easily portable to the assigned work areas are mobile tables and personal storage lockers, all on casters, which have been designed (in a collaboration of RMW and Knoll) with built-in rubber bumpers aligning with similar bumpers along corridors and fixed furnishings. In addition to the warmth of the anigré repeated in key locations, colors and materials are simple and industrial in character — metallic painted panels, custom casegoods and carpets, gray/beige backgrounds and jewel-toned accents. Not only has the design won further commissions for RMW; it has also been featured in Interior Design magazine, and has won the Grand Prize in the 1999 DuPont Antron® Design Competition.

Above, right: Lounge area adjacent to espresso bar.
Right: Work stations with mobile tables and storage lockers.

RMW Architecture + Design

**PeopleSoft
Headquarters
Pleasanton, California**

Left: *A bank of computer monitors introduces the company.*
Below: *Corporate visitor center ante area.*
Photography:
David Wakely and Steve Hall © Hedrich-Blessing

Right: Exterior view of the four-building complex.
Below: In a corridor, another video display wall.
Bottom of page: Glazed corner of a conference room along "The Lakeshore."

No "hoteling" concepts, shared spaces, or open workstations were wanted here! For their headquarters, the PeopleSoft computer software developers wanted a clear expression of their flat — rather than pyramidal — corporate hierarchy and their pride in their workforce. Translated into physical terms, that meant a requirement of 1,400 closed private offices for the company's 1,400 workers. These were to be accommodated in a complex of four new four-story buildings with a total square footage of 384,000. The four buildings, some placed at angles to others, are linked by a triangular circulation corridor wrapping around a central green space that has come to be known in PeopleSoft corporate lingo as "the lakeshore." Not surprisingly, a major design challenge was clear identification and pathfinding among the building elements. To this end, strong, easily identified coloration has been used in corridors and other public spaces, some of it visible from the exterior; signage and stylized

271

Left: One of the PeopleSoft presentation rooms.
Below: Employee cafeteria
Below left: Strong colors, simple graphics are orientation aids in circulation areas.

maps at key points are further orientation aids. Access to public spaces and to enclaves of private offices is all possible directly from "the lakeshore." There is more here, of course, than offices and corridors. Other facilities designed by RMW include a corporate visitor center, business partner demonstration suites, training rooms, server rooms, computer labs, and employee amenities such as a cafeteria and a fitness center. Beyond the strong primaries of the circulation system, colors are generally soft, dominated by deep earth tones with cool blue accents. Materials include stucco walls, wood flooring, linoleum, stained concrete, and loop carpeting. The indirect lighting employed throughout reduces glare on computer screens and gives a touch of residential character to the work spaces. As a PeopleSoft representative reports, the RMW design "supports our highly personal business style that we want our customers to experience."

RTKL Associates Inc.

1250 Connecticut Ave. NW
Washington, DC 20036
202.833.4400
202.887.5168 (Fax)
www.rtkl.com

Baltimore
Washington, DC
Dallas
Los Angeles
Chicago
London
Tokyo
Hong Kong

RTKL Associates Inc.

Virgin Atlantic
Upper Class Departures Lounge
Dulles International Airport
Loudoun County, Virginia

Right: The work table in the business services area.
Below: Principal seating area with bar and stair to mezzanine beyond.
Photography: Maxwell MacKenzie.

Dulles International Airport, near Washington, DC, is distinguished by its original terminal building designed by Eero Saarinen and finished in 1963. The Virgin Atlantic passenger lounge shown here — called "The Clubhouse" for short — enjoys a view of Saarinen's masterpiece through a double-height window wall. It provides plenty of visual interest inside, as well. Built for a capacity of 75 passengers plus a staff of six, it comprises seven key elements: the reception area for passenger check-in and storage for coats and luggage; the principal seating area; the bar; the dining area, located along the tall window wall and known as The Terrace; The Library, a quiet study area with extensive business services; The Pavilion, containing private showers and toilets; and The Mezzanine, a characterful perch with an overview of the whole 3,500-sq.-ft. facility. But these seven functional elements visually overlap and combine, due to shared vocabularies of shapes and colors. The shapes are simple and geometric, some of them with obvious aeronautical references to hangars, tailfins, and wings. The colors are vivid ones (red and purple) in combination with more subtle ones (gold and olive), the total effect quite lively compared to other parts of the terminal. And because The Clubhouse is used by passengers on Virgin Atlantic's overnight flights between Washington and London, particular attention has been paid to lighting and to comfortable transitions from daylight to artificial light; fiber optics are employed for the indirect lighting of high ceiling planes. RTKL's design has been awarded a 1998 Merit Award for Interior Design from the Washington chapter of the American Institute of Architects.

Top of page: View of lounge from reception area.
Middle: Entrance from the terminal. Red panels and white stripes convey Virgin's corporate identity.
Right: Terrace area and stair to mezzanine. Glass wall at left looks toward the original Dulles terminal.

275

RTKL Associates Inc.

MCI Telecommunications Corporation
Washington, DC

The new Washington DC offices of MCI Telecommunications Corporation comprise 105,000 square feet on seven floors of 1717 Pennsylvania Avenue, a recently renovated building in the heart of downtown. Built in three phases, the facilities include six floors of executive and administrative office space and one floor dedicated to reception, central services, and a conference center. To accommodate the fast growth and change within MCI. RTKL developed a flexible scheme that allows easy interchange of open and closed office configurations. To support the open plan, there are enclosed conference rooms and teaming areas on each level. In addition, the tenth floor has larger conference rooms and dedicated video teleconferencing rooms that are an instrumental part of the firm's communications system. The conference rooms, designated by frosted glass and horizontal metal rods, are intended to be beacons amid the office space; because circulation occurs around these enclosed rooms. They are set apart from the work areas and become the focal points of the open spaces. To create an illusion of height and depth within the extremely confined space, shallow changes in the ceiling plane and dramatic Illumination of the vertical surfaces create spatial rhythms that add interest and enrichment to the office area.

Above, left: Audio/visual teleconferencing room, part of the 10th floor's conference center.
Left: The 10th floor reception area; across the hall, a conference room behind panels of textured glass.
Photography: Maxwell MacKenzie.

Top left: An informal meeting area on a typical floor.
Top right: Within open plan areas, purple accent walls and glass panels identify conference rooms and meeting areas.
Above: Private offices along the building perimeter.
Right: Another part of the 10th floor conference center.

277

RTKL Associates Inc.

Concert Reston
Concert Global Communications
Reston, Virginia

Above: Separated by suspended glass planes, an open plan team area for informal meetings and work sessions.
Photography: Maxwell MacKenzie.

Below: Open plan workstations along the building perimeter give workers natural light.

Right: The "service hub" for reproduction services, food service, and more.

Bottom, right: Entry and reception area.

This 44,000-sq.-ft. expansion facility in Reston, Virginia, was designed by RTKL for Concert Management Services, a subsidiary of British telecommunications. It was completed for $34 per sq. ft. and on a "fast-track" schedule: only six weeks for conceptual design and construction documents, with just two months more for construction. On three floors, the unfettered plan responds to the client's desire to "hear and see a buzz of activity." Open plan workstations predominate and are given the choice perimeter locations. Among them are glass-walled team spaces and multi-purpose "service hubs." RTKL's accomplishment here has earned a 1998 award for Best Interiors from the National Association of Industrial and Office Properties, and has earned the firm subsequent work for Concert Management in multiple locations throughout the United States and Europe.

RTKL Associates Inc.

2000 L Street, NW
Washington, DC

Washington's 2000 L Street, NW, is an eight-story, 510,000-sq.-ft. office building with one level of streetfront retail, one level of below-grade office space, and two levels of below-grade parking. The building's broker, The JBG Companies, retained RTKL to provide new additions and — even more importantly — a new image. A ninth floor was added, some of the basement level was converted to new retail space, new building systems were installed, toilet rooms were made accessible to the handicapped, and, on all upper floors, elevator lobbies were given new finishes. Most obvious of the changes, however, are the building's new entrance with a glass bay above and the new entrance lobby within. RTKL also designed accompanying site improvements around the building: planters, lighting, and new stone paving.

Top of page, left: Retail component on L Street.
Top of page, right: Exterior view into lobby entrance.
Right: The elevator lobby.
Below: Main lobby and reception desk.
Photography: Alan Karchmer.

Sasaki Associates, Inc.

64 Pleasant Street
Watertown
Massachusetts 02472
617.926.3300
617.924.2748 (Fax)
e-mail info@sasaki.com
www.sasaki.com

900 North Point Street
Suite B300
San Francisco
California 94109
415.776.7772
415.202.8970 (Fax)
e-mail sanfrancisco@sasaki.com

Sasaki Associates, Inc.

Tufts Health Plan
Watertown,
Massachusetts

The client is a health maintenance organization that has been experiencing explosive growth. Thus the move of its customer service functions — consisting mostly of open plan office space — into new facilities. The location selected (with Sasaki Associates' assistance) was in a Boston suburb and consisted of a nine-story 1931 building in the Art Deco style and an attached warehouse structure from the mid-'50s. Together they provided 430,000 square feet for the HMO's more-than-2000 employees. A problem, however, was that the three-story warehouse had floors of 70,000 square feet each, so large that many areas were far from exterior light and views. Sasaki solved the problem by introducing a generous central atrium rising through the structure and capped with a skylight, creating a hub of employee interaction; a stair cascading along one wall gives easy access to this gathering spot from all floors. Another drawback was that the landmark 1931 building had been empty for more than a decade and had been stripped of most of its Art Deco features. Sasaki decided, nevertheless, to respect its heritage, devising modern interpretations of Art Deco chevron motifs to replace the missing ornament. These are seen in three-dimensional forms created from painted wallboard and also in painted trim, carpet designs, and lighting fixtures. In addition to the open plan offices, a conference center, training facility, data center, kitchen, and full-service cafeteria have been provided.

Top, left: Entrance with lighting pylons.
Top, right: Workstation cluster.
Left: Seating group in the lobby.
Opposite: The skylit central atrium with its "waterfall" stair.
Photography: Lucy Chen.

282

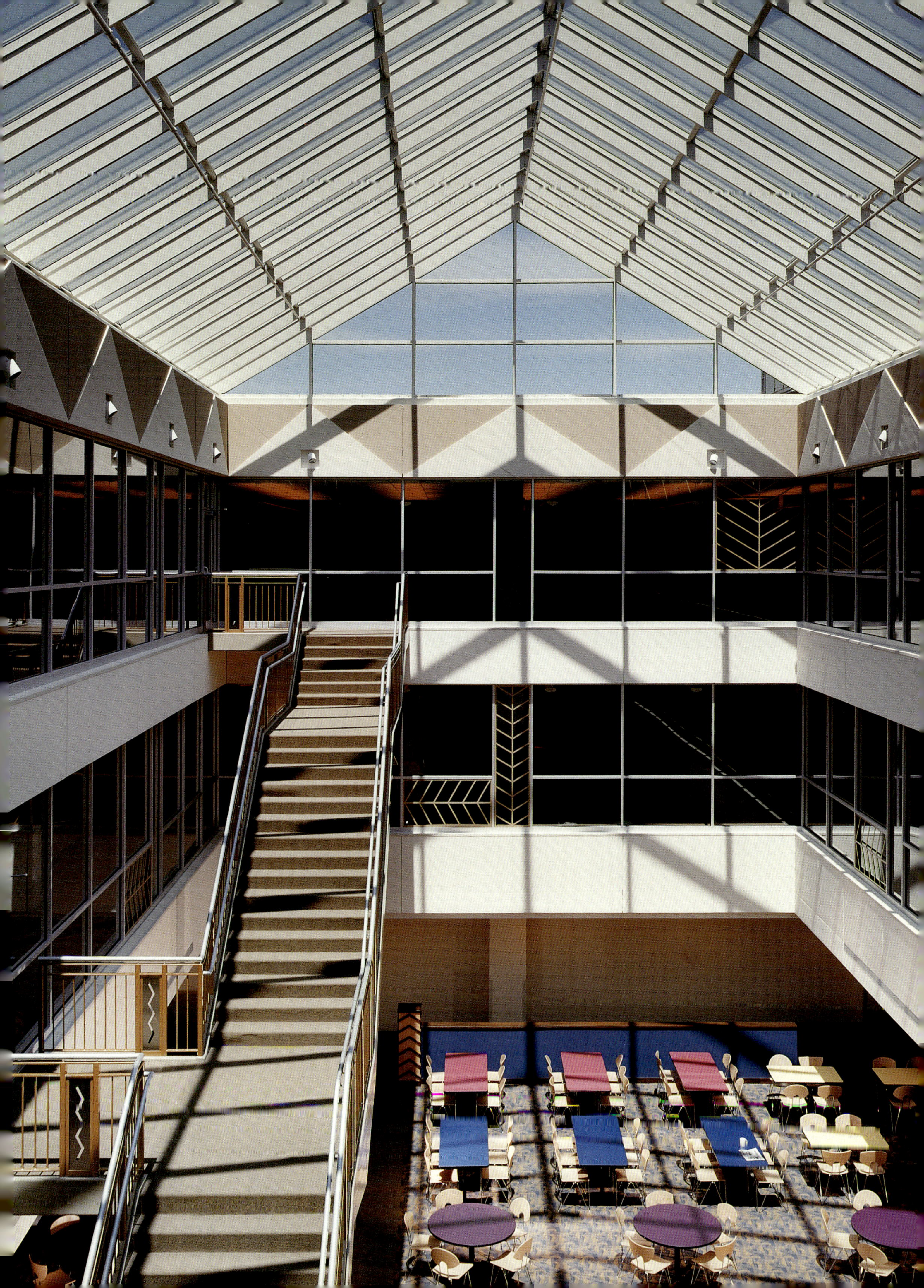

Sasaki Associates, Inc.

Scudder Mutual Fund Service Center
Salem, New Hampshire

Right: Exterior view (photograph by Christopher Barnes).
Below: The reception desk in the main lobby.
Photography: Richard Mandelkorn (except as noted)

For the Scudder financial and mutual fund management firm, Sasaki's mandate was a design that would communicate both an adventurous commitment to advanced business techniques and a conservative attitude regarding the use of shareholder assets — in other words, an environment with vigor but without extravagance. Also needed was a uniform space plan that could serve not only present needs but also future modifications. Scudder's commitment to technology was emphasized by the prominent placement of such facilities as a training center and an electronic "command cockpit" for customer service; these are visible from the building lobbies, which has a pierced, canted wall of artisan plaster suggesting an arcade. The three-floor, 114,000-sq.-ft. facility has been given orientation devices in the form of dropped luminous ceilings and burnished metal panels at key areas, and the materials and color palette throughout is more typical of a hospitality facility than of a corporate one. Wood veneer is used selectively in conference and dining areas. Staff amenities include a dining area, "coffee shops" on each floor, lockers, lounges, and an outdoor terrace.

Top, left: Commemorative plaque marks the building's opening and the years when embedded time capsules are to be opened.
Top, right: General training room seen from lobby.
Above: Technical training room.
Right: The cafeteria with custom lighting sconces of acrylic.

Sasaki Associates, Inc.

Scudder Shareholder Service Center
Norwell, Massachusetts

Right: Exterior view of curved entrance elevation.
Below: Reception desk at the base of the atrium.
Opposite: The central atrium.
Photography: Peter Vanderwarker

This project for a shareholder service center generated so much client satisfaction that it led to a second Sasaki commission for the same client (see preceding spread). It houses over 500 employees in 110,000 sq. ft., spread over three floors. The curving linear plan is centered on a building-high circular atrium lighted by a ring of clerestory windows, and each floor is further organized with a service core and six sub-cores, around which are clustered "neighborhoods" of open office landscape workstations. Interior space is therefore as flexible as possible. Sheltered in the concave side of the building's gentle curve is a terrace accessible from the employee cafeteria. Sasaki's work began with consultation on site selection and extended to programming, architecture, interior design, and landscape design.

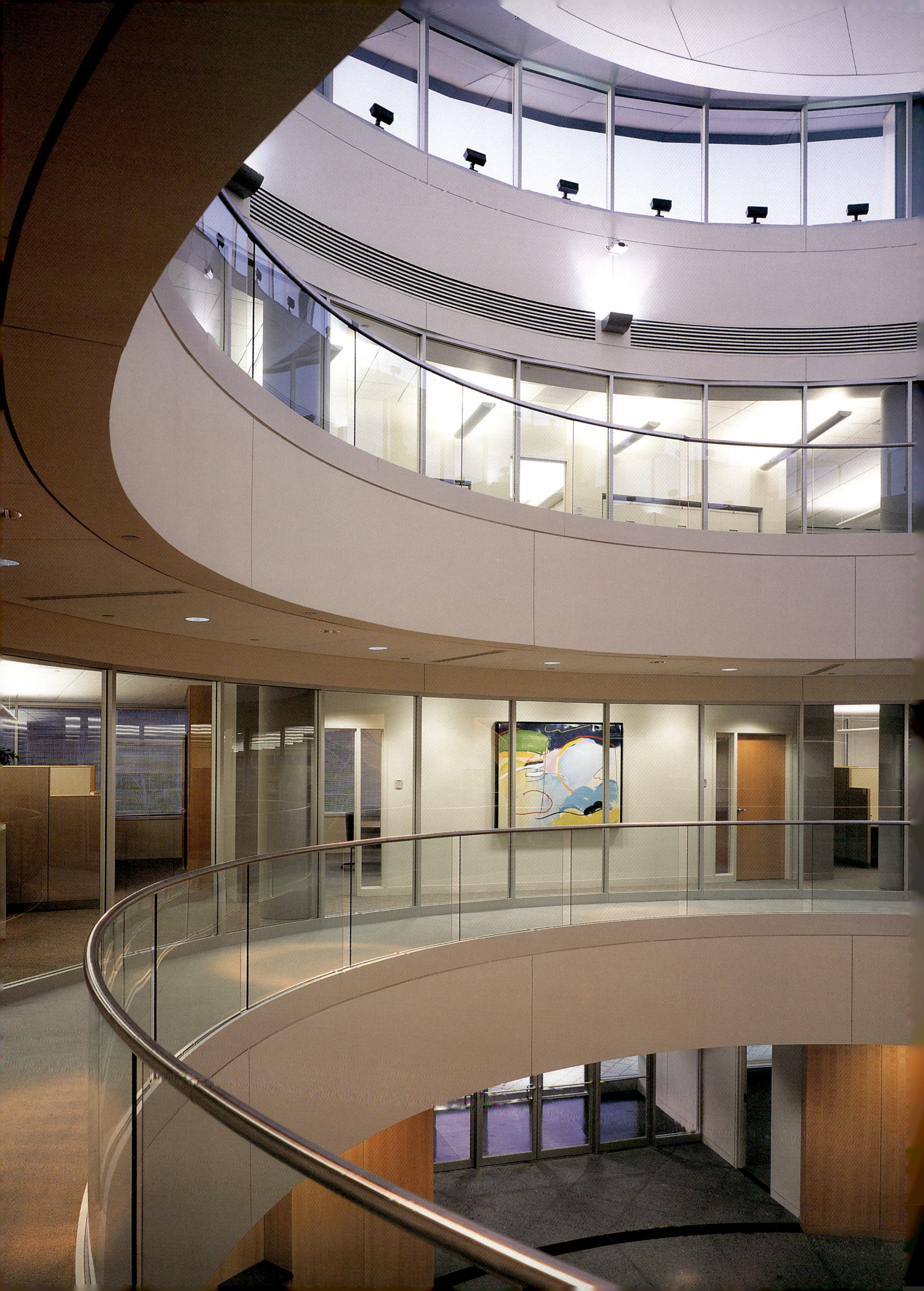

Sasaki Associates, Inc.

Sasaki Associates, Inc., San Francisco, California

For its own West Coast office, Sasaki wanted an open studio space that would promote collaboration among a diverse group of professionals. The chosen location was the 6,800-sq.-ft. top floor of a turn-of-the-century factory building in the historic Ghirardelli Square. The open plan capitalizes on expansive views of the city and the bay, and interior treatments respect the building's legacy of industrial materials. Scarred maple floors were uncovered, cleaned, and given a transparent finish; overhead, original metal trusses have been similarly cleaned and left otherwise undisturbed. Partitions stopping short of the metal-sheathed ceiling modulate space without blocking the flow of light, and a small core of closed rooms has been kept free of the exterior walls. In keeping with the building's character, sliding industrial doors are faced with zinc. A total of 35 employees are provided here with studio space, conference room, gallery, marketing area, and support services. The cost was $45 per sq. ft.

Right: Entrance area and reception desk in the firm's own San Francisco office. Original metal roof trusses were left exposed.
Photography: Chas McGrath.

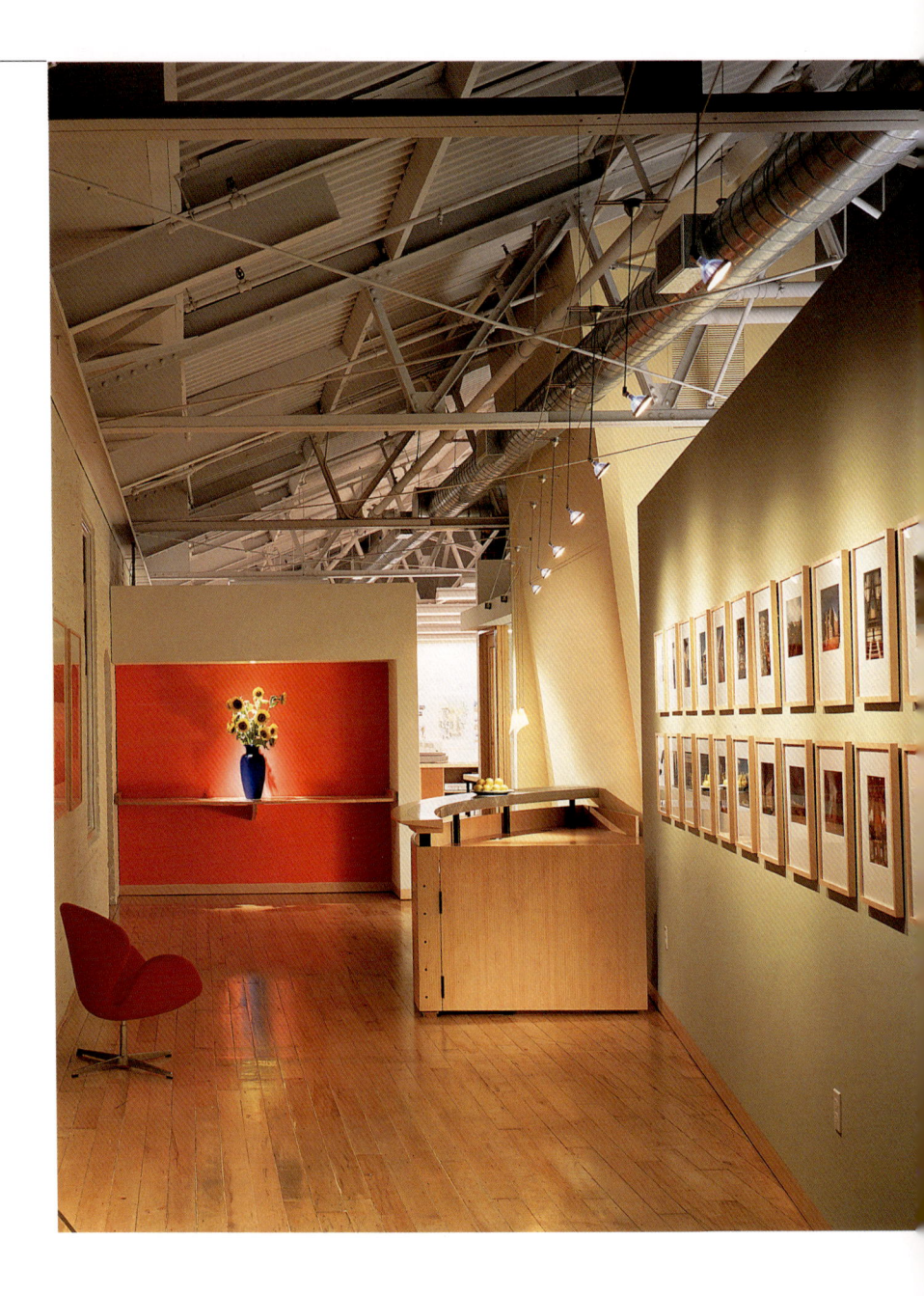

SCR Design
Organization, Inc.

305 East 46th Street
New York
New York 10017
212.421.3500
212.832.8346 (Fax)
www.scrdesign.com
info@scrdesign.com   Affiliates in Principal Cities of the World

SCR Design Organization, Inc.

MBIA (CapMAC)
New York, New York

Right: Interactive conference room.
Below: Room with some equipment in use.
Photography: Lynn Massimo.

This newly renovated 15,000 rentable sq.ft. floor is home to 120 employees of MBIA (CapMAC), a firm of municipal bond insurers. The building's elliptical floor plan presented a layout challenge - or, as the designers put it, "provided an opportunity to think out of the box." Rather than fighting the curves, SCR's design team worked with them to fashion an uninterrupted fluidity of space, most noticeably in a continuous interior corridor, roughly oval in shape, but articulated with a rhythmically spaced series of lighted display niches for the company's collection of fine Asian artifacts, some of them four centuries old. The corridor, therefore, becomes a gallery. Outside it are peripheral offices, sharing their daylight through translucent walls, and inside it are workstations, a trading room, and training and conference rooms. One of the conference rooms is equipped with the latest in audio-visual technology; its horseshoe-shaped table holds a series of computer stations that can be used for training seminars or collaborative work projects. This room and the trading room beyond share a wall composed of two panes of strengthened glass and, between the panes, a lamination of a special 3M film that, responding to an electrical charge, can make the wall either transparent or opaque; a desire for visual privacy can thus be accommodated at the flick of a switch.

Above, right: Art gallery corridor.
Right: Conference room with view into trading area.

291

SCR Design Organization, Inc.   **BMW of Manhattan, Inc.**
New York, New York

Left: *Evening view of the exterior.*
Below: *Showroom (first floor).*
Right: *BMW display beneath the angled glass wall.*
Right, below: *Sales/leasing showroom (second floor).*
Photography: Peter Paige.

SCR Design was awarded BMW's prestigious Manhattan headquarters project as a result of a design competition. This installation is more than just an auto showroom. Its five floors and 203,000 sq. ft. on Manhattan's West 57th Street also offer a service center, body shop, customer parking, new car storage, training facilities, a conference center complete with telephone and fax service, a European-style coffee bar, and executive offices. There is even a Lifestyle Boutique with gift items and memorabilia for BMW enthusiasts. About 100 employees are accommodated. The facility surpasses a typical showroom in stylistic character as well. Taking advantage of a vacant lot adjacent to the existing building, SCR designed a three-story atrium structure enclosing 3,000 sq. ft. within an angled wall of glass and steel, the structure not only giving the interior maximum visibility from the street, but also serving as a metaphor for the cutting-edge technology of the cars inside. This is now BMW's premier retail outlet in the United States, and, since completion of the SCR design, sales here are reported to have increased dramatically.

SCR Design Organization, Inc.

J. Muller International
New York, New York

Right: Reception area.
Below: Workstations with open conference area at left.

Above, right: A typical workstation.
Photography: Peter Paige.

J. Muller International is a leader in the design of bridges, a fact that is acknowledged in its company logo and in several aspects of these interiors designed for it by SCR. The space is a single floor of 10,000 rentable sq. ft. in a building on Manhattan's Park Avenue South, and it needed to accommodate 40 employees plus visitors. Included are private offices, placed in two rows along the sides of the windowed perimeter, workstations in a central open environment, a lunchroom, a conference room that can be divided easily into two smaller areas, a reception area, and service elements. These requirements were met on a strict budget and had to be inserted into an existing shell of little architectural distinction. SCR chose an economical but attractive materials palette of maple flooring, white-painted sheetrock, standard file pedestals, and plastic laminate work surfaces. Black columns punctuate the space, and halogen uplights mounted from the columns give a warm glow to the central open space. The custom-designed workstations are built within sheetrock panels that have been given a convex curve, emulating the arcs of bridge spans, and some of the metal furniture bases used throughout echo the same curve.

295

Above: J. Muller conference room with its movable wall in open position.

Conference rooms and private offices have dropped ceilings, while the central work spaces rise to the exposed building slab and supporting beams, and the reception area ceiling is pitched in an intriguing gabled effect. All these varying ceiling conditions, however, have been treated with restraint, all of them sharing the same white painted finish. The result is a sense of unusual spaciousness and simplicity. SCR's range of services for J. Muller included programming, space planning, design development, contract documentation, and administration of the construction process - in other words, from soup to nuts.

Silvester Tafuro Design, Inc.

Silvester Tafuro Design, Inc.
50 Washington Street
South Norwalk
Connecticut 06854
203.838.2436 (Fax)
STDICT@aol.com

Silvester Tafuro Bishop Design, Ltd.
Unit 7, 2nd Floor
Culvert House, Culvert Road
London SW11 5AP
United Kingdom
020.7498.5574 (Fax)
stbdesign1@compuserve.com

Silvester Tafuro Design, Inc.

US Airways Club
Philadelphia, Pennsylvania

Below: Overhead "beams" carry services and modulate the long space.
Right: A seating area beneath the suspended ceiling planes.
Photography: Tom Crane.

Within the Philadelphia International Airport, this 25,000-sq.-ft. lounge for USAir's frequent flyers posed some challenges in planning, design, and operational logistics: The space was eccentrically shaped, 400 feet long, entered at two separate points 250 feet apart, and ceiling heights varied from nine to 17 feet. A unified, cohesive look was desired, yet the long stretches of space needed to be divided into comfortably scaled seating groups. Above all, the arriving passengers needed to find what they needed without navigating the whole facility. Support functions such as restrooms, work carrels, television lounges, and coffee service areas were therefore duplicated several times along the lounge's length, as were the seating areas. The business center, however, has been kept at one end where ceiling heights are lowest, allowing those passengers not hard at work to enjoy the expansive window walls. Engineering requirements for HVAC and electrical access to the tall spaces resulted in the design of a series of horizontal beam-like elements that also serve to create the sense of individual spaces; between pairs of these beams, curved metal ceiling elements are suspended, and these hold downlights strategically positioned over the seating groups.

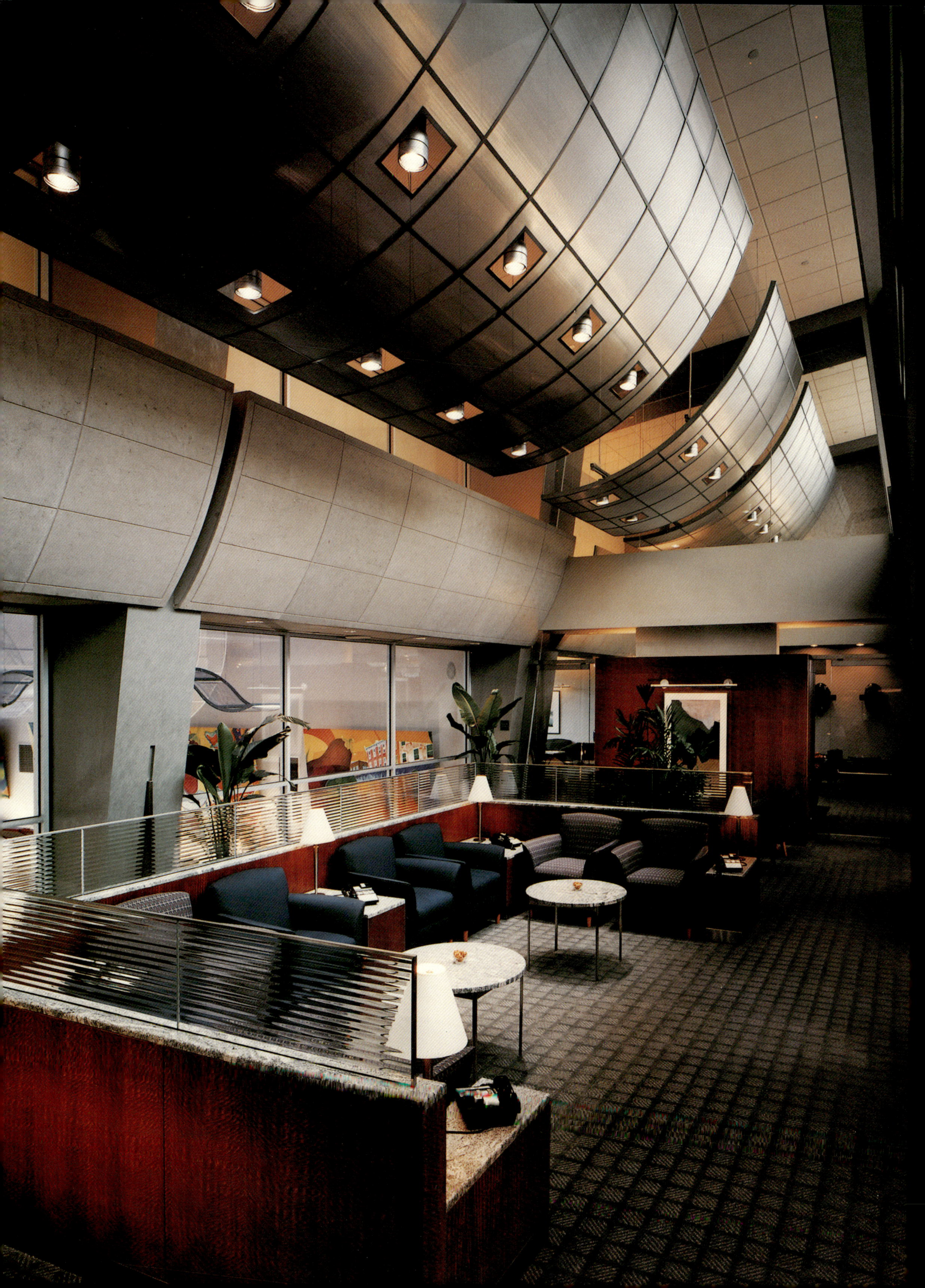

Silvester Tafuro Design, Inc.

Hudson News/Euro Café
Washington Dulles International Airport
Washington, DC

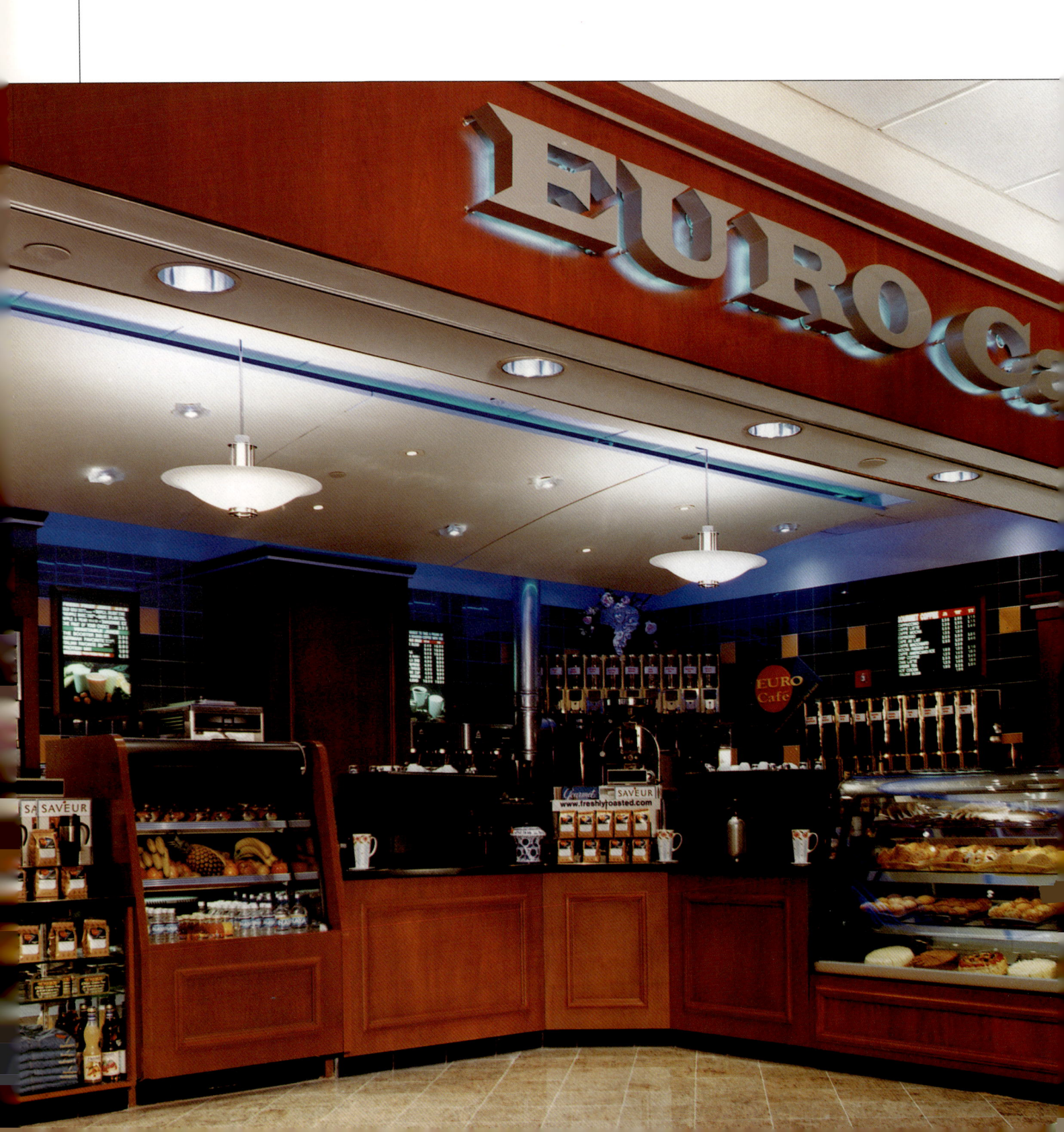

Described as a "very fast track" project, this 3,000-sq.-ft. installation had to fit within a long, shallow space in the Regional Airline Midfield Concourse and had to incorporate three distinct components, each with its own function. First, placed at one end of the space, was a coffee bar/café. Second, at the opposite end, was a Book Corner. And third, placed in the center, was a magazine, candy and cash/wrap counter. Unifying these three sections are the flooring of granite tile and the softly arched "floating" ceiling constructed of painted gypsum board. Other materials employed are star-patterned downlights, a blue neon strip, decorative Murano glass, carpet, metal trim, and — for cabinetwork — cherry wood. For the installation, Silvester Tafuro Design, Inc., provided the project conception, design development, construction documents, construction administration, graphics and logos. The colors, another unifying element, are described by the designers as "European, dark, and rich," adding an upscale look to the space.

Left: The Euro Café at the right end of the facility.
Right: Magazine and candy display.
Right, below: An overall view from the concourse.
Photography: Peter Paige.

Silvester Tafuro Design, Inc.

Hudson News
Grand Central Terminal
New York, New York

Left, below: The shop's rotunda-like central focus.
Bottom of page, left: A side view.
Bottom of page, right: Entrance seen from the terminal concourse.
Photography: Peter Paige.

Located behind the grand staircase of the beautifully refurbished main concourse of historic Grand Central Terminal, used by half a million people daily, is this Hudson News facility. At 3,000 sq. ft., it is the largest of three Hudson News outlets within the terminal complex, and it features over 3,000 magazine titles, including over 500 foreign publications. The organization of the space is dominated by a centralized focal point, a raised circular ceiling cove with indirect lighting. From this focus, radiating quadrants hold different display areas within makore and mahogany cabinetry, and the focus is enhanced by a centralized terrazzo flooring pattern recalling the cardinal points of a compass. The facility's role as an information center is also enhanced: Within the central rotunda, a continuous circular LED ticker provides up-to-the-minute stock market quotes and news stories, and four video monitors at the store perimeter broadcast the Fox News network. Bordering the ceiling and flanking the entry way are sepia-toned reproductions of classic magazine covers from decades past.

Silvester Tafuro Design, Inc.

LSG/Sky Chefs Sky Center
JFK International Airport
Jamaica, New York

With almost four million enplanements a year, it was determined that the American Airlines terminal at JFK International Airport was far below its potential concession space. The existing 20,000 sq. ft. was therefore expanded to 50,000, including food and beverage service, specialty retail, news and gift kiosks, and duty-free shops. Today, with rental agreements 95 percent complete, the expansion has more than doubled the per-passenger revenue. A design challenge was to create a cohesive program within two terminal buildings of very different character, and this was met by incorporating storefront facades of real and faux limestone and expanses of aluminum and glass, subtly echoing New York buildings of the 1930s. In the darker of the two terminals, large new vaulted skylights were added, and at night the lighting design reproduces the daylight effect. Reflective materials — stainless steel and glass ceramic panels — increased the light.

Above: Exterior view of a new concession area.
Right: Dining area under one of the new vaulted skylights.
Photography: Peter Paige.

Silvester Tafuro Bishop Design, Inc.

American Airlines City Ticket Office London, United Kingdom

Above, right: A sweep of seating at the curved counter.
Right: Looking back towards the Piccadilly entrance.
Photography: Pentagon Studios.

This facility provides American Airlines with a long-awaited presence on London's busy Picadilly. It occupies 3,000 sq. ft. on three floors of a "listed" building, in which exterior changes were severely limited, and security measures were another design consideration. Within these parameters, the ground floor ticket office, shown here, is completely new and vibrant in character, incorporating a long sweeping curve of counter separating sales staff from customers. Overhead, ceiling coves and curved track lighting over the counter repeat the movement. Prominent materials include American cherry, limestone, and granite, and the color scheme is a "hip" version of American's corporate red-white-and-blue. A staff room is in the basement below, and offices occupy the floor above.

Skidmore, Owing & Merrill LLP

14 Wall Street
24th Floor
New York
New York 10005
212.298.9300
212.298.9500 (Fax)

333 Bush Street
Suite 2300
San Francisco
California 94104
415.981.1555
415.398.3214 (Fax)

224 South Michigan Avenue
Suite 1000
Chicago
Illinois 60604
312.554.9090
312.360.4545 (Fax)

46 Berkeley Street
London W1X 6NT
United Kingdom
0171.930.9711
0171.930.9108 (Fax)

Skidmore, Owings & Merrill LLP

Financial Institution
New York, New York

Above left: Glazed wall of a typical office lets others share the Manhattan view.
Left: View from reception area to board room.
Above: The library for the firm's senior executives.
Photography: Marco Lorenzetti, Hedrich Blessing

Occupying a total of 50,000 square feet on two high floors of New York's Citicorp building, these offices for a rapidly growing investment firm demanded the utmost in flexibility. Working with the established grids of the building's structure, glazing, and ceiling modules, the SOM designers have responded with a universal lighting plan and a system of demountable partitions. Office enclosures that are largely of clear glass and doors of both clear and etched glass give most work areas a sense of openness and a share of the unparalleled views. The motivated staff works long hours in this environment, but their work is rewarded by — and their work spaces supplemented by — a number of on-site amenities: food service facilities offering breakfast-through-dinnertime food, meeting rooms both formal and casual, a library and magazine room, and a fitness center with changing rooms, lockers, and showers for men and women.

Skidmore, Owings & Merrill LLP

Chase Manhattan Bank Trading Facility
New York, New York

Having designed the Lower Manhattan landmark building at One Chase Manhattan Plaza back in 1960, SOM returned recently to insert new trading facilities into the tower. Two trading floors needed to accommodate 228 traders each, with all their requirements of space, computers, power, glare-free lighting, and the dissipation of generated heat, and infrastructure was also provided for the future addition of a third floor with another 228 positions. New generators were added on the tower's roof, served by new tanks and fuel lines, and the trading rooms were provided with Uninterrupted Power Supply, chilled water lines, cabling risers, and a new data center. A less technical — but equally important — requirement for such large areas was the maximizing of ceiling height, a problem made more difficult by the need for six-inch-high raised floors for the grids of cable routes. SOM achieved a new clear height of ten feet by removing the existing mechanical systems overhead and locating new fan coil units at the building's perimeter and core. In addition to the trading floors are associated amenities: offices, video conferencing areas, copy centers, coat rooms, and food service facilities. The materials palette, sympathetic to the original structure, includes stone, stainless steel, cherry paneling, and, on core enclosures, a highly durable polyester resin finish. A spiral stair of stone and steel connects the project's three levels. Total designed area is 73,200 square feet.

Above: One of the two trading floors.
Right: Stone and steel connecting stair.
Photography: Jon Miller, Hedrich Blessing

Skidmore, Owings & Merrill LLP

Goldman, Sachs & Co.
Superbooth at New York Stock Exchange
New York, New York

Right: *Goldman, Sachs Superbooth*
Photography: *Durston Saylor*

The first technologically upgraded trading station completed as part of a pilot program on the floor of the New York Stock Exchange, the Goldman Sachs "superbooth" brings the technical capabilities and design quality of Goldman Sachs's own trading desk to its traders on the floor of the exchange. A modular integrated datawall at the rear of the booth centrally houses all CPUs and peripherals and provides market data information from a variety of worldwide sources including NYSE ticker quotes, four video news service providers, and a continually updated data board. This same wall provides additional cooling capacity and storage areas for the eight trading positions that flank both sides. Two-way video connections linked to multiple Goldman Sachs trading facilities allow for seamless communication, and computer workstations are equipped with the same capabilities as those at the trading desk and enable brokers to execute orders more rapidly and efficiently. Multi-line phones with speed dialing and conferencing capabilities replace old single-line models, and experimental voice-activated order processors have been implemented. Comfortable, ergonomically designed seating placed at curvilinear synthetic countertops establish a level of design quality consistent with the Goldman Sachs headquarters. The superbooth is gently lit by diffused light reflected from the suspended curved ceiling.

Skidmore, Owings & Merrill LLP

Kirkland & Ellis Law Offices
New York, New York

The planning module is a frequently employed tool for bringing order and cohesion to today's corporate interiors, but seldom has it been used more pervasively or more persuasively than in the two-floor, 48,000-square-foot Manhattan offices for the law firm of Kirkland and Ellis. The resultant order is joined by a liberating sense of openness and light, with perimeter offices largely enclosed in glass. Where privacy was wanted for lawyers' offices, a pearlescent glass layer was laminated between two ribbed layers, blocking the view but still transmitting the light.

The heart of the office is a two-story law library, featuring a dramatic stair that, with open risers and laminated glass treads, continues the theme of lightness.

Left: Reception area under a metal grid.
Right: The double-height library and its glass stair.
Photography: Michael Moran

Skidmore, Owing & Merrill LLP

Financial Media Services Company
Princeton, New Jersey

SOM designed 16,000 sq.-ft. of temporary space on two floors to accommodate the expansion of this company's Multi-media Group. Adhering to a set of established design guidelines, the project design provides work space for 140 employees. Two groups of employees, the analytics department and the magazine department, are located on separate floors with shared informal meeting spaces.

Because of the unique composition of the company and the lack of an office hierarchy, the designers were able to incorporate many amenities on a limited budget. There was no requirement for private offices, and all work-stations are equal in square footage, which resulted in the creation of extra shared space and improved furniture and finishes standards. The program also includes two 70-person training rooms and a break-out room. Two conference rooms, located within the office area, are designed with revolving partitions that can also serve as pin-up space. A large multipurpose room located centrally within the office is available for employees and clients to exchange ideas; it features special computer workstations, cybercafe-style, that serve dual purposes, allowing employees an alternative place to work, in addition to showcasing the company's products and services.

Above: *Revolving partitions and view into conference room.*
Right: *Reception and seating area with view into servery and informal meeting/work space.*
Photography: *Durston Saylor*

**Staffelbach Design
Associates Inc**

2525 Carlisle
Dallas
Texas 75201.1397
214.747.2511
214.855.5316 (Fax)
www.staffelbach.com
sda@staffelbach.com

Staffelbach Design Associates Inc

Temerlin McClain
Las Colinas, Texas

Below: Double-height reception area.
Right: The chairman's office.
Photography: Nick Merrick © Hedrich-Blessing.

Temerlin McClain (formerly Bozell) is one of the 25 leading advertising agencies in the world. When the agency selected Staffelbach Design Associates Inc to design its corporate offices in Las Colinas, an executive park between Dallas and Fort Worth, the challenge was to create a contemporary but highly sophisticated environment that would reflect its increasingly global activities and would appropriately serve its clients, many of them members of the Fortune 500. The location, totaling 86,000 sq. ft., was spread over nine floors of an irregularly shaped structure that had a total of five entrances on various levels. Temerlin McClain moved several of its remote operations into the building, thus becoming its sole tenant, and Staffelbach simplified the situation further by reducing the number of entrances to two. One of these has been given a pronouncedly dramatic reception area, its previous finishes of brick and concrete replaced by a new composition of granite, glass, stainless steel, and black leather. The room's double height is emphasized by an array of dozens of pendant light fixtures highlighting — and

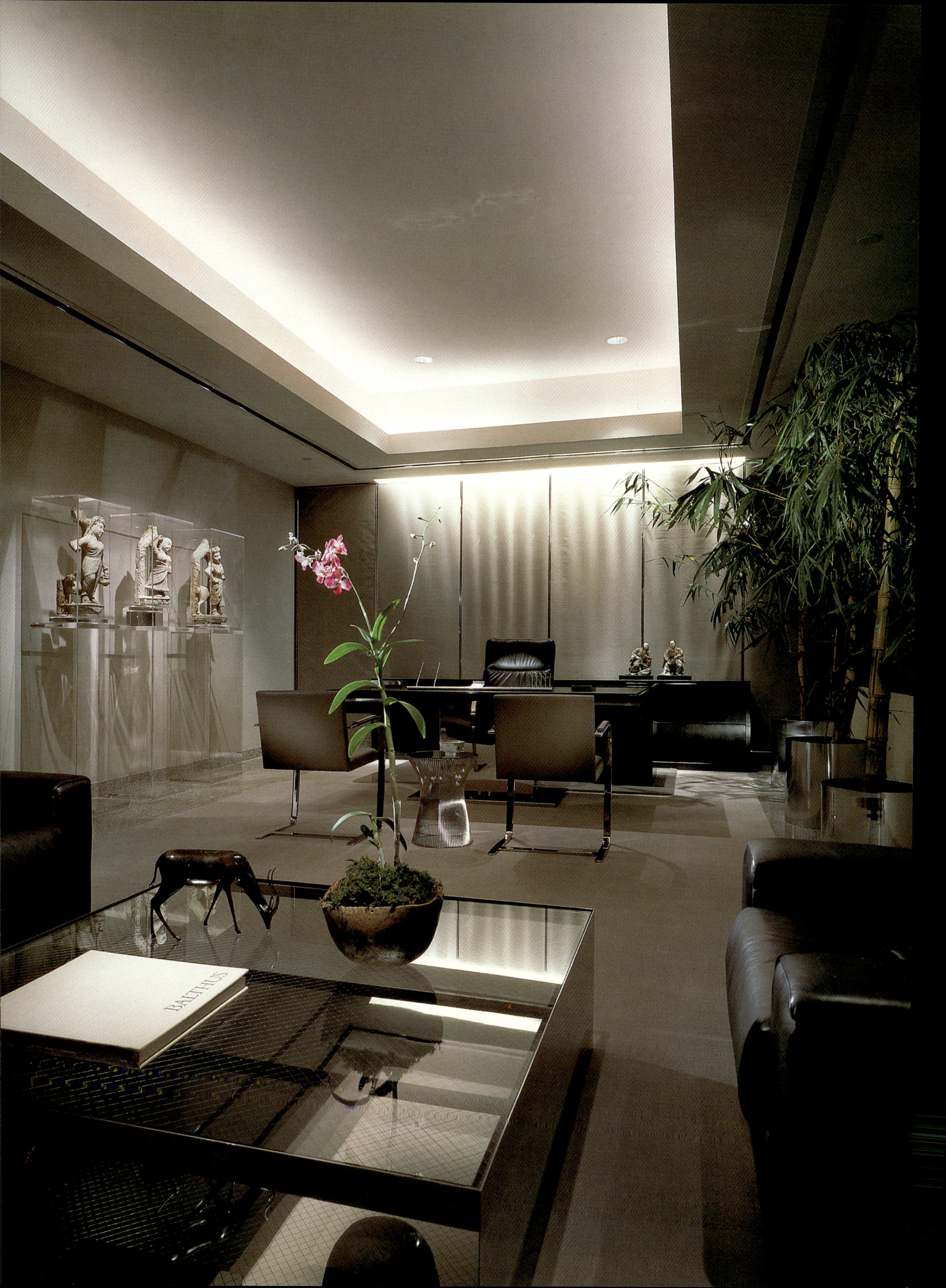
BALTHUS

Above: The president's office features antique chairs and art from his own private collection.
Opposite, top: The theater.
Opposite, below: Presentation room.

reflected in — the polished gray granite floor. The custom-designed reception desk is of black granite, and a projection of the earth's two hemispheres on the opposite wall reminds visitors of the scope of the agency's work. Other highlights of the installation are upstairs on the executive floor, where presentation rooms have been designed to complement — but not to upstage or interfere with — Temerlin McClain's impressive and progressive advertising presentations. Furnishings here are of chrome and leather, with subdued fabric facing the rooms' oval wall surfaces. Overhead, indirect lighting comes from recessed ceiling coves, and versatile technical equipment supports both on-screen and on-wall images. Also on the executive floor are the chairman's office and the president's office. Both feature ancient artifacts displayed in museum-quality vitrines, and both blend traditional art and antiques with new furniture and modern classics. Walls of glass block provide privacy while allowing a soft suffusion of natural light, and wall panels in the chairman's office are faced with stainless steel mesh. Every phase of the Staffelbach redesign was accomplished while the agency continued to conduct "business as usual."

Staffelbach Design Associates Inc

A.T. Kearney
Dallas, Texas

Left: View from elevator lobby into the reception area.
Photography: Jon Miller © Hedrich-Blessing.

Right: Corridor view, looking into a consultant's office.
Below: Administrative workstation, with two consultants' offices beyond.

This 30,000-sq.-ft. office on a single floor of an existing downtown Dallas highrise has been designed to accommodate the 90-person staff of A.T. Kearney, a firm offering professional consulting services. Also accommodated are the firm's consultants, for whom private and semi-private offices have been provided, and its visitors. These last are greeted by an impressive sequence of design features at the entrance, beginning with a custom-designed light canopy of aluminum and glass. This leads to a custom reception desk and, behind it, a "monument" wall faced with blue-gray slate. To either side are partially glazed walls enclosing a 22-seat board room and a 10-seat conference room, both provided with rear-projection audio-visual equipment. Flooring in the reception and conference areas is of Arabesco Fantastico marble and Grigio Perlato granite,

319

and walls are surfaced with Burlington stone slate. The boardroom floor is carpet, edged with granite. The color palette throughout is neutral and subdued, with rich accents of warm woods, natural stones, and stainless steel. Planning is open, and the sense of spatial flow is heightened by a generous use of glass. The installation's design has won for Staffelbach Design Associates Inc a corporate design award in a regional competition of the IIDA (International Interior Design Association).

Above: View into A. T. Kearney boardroom.
Right: The conference room adjacent to the lobby.

Sverdrup CRSS
A Division of Jacobs Facilities Inc.

1300 Wilson Boulevard	Arlington
Suite 500	Atlanta
Arlington	Boston
Virginia 22209	Chicago
703.351.4200	Costa Mesa
703.351.4366 (Fax)	Denver
	Houston
400 South 4th Street	New York
St. Louis	Orlando
Missouri 63102	Phoenix
314.436.7600	Portland
314.552.8005 (Fax)	Sacramento
	St. Louis
	Walnut Creek

Sverdrup CRSS

Sverdrup CRSS Offices
Arlington, Virginia

Below: *Reception desk and visitor waiting area.*
Photography: *Eric Taylor.*

Sverdrup CRSS (formerly Sverdrup Facilities, Inc.), now a division of Jacobs Facilities Incorporated, has major design and construction centers in Arlington, Virginia, and St. Louis, Missouri. Other offices are located in major cities throughout the United States. In Arlington, the staff of approximately 220 is housed on two floors of 23,000 sq. ft. each. Floor plates in the renovated Commonwealth Tower Building dictated the cruciform layout. Following this geometry, the design team located shared facilities around the central building core, and then created four separate office and studio areas on each floor. At the fifth floor lobby, a lacquered pearwood reception desk, accented with stainless steel and glass, serves as the focal point for the space. Other materials include granite tile floors, painted drywall partitions, and suspended ceilings with direct and indirect lighting fixtures. Furnishings and colors have been kept simple and timeless, in order to emphasize project presentations. A generous use of clear and etched glass partitions throughout the office spaces creates an open feeling, transmitting natural light to studio areas and fostering communication among managers and staff. Accents of pearwood, stainless steel, and black granite and black leather repeat throughout the office spaces, as well as in the executive offices and conference rooms. Workstation areas utilize indirect lighting, selected to enhance the computer work environment. The systems furniture pallette repeats the monochromatic scheme of medium-grey finishes against a black-and-grey pinstripe carpet, accented with black borders. Nicholai Kolesnikoff, vice president of the firm, explains that the design goal was to create "space that presents a sophisticated yet cost-conscious appearance to our clients." He reports that some clients of the firm have requested that the environment be duplicated in their own facilities. For their office facility in Arlington, Sverdrup CRSS provided programming, space planning, interior design, graphic design, lighting design, data and telecommunications design, and construction services.

Above: Studio area with views into private offices.
Right: The internal stair between studios.

Sverdrup CRSS

Ernst & Young LLP
Austin, Texas

Right, above: Looking towards the reception area from the elevator lobby.
Right: Client presentation/conference room.
Right, below: A partner's 150-sq.-ft. office.

Sverdrup CRSS began work for the accounting and consulting leader Ernst & Young with the Dallas office of the firm (seen on the following pages). Many of the design principles developed for the Dallas project were adopted for the Austin facility, which accommodates 100 employees and their visitors in 18,000 sq. ft. of space. Although smaller, Austin is similar to Dallas in functional and operational requirements. Together, the two offices provided Sverdrup CRSS the opportunity to develop a new office prototype for Ernst & Young. Goals developed with the Ernst & Young management team included maximizing flexibility while minimizing occupancy costs. Also key was the presentation of Ernst and Young as an efficient, client-driven organization, with integrated services and easy interaction among groups. Typical office space is interchangeable, not hierarchical. Voice and data technologies are highly connective ("networked") and integrated into workspace while remaining portable. Such technology is able to support a variety of alternative workplace strategies, including hotelling. For this prototype facility in Austin, Sverdrup CRSS provided programming, space planning, interior design, graphic design, lighting design, and communications technology solutions.

Above: Corner office of a managing partner.
Photography: Anthony Carosella and Peter Wilson, Sverdrup CRSS.

Sverdrup CRSS

Ernst & Young LLP
Dallas, Texas

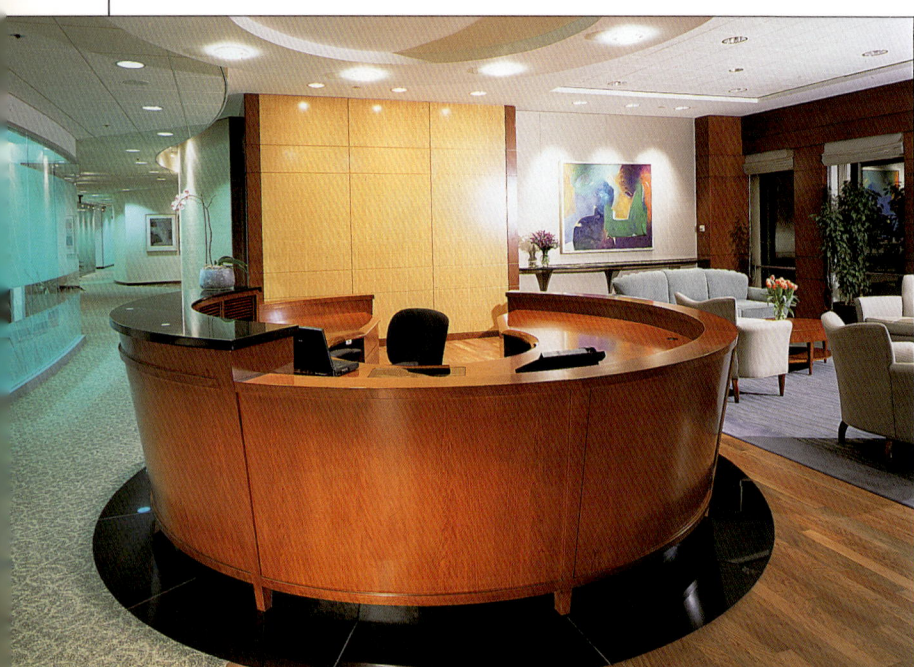

Above: Elevator lobby, with view into the reception area.
Left: Reception area with "Main Street" beyond.
Left, below: A mini-meeting room.
Photography: Anthony Carosella and Peter Wilson, Sverdrup CRSS.

Dallas offices for the accounting and consulting firm Ernst & Young occupy 180,000 sq. ft. on six equal floors, and accommodate 1,000 employees. A variety of office spaces were required, including private offices, meeting and client presentation rooms, teaming and training rooms. Employees also needed access to shared resources areas, including break rooms, high-density file rooms, a library resource center, a file server room, and a center for copy, mail, supplies, word processing and graphic design work. To organize these areas both functionally and spatially, the designers created a "Main Street," wider than the typical office corridor. Similar to a small town main street, this highly interactive area provides employees with telephone booths (30 sq. ft. each); mini-meeting rooms (120 sq. ft.); and "huddle" rooms

Right: The teaming room.
Below: The client presentation/conference room.

(120 sq. ft). Also available are teaming rooms; conference rooms; coffee/snack rooms with lap-top and lunch tables; and all of the typical services including copy centers, hotelling lockers, and reference material collections. Curving walls along this thoroughfare provide a changing series of vistas and reinforce the notion of fluidity through movement. Along the way, the aniline-dyed movingue walls house touch-screen monitors framed in tulipwood. For work requiring heads-down concentration, employees leave the bustle of "Main Street" through entrances or portals and retreat to quieter work areas, including study carrels, "cockpit" offices (75 sq. ft), and private offices (150 sq. ft.). A month after occupancy, the management of Ernst & Young reported that the design of the facility was helping them attract new employees.

Right: "Main Street" with reception desk and view into a client conference room.
Below, left: Also off "Main Street," one of the "huddle" rooms.
Below, right: A 75-sq.-ft. "cockpit" office.

Swanke Hayden Connell Architects

295 Lafayette Street
New York
New York 10012
212.226.9696
212.219.0059 (Fax)

1030, 15th Street, NW
Suite 1000
Washington, DC 20005
202.789.1200
202.789.1432 (Fax)

First Union Financial Center
200 South Biscayne Boulevard
Suite 970
Miami
Florida 33131.2300
305.536.8600
305.536.8610 (Fax)

84 West Park Place
Stamford
Connecticut 06901
203.348.9696
203.348.9914 (Fax)

25 Christopher Street
London
England EC2A 2BS
44171.454.8200
44171.454.8400 (Fax)

Kore Sehitleri Cad.
No. 34/2 Deniz Is Hani
80300 Zincirlikuyu
Instanbul
Türkiye
90.212.275.4590
90.212.275.3780 (Fax)

Swanke Hayden Connell Architects

SBC Warburg
New York, New York

Right: View from one conference/dining area into another.
Below: The reception and client contact area.
Photography: Gayle Gleason.

For SBC Warburg, an investment banking firm, Swanke Hayden Connell Architects has designed a complete tenant fit-out for 160,000 sq. ft. on two floors of a New York building. In addition to private offices and open workstations, client requirements included a trading floor, conference rooms, reception and client contact areas, an employee cafeteria, and a suite of private dining rooms. Requirements for the character of these spaces were of two types: first, SBC desired a reinforcement of its established image and an appropriate backdrop for its collection of antique furniture; but second, there was also a desire for expression of the company's progressive outlook and its use of innovative telecommunications technology. Swanke Hayden Connell therefore blended traditional, transitional, and contemporary imagery: a wood-paneled lobby, tapestry-like upholstery fabrics, and doors and door frames of Makore mahogany veneer nod to the past, while detailing throughout is minimal and crisp, and carpet tile is arranged in modernist patterns. Further client needs were for quick-as-possible occupancy, and to this end the designers worked closely with the building staff and construction manager to develop a series of mini-phases contributing to a fast-track construction schedule.

Top of page: The trading floor.
Right: Stair leading to reception area.

Swanke Hayden Connell Architects

**Mobil Oil Company Limited
Witan Gate House
Milton Keynes, United Kingdom**

Right: The employee coffee bar.
Below: The cafeteria with servery beyond.

In 1993, Swanke Hayden Connell International Limited (SHCIL) was asked to assist Mobil Oil's corporate real estate division in moving its U.K. headquarters from London to a site near the M25 motorway. SHCIL provided an analysis of space requirements and appraised a number of new buildings for their appropriateness, and eventually the Witan Gate House at Milton Keynes was chosen. It provides four floors of space totaling 125,000 sq. ft. Following the selection process, SHCIL provided design services, the preparation of construction documents, and on-site construction monitoring. The firm also proposed the early appointment of a Construction Manager and of various trades in order to meet the client's requirement for speed. For the 500 Mobil employees brought to Milton Keynes, a variety of amenities were provided, including a coffee bar as well as kitchen facilities and a full-service dining room that has won an award for the best new catering facility in the region. There are also meeting rooms, a training center, and a mail room with reprographic equipment. General offices, including clusters of team rooms and other communal spaces, occupy the building's upper three floors. The entire project was conceived as a possible model for Mobil's worldwide redefinition of its space use strategy; considered a success, the Milton Keynes design and its occupational standards are now being applied throughout Europe. All work was accomplished within a period of eight months.

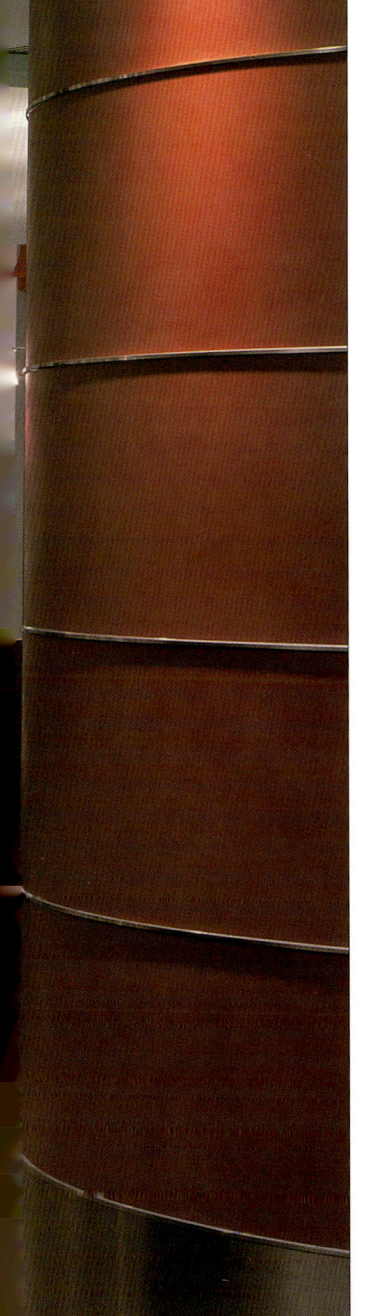

Right: *The boardroom.*
Photography: *Jeremy Cockayne.*

Swanke Hayden Connell
Architects

Citigroup Corporate Center
New York, New York

Opposite, top: A view across the atrium.
Left: A flexible area that can be used for meeting breakouts or for dining. Ginger jar lamps add a non-institutional touch.
Top of page, left: Corridor with secretarial workstations.
Top of page, right: Executive bath with marble counter.
Above: Library (one of a pair) has a bowed wall of wood and glass.
Photography: Peter Aaron/ESTO.

Before Citigroup was formed by the merger of the Citibank banking giant and the Travelers Group, Swanke Hayden Connell Architects had done work for both its components: an executive suite for Citibank's chairman and headquarters for Travelers. A natural, then, that they be chosen to design the new entity's corporate center in the namesake Citigroup Center at Lexington Ave. and 53rd St. The occupied space, divided among three equal levels (floors three, four, and five), totals 90,000 sq. ft., and housed here are approximately 165 Citigroup workers, including some top executives of the corporate leadership. The middle floor is linked to the upper one by an open elliptical stair detailed in sycamore —an important material throughout the interiors — detailed with stainless steel railings; the middle floor is linked to the lower one by a less flamboyant enclosed stair. Private offices and open workstations for support staff are found on all levels, as are reception areas; only the top level boasts the boardroom suite, the dining areas, the fully equipped kitchen, and the generous breakout area, this last furnished with groupings of lounge chairs but able to function also as additional dining space. Several of the many conference rooms are unconventional and informal in character and referred to as libraries with chairs around clusters of small tables. Conference rooms of more typical design are also available, of course. Materials have been chosen to bring warmth to the center, notably the aforementioned sycamore. Complementing it are sisal wallcovering, flooring of natural cleft slate, and panels of carved glass. An extensive art program, carefully lighted, includes a three-story red-and-gold atrium triptych painted by Valerie Jaudan.

Above: Citigroup's elliptical stair is sheathed in sycamore and has an open railing of brushed stainless steel.
Right: Conference room has sisal wall covering and an onyx counter; the table is veneered in sycamore and cherry.

Ted Moudis Associates

305 East 46th Street
New York
New York 10017
212.308.4000
212.644.8673 (Fax)
tma@tedmoudis.com
www.tedmoudis.com

Ted Moudis Associates

Tiffany & Co.
New York, New York

Left: Room has multiple seating groups interspread with jewlery vitrines. The windows overlook East 57th Street.
Photography: Christopher Barrett © Hedrich-Blessing.

The 9,000-sq.-ft. mezzanine level is located in Tiffany's famous Fifth Avenue retail store. The mezzanine is home to Tiffany's customer service department, it's venue for promotions and social events, and their most exclusive jewelry collection. To follow suit with the store's main floor, the character and feel of the mezzanine floor is that of quiet elegance. Ted Moudis Associates' cohesive plan links the floor's functions with inviting vestibules, display niches, and quiet anterooms that act as areas of interest as well as versatility. The customer service area is planned in a logical and accommodating manner. The focal point is a prominent reception desk, flanked on either side by comfortably furnished waiting areas and a series of private consultation bays. Each bay is lined in mahogany, fitted with generous, cantilevered limestone counters, and adorned with upholstered guest chairs. The Tiffany Room is a divisible room able to be configured for a variety of events, and is equipped with a full service kitchen for all catering needs. Due to its central location on the floor, the Tiffany Room also acts as additional gallery space connecting the customer service area and the Diamond Salon. The room's sophisticated palette combines beige-toned walls, rich mahogany wood, stainless steel accents, and chocolate and beige wool carpeting. The Schlumberger Room is a smaller and more intimate room designed by Tiffany's in-house Store Planning and Visual Merchandising departments. It is here that Tiffany's most exclusive jewelry collection is shown. Custom vitrines, neutral wall color, elaborate wood moldings, and soft wool drapes, together with the help of Ted Moudis Associate's lighting suggestions combine to give the room a warm and inviting feeling. With a phased project schedule, Tiffany's customer service department was able to maintain business during construction. Together, with Tiffany's in-house design departments, Ted Moudis Associates' helped create the versatile and elegant space that reflects the Tiffany image so well.

Above: The Schlumberger Room overlooking Fifth Avenue.
Above, right: Seating area in the Diamond Salon. The Tiffany Room is beyond.
Right: Private consultation bays in the customer service area.

Ted Moudis Associates   Deutsche Telekom
New York, New York

German-based Deutsche Telekom is one of the largest telecommunications companies in the world. For it's North American headquarters, Ted Moudis Associates was asked to design two floors totaling 37,000 square feet in a Park Avenue tower with views of Rockefeller Center, St. Patrick's Cathedral and the Hudson River beyond. Within this archetypal Manhattan setting, the client's desire was to reflect their European roots. A unique requirement, was the need for a space that would act as an interactive-showroom and educational facility to aid clients in understanding the capabilities Deutsche Telekom has to offer. Clustered together in a showroom, large graphic images advertise various products or services. Each panel has an accompanying interac-

Right: View from elevator lobby towards reception area.
Below: Interconnecting stair, with glimpses of the reception areas on both floors.
Right, below: Videoconference area in Customer Service Room.
Right, bottom of page: Reception area with stair in foreground.

tive area, whereby the client is able to log-on to the flat screen computer to research, investigate and gather pertinent information about the particular product. The product and services stations are housed in an appropriately "high-tech" environment, consisting of a stainless steel ceiling plane, motorized solar shades, black theatrical track lighting, and structural columns sheathed in aluminum. This modern, "techy" feeling is consistent throughout the space and includes the reception areas, video conference rooms and other public spaces. A variety of shades of gray and silvery whites dominate the interior and are warmed by repetitive accents in pear wood. An inter-connecting custom designed staircase has railings and parapets of flat stainless steel members, and horizontal industrial cables between. The European influence is evident in the selection of the reception furniture with recognizable modern classics in shiny chrome and soft, black leather. Ted Moudis Associates designed a floor plan in layers, with the outermost perimeter along the windows consisting of private offices, offices for visiting European employees, conference rooms, and the product and services showroom. Adjacent to the outermost layer is a secretarial layer with large built workstations located directly adjacent to each private office. The innermost layer is for support, which includes the reception areas, copy and equipment spaces, pantries, and a server room. A generous use of glass throughout the project allows an tremendous amount of natural light to infuse and warm the interior.

Above: Looking from the videoconference area towards the interactive product and service showroom.
Photography: Christopher Barrett © Hedrich-Blessing.

Ted Moudis Associates

Ted Moudis Associates' Own Offices
New York, New York

For the design of their own space on adjoining floors in a mid-town Manhattan office building, (7,500 sf on the 16th floor and 5,000 sf on the 17th floor), the architectural and interior design firm of Ted Moudis Associates instituted a firmwide design competition. Each employee, including the administrative staff and accounting department was included on a design team. Each team was charged with analyzing needs, developing concepts and expressing their "wish lists" to include in a new environment. This new office environment would not only be where they would all work, but would act as a representation of the type of interiors they are capable of creating for

Above: Main conference room with glass sidelight facing reception area.
Right: Looking from elevator lobby into reception area.
Photography: Christopher Barrett © Hedrich-Blessing.

future clients. This firm-wide involvement fueled imaginations, generated tremendous energy and created a cohesive spirit. The end result, culled from the best contributions of all the teams, is an open work environment infused with tremendous amounts of natural light. A prominent, custom staircase was designed not only for ease of circulation between the two floors, but to encourage communication. Having only a few necessary closed spaces, the interior is primarily open, taking full advantage of its bright location and unobstructed views on the banks of the East River. Together, the low, built workstation partitions, combined with the high, exposed ceilings of this former factory, maximize

Above: Open workstations in a loft-like area. In the background are the open resource library and a team room.
Right: View into reception area, with an open area workstation at left.

Right: *The Ted Moudis Associates team room with a view over New York's East River.*

openness and the distribution of natural light throughout the space. To offset these permanent architectural features, the satellite meeting spaces and conference areas are comprised of lightweight furniture that is easy to reconfigure and allows for maximum flexibility. The materials and finishes selected reflect the firm's strength and sense of timelessness. The carpet's subtle pattern of tan and gray offset stripes, and the walls' ivory toned paint establish a neutral backdrop that is enriched by a warm glow of pear wood feature walls, cabinetry and other architectural details. Frosted glass sidelights, stainless steel accents, and chrome highlights are used throughout the space, adding a touch of sparkle and contrast in the neutral interior. The success of Ted Moudis Associates' collaborative design effort is attested by a number of the firm's clients, who have admired the environment and have requested "Exactly the same!" for their own space.

van Summern Group

422 Summer Street
Stamford
Connecticut 06901
203.327.4141
203.327.2233 (Fax)
architects@vansummern.com

van Summern Group

Fort James
International Headquarters
Deerfield, Illinois

Fort James is the world's second-largest towel and tissue paper company worldwide. The goal for this 125,000-sq.-ft. International Headquarters in Deerfield was twofold: first, Fort James wanted to project an image of confidence and forward vision, reflecting the strength of its recent mergers; and second, it sought the creation of a visual language that would serve as the catalyst for the emergence of a new corporate culture. This language, in the hands of the van Summern Group, is grounded in paper products, their manufacture, their character, and their ecological impact. Wood—the source of paper—is used throughout; maple and cherry were chosen because they are both unendangered and renewable. These woods appear not only in the furniture and flooring but also in wall panels and a variety of custom-designed suspended ceiling elements. Artwork is similarly related to Fort James's business. In the gallery adjacent to the boardroom, for example, common handmade papers from around the world are delicately suspended in hand-rubbed black lacquer frames. The entire project, from design concept through construction, was accomplished in less then four months.

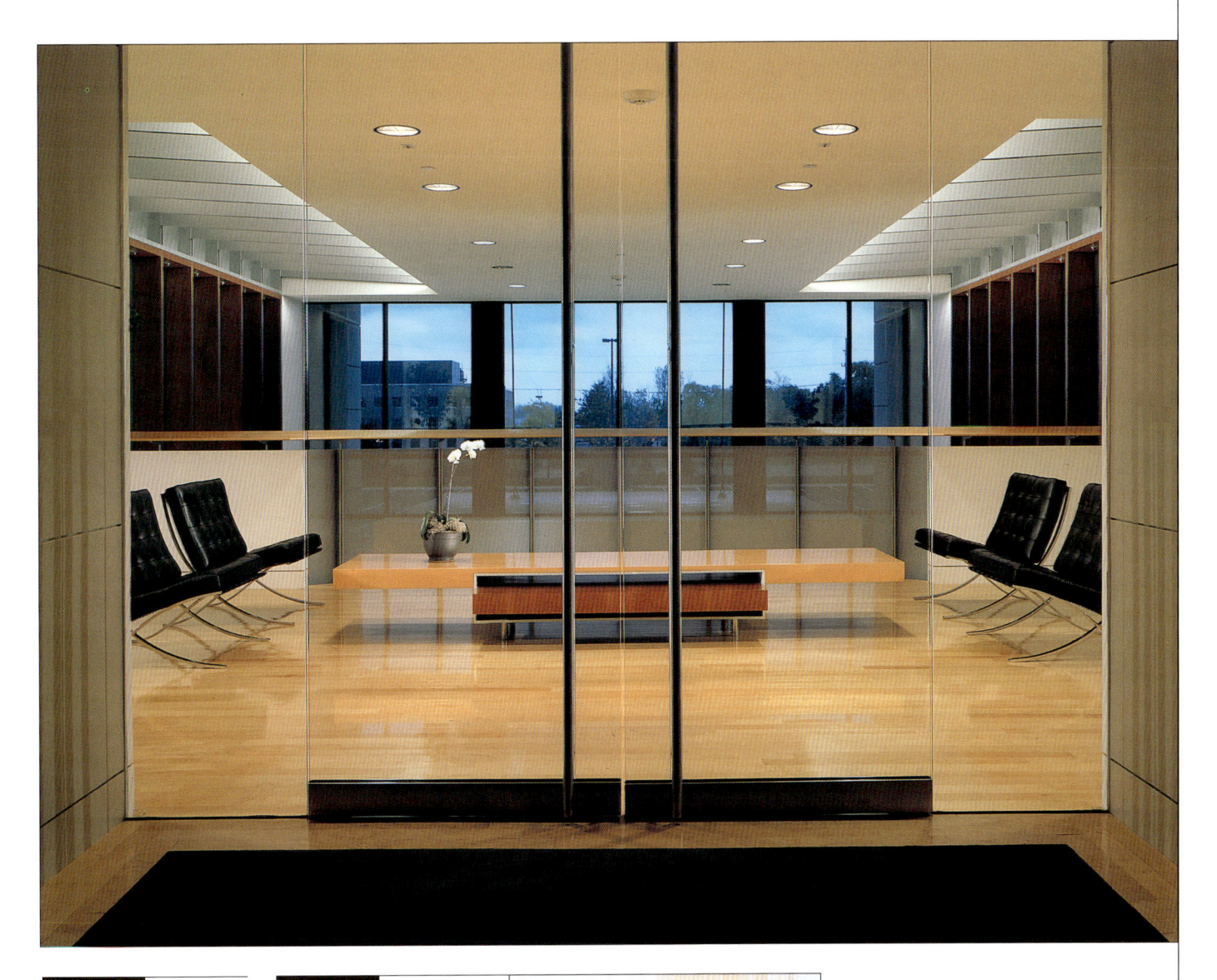

Opposite: Double-height main entrance lobby designed to make use of an existing developer-spec lobby space.
Above: Mezzanine seating area overlooking the main lobby.

Right: Detail of custom table design in mezzanine seating area. *(Photography: Robert Allen, vSG)*
Photography: Scott McDonald © Hedrich-Blessing, except as noted.

Right: The reception area of the executive floor.
Below, left: Executive dining room, with boardroom beyond. (Photograph: Robert Allen, vSG)
Below, right: Boardroom, with gallery at left.

Right, above: View down office suite hallway.
Right: View out of typical executive office.

van Summern Group

Fort James
North American Headquarters
Norwalk, Connecticut

As with its International Headquarters, seen on the previous pages, Fort James wanted its North American Headquarters to express a fresh attitude towards the company's business future and to reinforce the new language of its culture. This project, too, was completed, in less than four months, which included both the Thanksgiving and Christmas holidays. Again, warm woods dominate the materials palette, and artwork relates to paper and its sources. Twenty photographs commissioned from Paul McGuirk are displayed in niches throughout the installation. They depict the stark realities of the paper manufacturing process, its workers and machinery. Prominently flanking the open conference room area are two tall lighting fixtures from Spain that evoke giant pieces of paper wrapped around single shafts of light. Corridor lighting is diffused through rice paper laminated between sheets of glass, and walls are covered in random-weave rice paper. The headquarters in Norwalk, Connecticut, totals 160,000 sq.ft., including the 18,000-sq.ft. executive floor.

Opposite: The reception area on the executive floor.
Top: Central space leading to conference area is sparely furnished to accentuate the effect of the light fixtures and custom table beyond.
Right: Corridor ceiling diffuses light through laminations of rice paper and glass.
Photography: Paul Warchol.

van Summern Group

Fraser Papers
Stamford, Connecticut

Left: The main reception area.
Below: Detail of display case featuring fiber-impregnated paper diffuser at back of case.
Photography: Robert Allen, vSG.

As part of its relocation and fitout of a 30,000-sq.-ft. space in Stamford, Connecticut, Fraser Papers asked the van Summern Group to design a reception area that would communicate its new corporate identity and strategic positioning in the paper industry. Working closely with the Marketing and Corporate Communications Department, the designers created a welcoming space that tells the company's story at-a-glance. Behind the receptionist's desk, custom-designed in multiple woods, is a high-contrast floor-to-ceiling abstracted photograph of a forest scene. On the facing wall, shown here, a wall display illustrates the company's products. Each of Fraser Papers' six divisions is represented by a graphic image, while cantilevered wood-and-glass light boxes display individual paper types and products from each division. The space has consolidated the entire product line into a comprehensible, confident whole, and has becomes a source of pride for those who represent Fraser Papers.

WPG Design Group

85 John Street
New York, NY 10038
212.566.5048
212.566.5854 (Fax)
www.wpgdesign.com

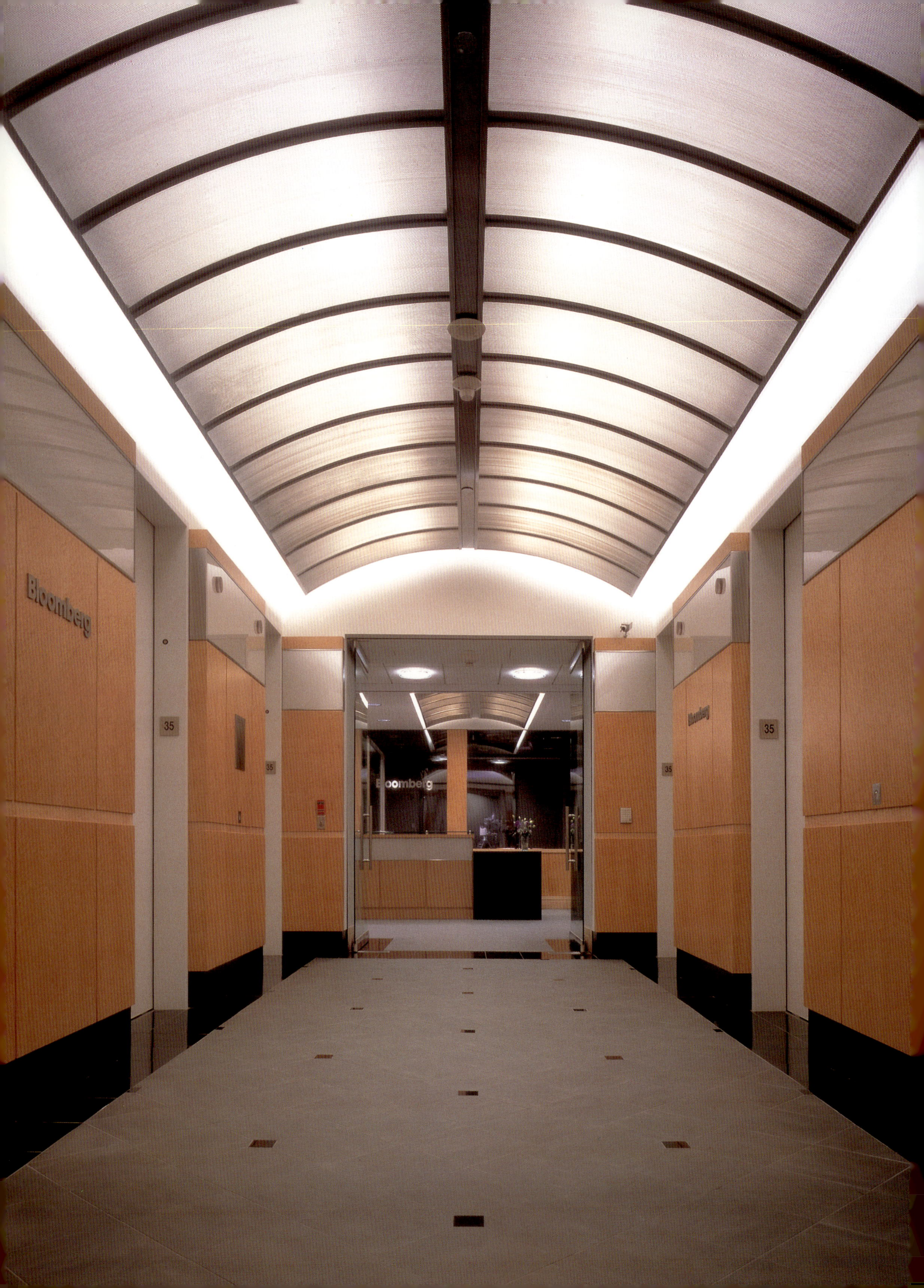

Bloomberg
35
35
Bloomberg
35
35
Bloomberg

WPG Design Group

Bloomberg, L.P.
San Francisco, California

Opposite page: View from the wood-faced elevator lobby into reception area.
Below: Conference room with a "Bloomberg screen" giving a variety of financial data.
Photography: David Wakely.

This new 18,000-sq.-ft. facility serves as the west coast sales office for Bloomberg, L.P., a financial services company with international connections, with South American headquarters in São Paulo, Brazil, and with satellite locations in a dozen cities in the United States, Canada, Mexico, and Malaysia. The San Francisco sales office is also a Bloomberg flagship, however, prominently located on a single floor of a landmark office building with dynamic views of the city, its bridges, and its bay. The visitor is directed from the elevator lobby, with paneled walls of birdseye and straight grained maple, beneath a translucent stainless steel mesh ceiling vault and into the reception area; from there, two other key spaces are visible: the first is a lounge and food service area, where employees and their guests are entertained not only by the views but also by a collection of exotic fish in a large aquarium; the second is a broadcast studio used for live television and radio productions, reports and interviews. In this studio, the various conference rooms, and elsewhere throughout the office, Bloomberg's own terminals provide visitors or staff with the opportunity to check current market activity and other financial information.

Seminar rooms and a large training facility are equipped with advanced broadcasting equipment. An open plan area has been designed for 88 workstations with a number of video display columns interspersed among them. There are private offices as well, and the usual complement of support services. The manifestations of Bloomberg's technical expertise that are evident throughout the office have been emphasized by the designers, not by enclosing them in a "high-tech" environment, but by contrasting them to surroundings that are calm and orderly, contemporary but warm. Surfaces have been kept simple, the materials palette features glass, maple, and painted drywall, the lighting design is a careful combination of cove, ambient, and conventional fixtures, and the color scheme is based on recessive neutral tones with natural wood accents. Within this serene shell, Bloomberg's impressive electronic and broadcasting capabilities have been effectively showcased.

Below: Bloomberg's lounge and pantry area. At right is the aquarium of exotic fish.
Right: The terminal training room.

357

WPG Design Group

Perfumes Isabell
Corporate Headquarters
New York, New York

Right: Conference table with an array of products.
Below: Lounge seating in the reception area.
Photography: Roy Wright.

The pleasures of perfume are largely olfactory, but not entirely: There are also sensuous visual effects associated with perfume's packaging and presentation. Such effects have been fully acknowledged and applied by WPG Design Group in this 6,500-sq.-ft. corporate headquarters for Perfumes Isabell. Fittingly located in the heart of Manhattan's famed "flower district," the headquarters houses corporate and sales functions in a streamlined version of a loft-like environment. Ceilings have been left open to their full height, exposing overhead ducts and sprinkler lines, and the space's hardwood floors and pendant light fixtures complement the loft atmosphere. Within this eminently practical shell, however, the designers have created an elegant display of the client's sophisticated wares. These include not only the perfume bottles themselves, but also the finely crafted brushed aluminum vitrines and kiosks used to display the bottles in retail locations. Also highlighted are striking backlit panels that emphasize the floral origins of the

359

floral origins of the company's scents. Comfortable seating in the reception area and conference room allow relaxed contemplation of the displayed wares. Even in the open workstation areas, the designers have adapted furniture systems and custom elements to create additional areas for both conferences and display. Flexibility for future growth has also been an important design determinant. And effectively mediating between the casual character of the loft environment and the elegance of the displays are tabletops, doors, and wall panels utilizing glass in differing degrees of translucency.

Above: One of the workstations custom designed for Perfumes Isabell.
Right: Receptionist's desk with product display.

360

"I told my architect we wanted a place where ideas can't help but collide. A space that gives us an edge on the competition. Where the techi and the artist both feel at home. And work is what you escape to, not from." When you want an architect to build on your vision, call a member of The American Institute of Architects.

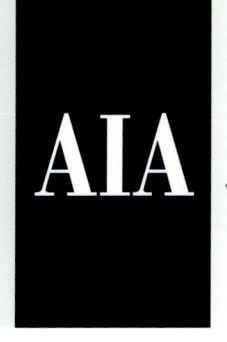

AIA

Building on Your vision.

THE AMERICAN INSTITUTE OF ARCHITECTS

aiaonline.com

Buildings that engage.

Geiger BRICKEL

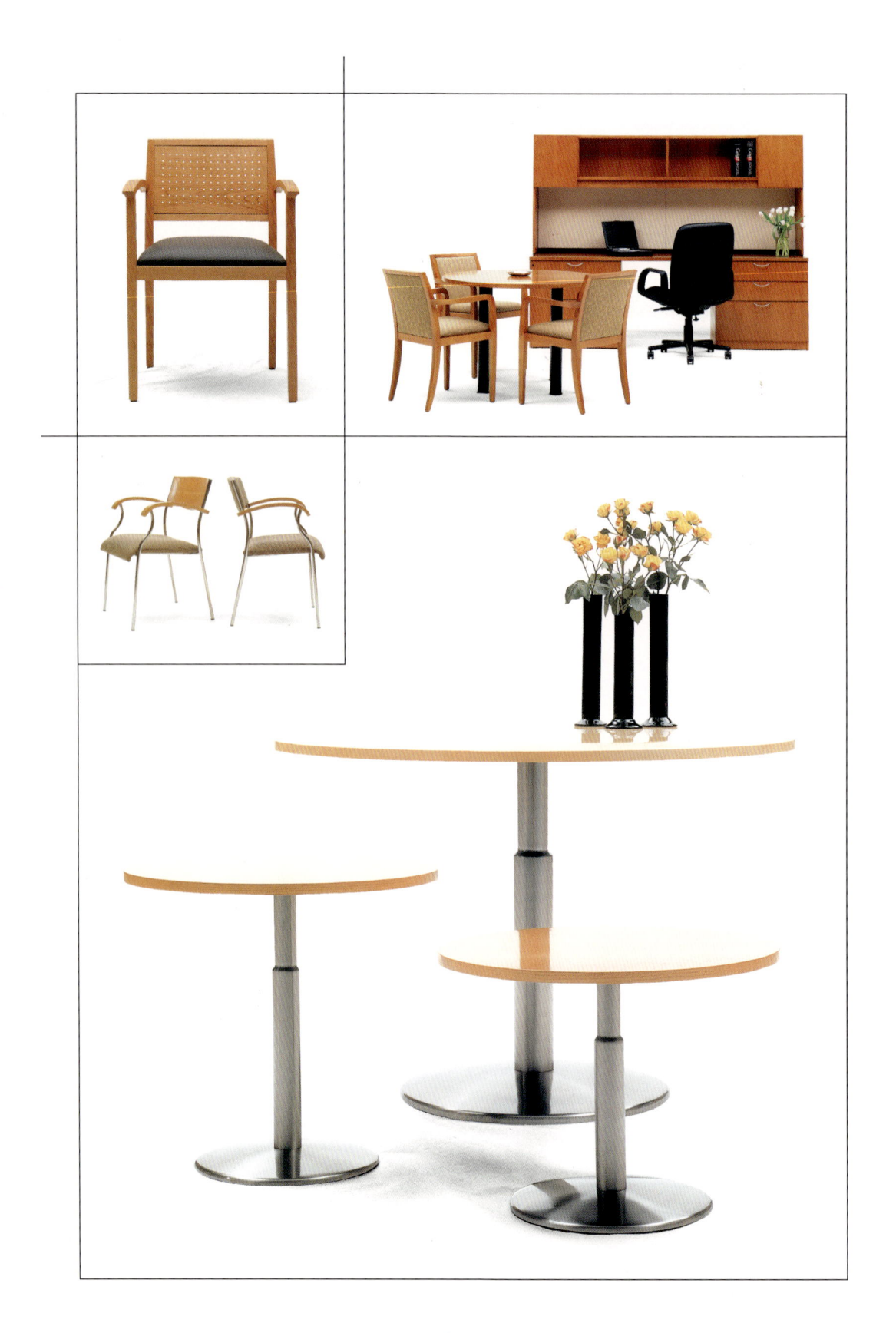

A HERMAN MILLER COMPANY   800.444.8812   WWW.GEIGERBRICKEL.COM
ATLANTA   CHICAGO   HOUSTON   LOS ANGELES   NEW YORK   SAN FRANCISCO   LONDON

Geiger BRICKEL

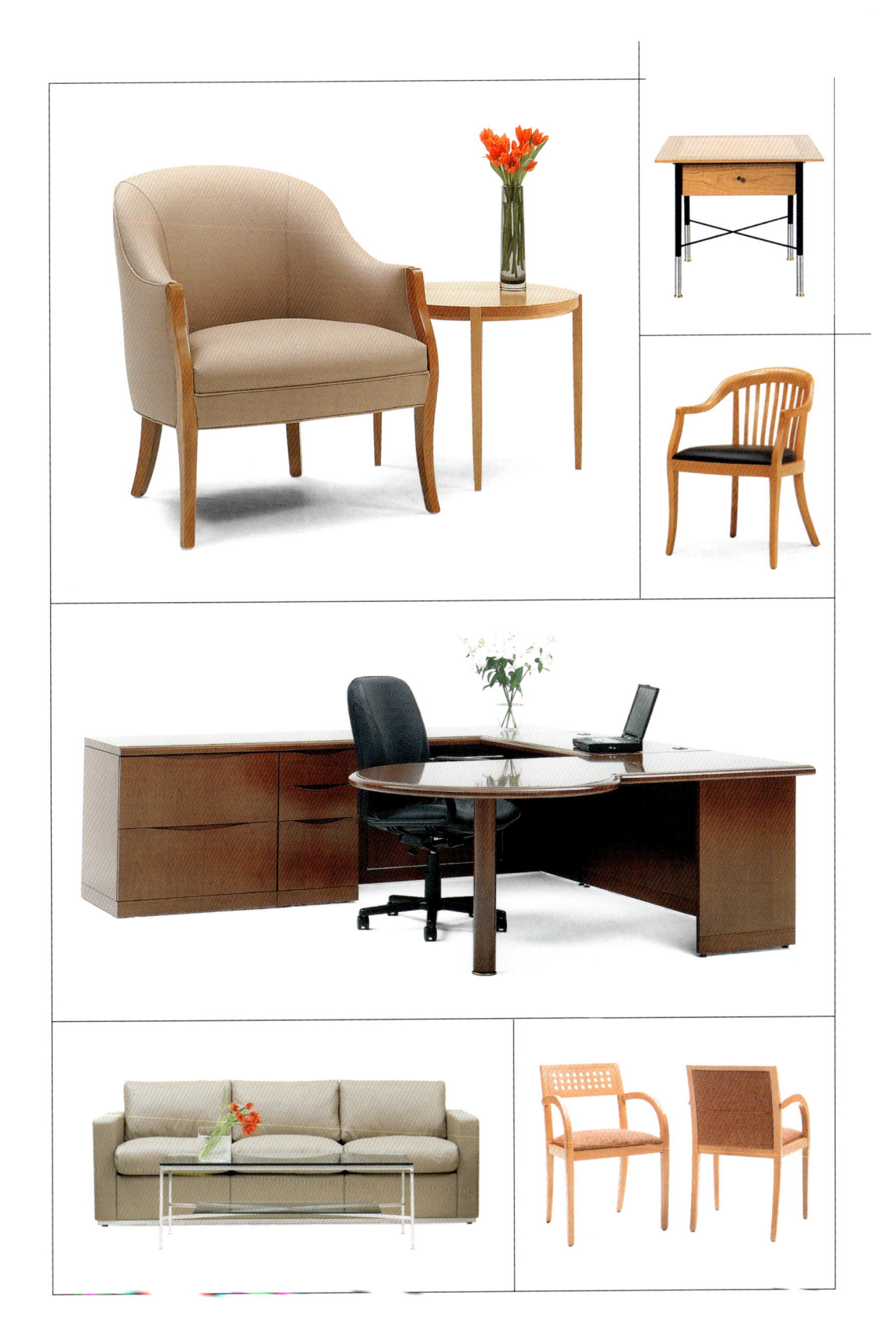

FURNITURE FOR ARCHITECTURE   800.444.8812   WWW.GEIGERBRICKEL.COM
ATLANTA CHICAGO HOUSTON LOS ANGELES NEW YORK SAN FRANCISCO LONDON

ICF

THE PLANK CHAIR IN ZEBRANO OR EBANO TECHGRAIN

ICF|group

ICF • Unika Vaev • Nienkämper • Helikon
800 237 1625
www.icfgroup.com

Carnegie creative textiles for contract interiors

carnegiefabrics.com 800.727.6770

JM Lynne Corporate

Specify exclusive wallcoverings from JM Lynne's Vinyl Resource collection for your next corporate interior, including designs by Patty Madden. 1.800.645.5044. www.jmlynne.com

high tech humanity

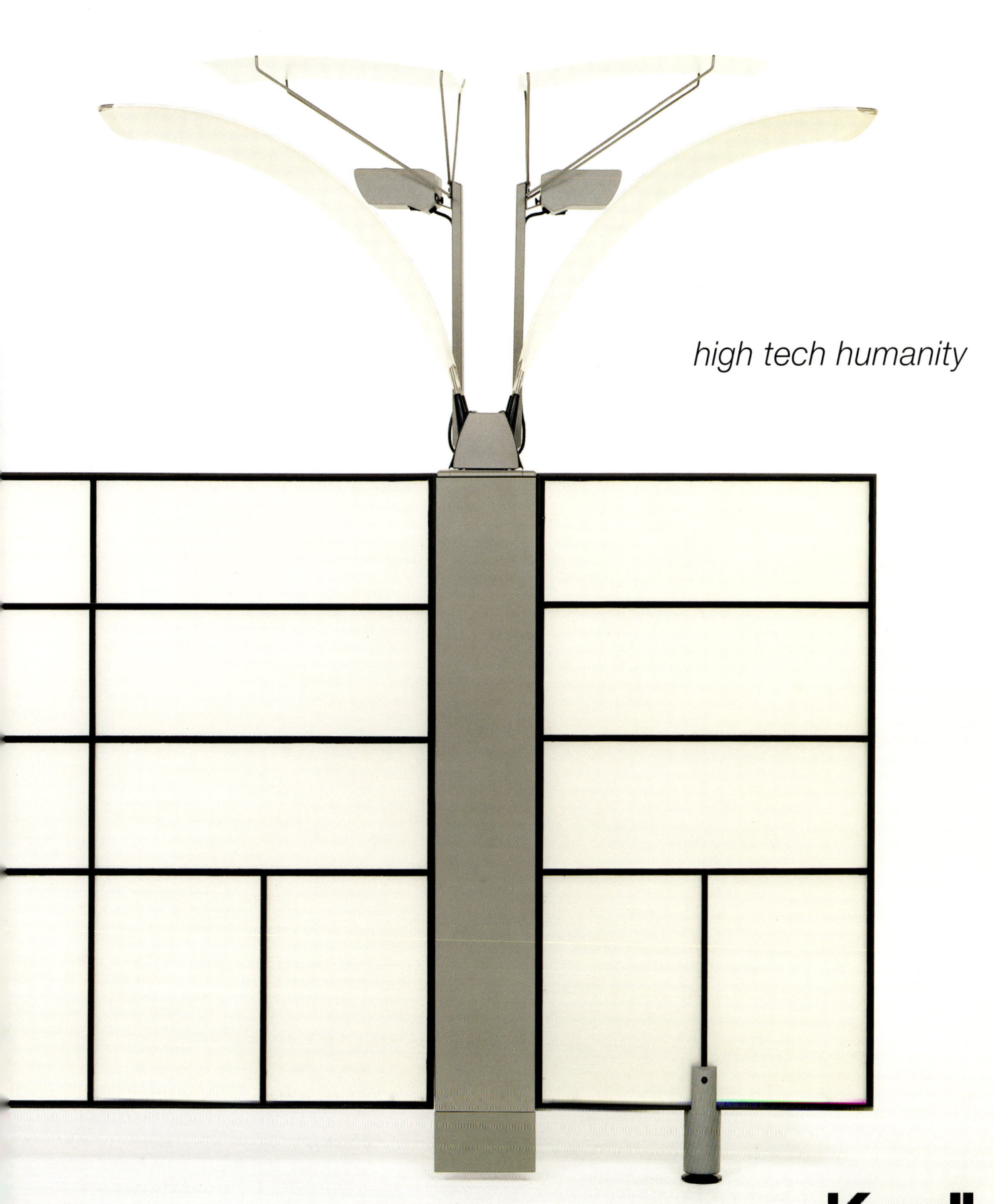

Knoll

F

FIXTURES FURNITURE

A Jami Company

Tough room, tough crowd, tough furniture.

| The D Chair | The Round Wave base | The Bola | The Saturn base | The Encore |

FIXTURES FURNITURE

Pretty tough stuff.™

1-800-821-3500

IIDA
INTERNATIONAL INTERIOR DESIGN ASSOCIATION
CHARTER CORPORATE INDUSTRY MEMBER

©1999 Burlington Industries, Inc.

EARTHY
RABL
TIMELESS
TURE

From a series of collections designed by Clodagh for Lees. For information - 800•545•9765 www.leescarpets.com

Clodagh for Lees

A Division of Burlington Industries, Inc.

Poetry in Motion

Its upper back
moves
as your upper
back
moves.

Its lower back
moves
as your lower back
moves.

Its seat
moves
as your seat
moves.

Its arms
move
as your arms
move.

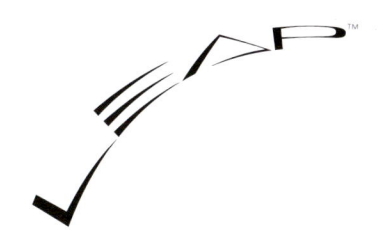

Leap is the first chair that contours to you and your spine…and not the other way around.

See for yourself. Test sit Leap at a Steelcase dealer near you…just for the health of it.
For a Leap CD call 1.800.333.9939, or go to steelcase.com.

Steelcase

SCHUMACHER

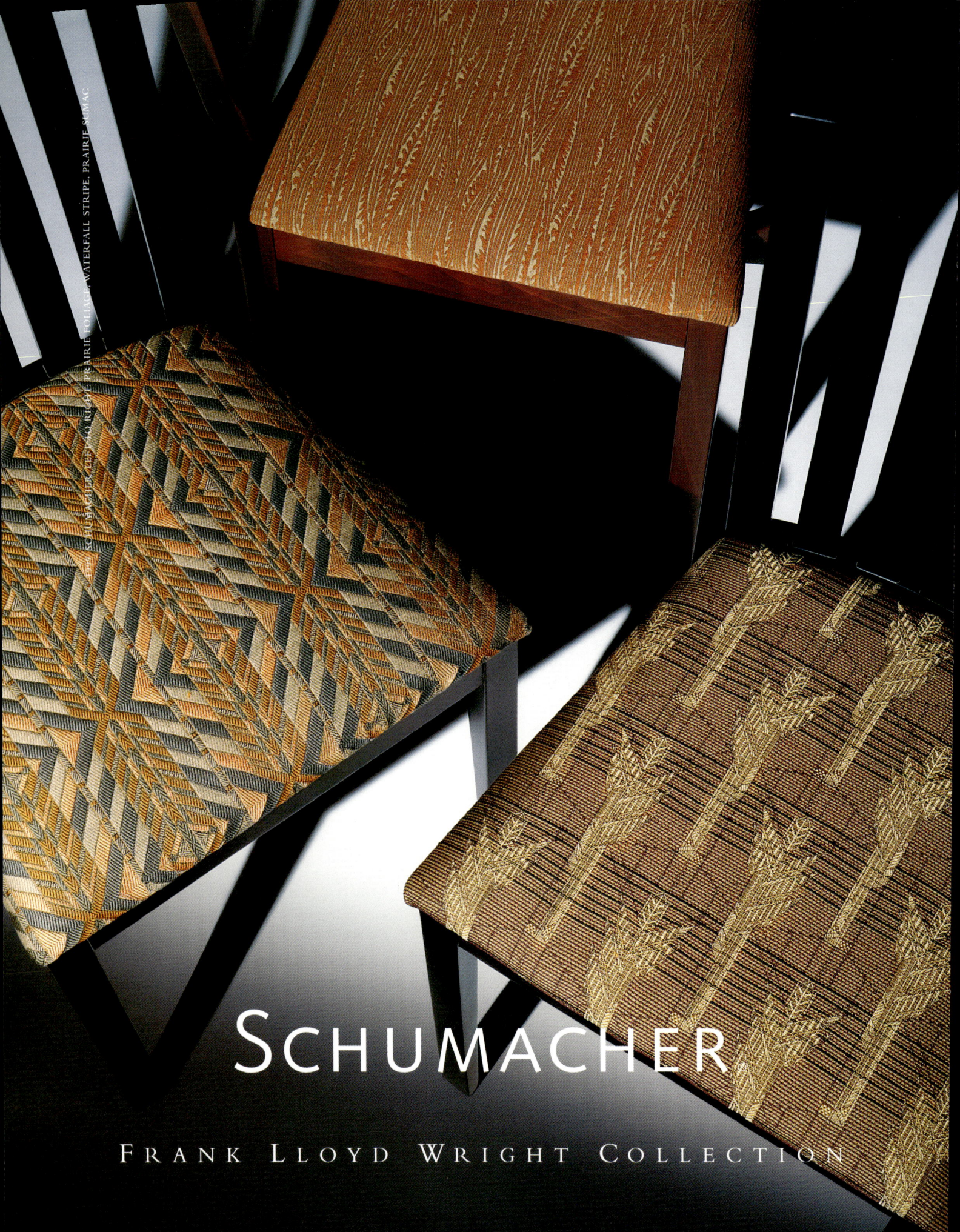

FRANK LLOYD WRIGHT COLLECTION

345 CALIFORNIA • AWAHNEE HOTEL • AAMES FINANCIAL • ABBOTT LABORATORIES • ACCLAIM ENTERTAINMENT • AIG PROPERTIES • AIR JAMAICA • AIR SHAMROCK • AL BATEEN PALACE • ALABAMA FARMERS FEDERATION • ALAN JACKSON MUSEUM • ALAINT BANK • ALLIANCE CAPITAL • ALLSTEEL, INC. • ALLTEL SERVICE CORPORATION • AMERICAN AIRLINES • AMERICAN BROADCASTING COMPANY • AMERICAN EXPRESS • AMERICAN MUTUAL INSURANCE • AMERITECH • AMSTED INDUSTRIES • ANSETT AIR • ARAMCO • ARKANSAS CANCER RESEARCH • AT&T • ARNOLD & PORTER • ARTHUR ANDERSON • AUTO ONE • BANCO MERCANTILE • BANPAIS • BARGER & MOSS • BARON CAPITAL BAXTER • BEAU RIVAGE • BECTON DICKINSON • BELAGIO HOTEL • BERTLESMAN • BLUE CROSS BLUE SHIELD • BOEING COMMERCIAL AIRPLANE CO. • BOEING EXECUTIVE LOBBY • BRADLEY, ARANT, ROSE & WHITE • BRISTOL MEYERS • CANTOR FITZGERALD • CAPITAL GROUP • CAPITAL RECORDS • CARTER WALLACE • CHAPMAN EXPLORATION • CHASE BANK OF TEXAS, N.A. • CHASE MANHATTAN BANK • CHEMICAL BANK • CHICAGO MERCANTILE EXCHANGE • CHURCH OF THE NATIVITY, EPISCOPAL CHURCH • CITIBANK • CITIBANK MEADOW BANK GOVERNMENT CENTER • CITICORP • CITIFLIGHT • CLAYTON CENTER • COCA COLA • COLE-HAAN • COWEN & CO. • CREDIT SUISSE • COMMERZBANK • CROWN PRINCESS • CUSHMAN & WAKEFIELD • DALLAS CONVENTION CENTER • DALLAS COUNTRY CLUB • DALLAS MUSEUM OF ART • DAVIS POLK WARDWELL • DAWN PRINCESS • DEAN WITTER • DEAN WITTER DRAGORO • DEL WEBB CORPORATION • DEWEY BALLANTINE • DIME SAVINGS BANK • DOCTOR'S CENTER • DOMINO'S PIZZA • DRAGOCO • DUKE ENERGY • E.A.J. CORPORATION • EASTMAN KODAK • ELEVEN HUNDRED UNION PACIFIC • ELI LILY • ENPRO INTERNATIONAL • ENSAFE • EQUITABLE LIFE • EQUITY OFFICE PROPERTIES • ESSENCE COMMUNICATIONS • ETHIOPIAN AIRLINES • EXXON • F & M BANK • FAISON STONE • FANNIE MAE FOUNDATION • FEDERAL RESERVE BANK OF NEW YORK • FIRST BANK • FIDUCIARY TRUST • FIRST CHICAGO BANK • FIRST NATIONAL BANK OF OMAHA • FIRST USA • FMC FULTS COMPANIES • FMF REALTY • FOOTHILLS CHURCH • FORD MOTOR COMPANY • GARDERE & WYNNE • GENERAL CORPORATION • GENERAL ELECTRIC • GIANT GROUP • GIVENCHY HOTEL & SPA • GLOBAL INDUSTRIES • GOLDCREST CONDOMINIUMS • GOLDMAN SACHS • GOVERNMENT OF ARGENTINA • GOVERNMENT OF THE KINGDOM OF SAUDIA ARABIA • GRAND CASINO COUSHATTA HOTEL • GRAND PRINCESS • GULFSTREAM • GREENPOINT SAVINGS BANK • GULF STATES TOYOTA • GULFSTREAM DEMONSTRATOR • HALL, DICKLER • HARBERT INTERNATIONAL • HARBOR COURT • HARRIS BANK • HARROD'S • HARVEY HOTEL • HEINZ USA • HENRI BENDEL • HERSHEY TRUST COMPANY • HEWLETT PACKARD • HOFFMAN LA ROCHE • HOLIDAY INN • HOUSTON DOUBLETREE GUEST SUITES • HOUSTONIAN HOTEL CLUB & SPA • HUDSON FOODS • IBM • INDIAN RIDGE • INGERSOLL RAND • INTERNATIONAL PAPER • ISK CONCERT HALL • ISLAND PRINCESS • ITT • JACKSON MISSISSIPPI AIRPORT OFFICES • JENNISON ASSOCIATES • JOHNSON & JOHNSON • JOHNSON PUBLISHING • JORDAN INDUSTRIES • J.P. MORGAN • JPI • KAPPA SIGMA FRATERNITY • KEY INVESTMENT • KK & R • KOCH INDUSTRIES • KONFARA • LA TOUR CONDOMINIUMS • LANCASTER HOTEL • LANGLEY FEDERAL CREDIT UNION • LASALLE PARTNERS • LATTICE • LAZARD FRERES • LIBERTY MUTUAL • BELL ATLANTIC • LIBERTY SPORTS • LIMITED • LINCOLN PROPERTY COMPANY • LINCOLN TOWERS • LITTLE NELL HOTEL • LOCKHEED ENGINEERING • LOUISIANA GOVERNOR'S MANSION • LUCASFILM • MARATHON OIL • MARRIOTT'S TAN-TAR-A-RESORT • MARRIOTT CUSTOM HOUSE HOTEL • MARY KAY COSMETICS • MASTERCARD • MAUNA LANI BAY • MCKINSEY & COMPANY • MCKOY PEAK LODGE • MCWANE COMPANIES • MEADOWBROOK CARE CENTER • MEDPARTNERS • MERCK • MERRILL LYNCH • MET LIFE • MILBANK, TWEED, HADLEY & MCCLOY • MILLER-BOYETT PRODUCTIONS • MONTGOMERY ASSET MANAGEMENT • MUSEUM OF SCIENCE AND INDUSTRY • MUTUAL OF AMERICA • NATIONS BANK • NEW YORK STATE DORMITORY AUTHORITY • NEW YORK STOCK EXCHANGE • NEWS CORPORATION • NIKE • NOMURA SECURITIES • NORTHWOOD CLUB • OAKTREE CAPITAL MANAGEMENT • OFFIT BANK • OLYMPIC AIRWAYS • OMNI ROYAL ORLEANS • ORACLE NASHUA • OXY CHEM • PACIFIC PRINCESS • PACIFIC TELESIS • PAGENET CORPORATION • PAN AMERICAN LIFE • PAUL STUART CHICAGO • PEBBLE BEACH COMPANY • PEPSICO • PETROLA HOUSE • PFIZER • PHILLIP MORRIS • PORT AUTHORITY OF NEW YORK AND NEW JERSEY • PRESBYTERIAN HOSPITAL DALLAS • PROTECTIVE LIFE INSURANCE COMPANY • PULSAR • QUAIL CREEK GOLF & COUNTRY CLUB • QUANTAS AIRLINES • QUAKER RIDGE COUNTRY CLUB • REESE DESIGN INTERNATIONAL • REESE DESIGN LIMITED • REGENT NEW YORK • REYNOLDS & REYNOLDS • RITZ-CARLTON • RITZ-CARLTON, SAVANNAH • RODEN & HAYES • ROUSE & COMPANY • ROYAL PRINCESS • SAFRA NATIONAL BANK • S.M. PHELPS REALTY • SANFORD C. BERSTEIN & COMPANY INC. • SANTA MONICA BANK • SAUDI ROYAL FLIGHT • SEA PRINCESS • SEAFLITE • SEAGRAM'S • SHAW COMMUNICATIONS • SILBER PEARLMAN • SILVER STAR CASINO • SINCLAIR OIL COMPANY • SKADDEN, ARPS, SLATE, MEAGHER & FLOM • SKIDMORE OWINGS & MERRILL • SKOKIE COUNTRY CLUB • SOCIETE GENERAL • SOKA UNIVERSITY OF AMERICA • SONY MUSIC • SOROS FUND MANAGEMENT • SOUTHERN CALIFORNIA GAS COMPANY • SOUTHERN HILLS COUNTRY CLUB • SOUTHERN STAR • ST. LUKE'S EPISCOPAL CHURCH • STAR PRINCESS • STATE OF NEBRASKA GOVERNOR'S MANSION • STERLING SOFTWARE • SUNSET CLUB • SWISS BANK CORPORATION/SWISS RE • T.X.I. • TENNESSEE VALLEY AUTHORITY • TEXTRON • THE BREVOORT • TORRAY • TRAVELERS GROUP • TRITON • TROPWORLD HOTEL • TRUST INVESTMENTS • TURTLE CREEK CENTRE • TWO ALLEN CENTER • TWO UNION SQUARE • U.S. AIR • U.S. DEPT. OF STATE • U.S. SURGICAL • U.S. TRUST • U.S.T. & C. • UNION PACIFIC RESOURCES • UNITED SAUDI COMMERCIAL BANK • UNIVERSITY OF ALABAMA, BRUNO LIBRARY • UNIVERSITY OF CHICAGO • UNIVERSITY OF MICHIGAN RARE BOOKS • USX • UNITED STATES EMBASSY (CARACAS) • UNITED STATES EMBASSY (SINGAPORE) • VAIL CASCADE HOTEL • VALERO CORPORATE SERVICES COMPANY • VITRO • WALT DISNEY WORLD • WEBSTER BANK • WEIL GOTSHAL & MANGES • WELLS FARGO • WESTINGHOUSE • WESTSIDE LEXUS • WHITE & CASE • THE WHITE HOUSE • WILLIAMS SQUARE, LAS COLINAS • WOMEN'S ATHLETIC CLUB OF CHICAGO • WOODMARK HOTEL • WORLD BANK • WORLD SAVINGS BANK • WUNSCH/MCREADY • WYNDHAM HOTELS

The executives, employees and customers of work and walk on carpet by EDWARD FIELDS

232 EAST 59 ST. • NEW YORK, NY 10022 • 212-310-0400

BOSTON • CHICAGO • DALLAS • HOUSTON • DANIA • LOS ANGELES • NEW YORK • SAN FRANCISCO

http://www.dir-dd.com/edward-fields.html/

The New York Design Center

Fine Furnishings Through Design Professionals Since 1926

"The NYDC is a great building and a terrific resource."
—Michael Vanderbyl

THE NEW YORK DESIGN CENTER SERVES A LOYAL CLIENTELE OF DESIGNERS, ARCHITECTS AND SPECIFIERS WHO BELIEVE THAT 200 LEXINGTON AVENUE IS AN INVALUABLE RESOURCE FOR CONTRACT FURNISHINGS.

Unlike most design trade buildings, **THE NEW YORK DESIGN CENTER** is operated by industry professionals. With this "insiders" perspective we have developed services and facilities that create a functional, user-friendly environment. With nearly 100 showrooms, Manhattan's premier design resource center offers a sophisticated and unparalleled international mix of furnishing styles from Italy, England, France and of course the United States. From furnishings and flooring to wall coverings, fabrics and accessories, the NYDC is the one-stop-shop for contract as well as residential products.

NYDC

200 LEXINGTON AVENUE,
NEW YORK, NY, 10016

(212) 679-9500

WWW.NYDC.COM

The New York Design Contract Center Resources

American Seating
Amtico Design Floors
Arnold Group
Anderson Hickey
Atlas Carpet Mills Inc.
Baker Contract
B.P. Associates
BPI
Bright Chair Company
Carmel Furniture
Carolina
Cartwright Inc.
Chairworks
Charles Braham Associates (CBA)
Chromcraft Contract
Classic Tile, Inc.
Cleator
CN Associates/IEI
CCN International
Cymann2
Dar Ran
Design Options
E/2
Eck Adams
Eco-Tech Resources
Ekitta Tables
Egan
ERG Int'l & Corporate
Ergonomic Concepts
Ergo Systems
Eurocraft Corp.
Falcon
Farallon
FCI, Inc.
Fireking/Meilink
First Source
Fixtures Furniture
Garrett Leather
Gautier
GF Office Furniture, Ltd.
Gin Nes, Inc.
Gianni
Globe Business Furniture
Gordon, Arthur Associates
Gordon International
Gregson
Hag, Inc.
Harden Contract
HBF Hickory Business Furniture
HBF Textiles
HLC-Hickory Leather Co.
Integrity Flooring Inc.
Jackson of Danville
J. Norman Assoc., Inc.
JOFCO
Jasper Seating/Community
Kaufman Contract
Keilhauer
Ken Gibson & Assoc., Ltd.

Koch Originals
Krug
La-Z-Boy
Levine Calvano Furniture Group
Lincora/KMI
Lowenstein
Lucia Cassa Textiles
Mannington Comercial Carpets
Marvel
Memmo & Freschi, Ltd.
Metrogroup Representatives
Miller Desk
Monterey Carpets
Nessen Lighting Contract
Nestler Enterprises, Inc.
Neutral Posture Ergonomics
Nevins International
Nemschoff
Newell
Northwood
Office Specialty
One Angell Collection
OSI-Signatures in Fine Wood
Packer and Associates
Pande Cameron & Co.
Patrician
Primason Symchick, Inc.
Prismatique
Quartet/GBC
Sales Associates
Sashi Caan Textiles
Seating Systems Intl.
SIS/Human Factors
Sligh
Softcare Innovations
Spacenow!
Standard Desk
Stylex, Inc.
Teamboard
Trosby
United Chair
Viking Acoustical
Vogel Peterson
Workstream Laminate Casegoods

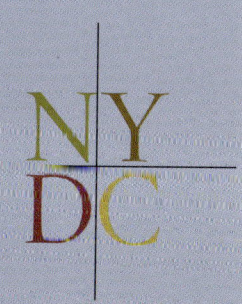

NYDC

200 LEXINGTON AVENUE
NEW YORK, NY 10016
212-679-9500

GORKA
Designed by Jorge Pensi

Impressively solid and architecturally sound

• RECYCLABLE • FUNCTIONAL • VERSATILITY • STACKABLE • UNIQUE •

AGI

AGI • High Point, NC • 336.434.5011
a division of KI

Charleston

Introducing the Charleston Collection from Gianni. Classically styled and crafted to reflect the architecture of Southern gentry, this furniture exudes charm with light wood shading in tones of cherry, maple or anigere. Various inlay options and dentil molding add to its elegance. And to embellish its functionality, design elements have been tastefully incorporated to house a laptop, keyboard, wire management and CD-ROM storage. Charleston. Classic and contemporary.

GIANNI
Distinction At Any Price

FOR MORE INFORMATION PLEASE VISIT US AT WWW.GIANNI.COM OR CONTACT YOUR LOCAL REPRESENTATIVE OR DEALER.

Forma Kristall.
ONE OF SEVEN CONTEMPORARY COLLECTIONS.

FREZZA *by* JOFCO

JOFCO IS THE EXCLUSIVE IMPORTER AND
DISTRIBUTOR OF FREZZA PRODUCTS IN THE USA.
1-800-23-JOFCO   WWW.JOFCO.COM

Foto: Mario Carrieri

UNIFOR

Less
designed by
Jean Nouvel

Progetto 25
designed by
Luca Meda

Unifor
149 Fifth Avenue
New York, NY 10010

Telephone: 212.673.3434
Facsimile: 212.673.7317
E-mail: unifor@uniforusa.com

SLYM JYM
STACKABLE

DESIGNED BY
STANLEY JAY FRIEDMAN

BONAVENTUREUSA
A DIVISION OF BRUETON ®

REPRESENTED THROUGHOUT THE GALAXY • ON EARTH 1 800 221-6783

Highland Weave   Dupont Antron® Legacy

Masland
contract

Our past. Our presence.

130 years of dedication, innovation, and creative integrity.

An enduring legacy of craftsmanship, style, and quality.

integrity

craft

accomplishment

888.633.4770
maslandcontract.com

Over 75 years in the furniture business, and we're still green. The General Services Administration just gave us their Green Award for environmentally

thumb

Peace

peas

Hornet

grass

Bay

tea

light

Eggs & Ham

house

Acres

issues

sensitive products and business practices. Herman Miller digs green things.

HermanMiller Things that Matter

www.hermanmiller.com

Herman Miller® and Things that Matter™ are trademarks of Herman Miller, Inc. Zeeland, MI ©1999

FUTURE PROOFING THE WORK SPACE

By Roger Yee

Where on earth did the modern office come from? In the late 20th century version, clusters of cubicles are ringed by private offices and conference rooms and dotted with islands of lounge furniture. The smell of freshly made cappuccino fills the air, while the murmurs of quiet conversation are punctuated by the rings of telephones and the beeps, clicks and whirls of a menagerie of computer-driven office machines. Jack Lemmon, playing an insurance clerk adrift in a sea of desks in Billy Wilder's 1960 comedy film, The Apartment, would have stared in surprise. How and why the office has arrived at its current form is not a mystery, however. Office workers make the office as much as the office makes the office workers. Office design continues to evolve to reflect the organization, activity and composition of the white collar population, which is now making the transition from the industrial age to the information age.

Of course, anyone who grew up early in the second half of the 20th century could easily think today's office came from outer space. In the 1950s, the typical big city CEO occupied a spacious corner office with fine wood furniture and carpet on the floor, hard to miss when everyone else had metal desks on linoleum floors. The CEO himself—and "he" was inevitably a man—was the silver-haired gentleman in the tailored suit and four-in-hand cravat followed by anxious aides carrying his folders.

In the 1990s, that pizza delivery guy with the surfer dude tee-shirt, khakis, running shoes and laptop computer in a backpack you nearly ran into at the door is the twentysomething CEO of the Internet IPO of the hour—though "he" might easily be a "she" such as Carly Fiorina of Hewlett Packard, Ann Winblad of Hummer Winblad Venture Partners or Margaret Whitman of eBay. Don't waste your time searching for the CEO's corner office, by the way. It's quite possibly a modest private office or cubicle that looks like everyone else's except that it's the one closest to the parking lot.

WHY SHOULDN'T AN OFFICE BE RUN LIKE A FACTORY?

The primary force for change in office design is the new way clerical, managerial and professional employees are working as we enter the 21st century. Businesses are shifting from production-centered, command-and-control office operations, characterized by superiors directing their subordinates in neatly prescribed rote tasks, to information-centered, horizontal office operations, characterized by teamwork and reasoned tasks that defy conventional job descriptions. Consequently, more people at lower levels of the organizational hierarchy are being paid to think for themselves, fast, frequently and as effectively as they can justify, and their working environments are evolving to help them handle their growing autonomy and accountability.

Yet we citizens of the World Wide Web should not feel too smug about our advances. Many of today's offices still display the traits of their lineage from the last turn of the century, when the industrial age grew rapidly in the Western world and began spilling over into non-Western societies. When architect Peter Ellis designed the Oriel Chambers in Liverpool in 1864, he created a long, narrow, four-story structure of small, repetitive suites of rooms for two to three persons lining both sides of a hallway that ran the full length of the building. Each suite resembled a residential apartment. By the 1890s, architect Louis Sullivan had conceived a 10-story skyscraper followed quickly by a 12-story skyscraper—the Wainwright Building of 1892 in St. Louis and the Guaranty Building of 1894 in Buffalo—that simply repeated the pattern of small suites in a U-shape, stacked higher and deeper thanks to the invention of the

Kroin

Kroin Incorporated
180 Fawcett Street
Cambridge, Massachusetts 02138
Telephone 800 OK KROIN
Telefax 617 492 4001
Online www.kroin.com

Birds of a feather...
Kroin sanitary fittings and
polished stainless steel basins
flock together.

Design: Prof. Arne Jacobsen, MAA
Selected for the Design Collection, MoMA.

elevator by Elisha Otis in 1852 and the electric light by Thomas Edison in 1879.

Housing administrative work in office suites on floors of 10,000 sq. ft., more or less (surviving examples of the four- to-six-story "office blocks" that preceded skyscrapers can be found in many American cities and towns) made sense when businesses were small, managers struggled just to make industrial products reliably and cheaply, and markets were constrained by geography and infrastructure. Rapid expansion of the magnitude, complexity and geography of business activities by such ambitious late 19th century and early 20th century entrepreneurs as Andrew Carnegie, Henry Ford and John D. Rockefeller dramatically redefined the business organization and stretched the concept of the office suite to the breaking point. The burgeoning office work force soon evolved into three well defined functional groups, production, finance and sales, that would manage the basic operations of business in this century as companies turned to the nation and the world to draw their resources and distribute their products.

Visitors to industrial enterprises of the era could not fail to notice the devotion to clarity, proficiency and efficiency in both factories and offices. Breaking critical tasks into manageable components and training employees to specialize in processing small increments of these tasks, the "division of labor" that was key to mass production, would simplify work to the point of tedium and disengagement for individual workers. But in the first half of the 20th century, this narrowing down of the definition of work let organizations become extremely efficient in their operations. If social critics like Ida Tarbell, Upton Sinclair and Frank Norris and union leaders like Terence Powderly and Samuel Gompers decried the human cost of such grueling endeavor, industrial experts like Frederick Winslow Taylor—the engineer who invented the "time and motion study" of efficiency—assured the captains of industry that such was the inevitable cost of progress.

BOARDING AN ELEVATOR TO REACH YOUR OFFICE IN THE SKY

By 1905, Frank Lloyd Wright broke the architectural mold for office design in Buffalo with the Larkin Building, an airy, spacious environment in which multiple rows of desks stretched towards the horizon on spacious floors bathed in the skylit glow of a four-story atrium. Then, despite the appearance of fluorescent light, central heating and air conditioning, acoustical suspended ceilings and movable, demountable wall partitions, the form of the office stopped evolving and froze—for decades. Whether an organization preferred totally open spaces or "bullpens," neat, factory-inspired grids of desks and chairs for clerks and supervisors, or rabbit warrens of private window offices for senior managers and interior offices for junior managers, where size might symbolically increase with the occupant's status, the die had been cast. Even the office furniture that prevailed since the turn of the century, including the desk, the credenza, the filing cabinet, the conference table and a host of office chairs of varying degrees of discomfort, accompanied the white-collar work force like a faithful pack of dogs wherever it went for over half of the 20th century.

Who could argue, after all, with the success of the business organization that built and occupied this hierarchical, compartmentalized and well-groomed facility with floors that could engulf 30,000 to 45,000 sq. ft. or more? Corporate payrolls grew in step with business operations, and each new layer of management was added to oversee the layer below it as the overall enterprise expanded. Young people—again, mostly men, since women stayed at the clerical

[T . L . C .]

Tables Lovin' Chairs.   Only at Versteel.

VERSTEEL™

800.876.2120

level only long enough to marry, resign and start families—were inducted into the system as life-time employees.

Employers and employees mutually understood that the reward for loyal service, meticulous conformity and hard work would be a steady rise through the ranks from clerical to supervisory to managerial positions, so memorably portrayed in the classic management study, The Organization Man, of 1956 by William H. ("Holly") Whyte. So what if everyone reported for work in the same white shirt, blue tie and gray flannel suit? The top-down model of business administration carried the United States successfully through World War I, the Depression and World War II to the 1960s, giving rise to such corporate giants as General Motors, AT&T and IBM, and endowing the American family with a standard of living that was the envy of the world.

Indeed, the structures designed to house this archetype were often quite splendid as landmarks, taking their place alongside great railroad stations, post offices, court houses and other pillars of their communities. Many of the world's great architects, especially Americans, have had a go at shaping the office building as a vertical, high-rise tower (the skyscraper is the nation's unique contribution to world architecture) or a horizontal, low-rise campus-style basilica. Among the noted individuals who have made distinguished contributions to this building type in America are Louis Sullivan, Daniel Burnham, Cass Gilbert, Frank Lloyd Wright, Raymond Hood, Mies van der Rohe, Walter Gropius, Marcel Breuer, Pietro Belluschi, Eero Saarinen, Philip Johnson, Skidmore Owings & Merrill, I.M. Pei, Kohn Pedersen Fox, Helmut Jahn, Kevin Roche, Gunnar Birkerts, Arata Isozaki, Robert Stern and Aldo Rossi.

THE OFFICE AS FORTRESS SURRENDERS—TO AN AQUARIAN AGE "KIT OF PARTS"

To be fair to our parents, grandparents and great grandparents, the impact of the information-driven society on the design of the office probably got its start in the Depression, long before computers became commonplace, when the great industrial machinery of the developed world came to a screeching halt. Suddenly manufacturers with greatly enlarged and highly productive factories became desperate for ways to distinguish their products from those of competitors to attract scarce customers. Modern marketing was born, and industrial design as well as the Depression nurtured such talented U.S. product designers as Walter Dorwin Teague, Raymond Loewy, Henry Dreyfuss and Donald Desky. America's new awareness of the power of creative design might have reshaped the office, but chronic unemployment and the outbreak of World War II kept everyone's attention focused on production problems, and the assembly line look stayed put.

By the 1960s, however, the United States was prepared to reconsider the fate of the bullpen and the rabbit warren. One key agent of change came from abroad when the Quickborner Team of management consultants transplanted the concept of office landscaping or bürolandschaft from Germany to the United States. Visitors to duPont's Freon Division in Wilmington, Delaware, in 1967 sensed that a new age of enlightenment—or madness—had dawned. Furniture and freestanding screens were arranged in organic, free-form patterns to mirror prevailing communications patterns or "bubble diagrams" rather than standard, calibrated grids.

Bürolandschaft soon proved to be a dazzling yet false start, despite or perhaps

vesa collection

Tuohy

42 Saint Albans Place   Chatfield, Minnesota 55923   800.533.1696   email: info@tuohyfurniture.com
Design: Manuel G. Vesa

because of its radical departure from existing norms. Occupants and visitors alike found navigating the irregular paths around work stations to be much too disorienting. Worse still, workers distracted each other excessively in the absence of physical barriers to block the constant barrage of extraneous sights and sounds.

One radical idea survived nonetheless. If what you did was more important than who you were, offices and office furniture could be chosen to suit your task and not your title. The stage was set for open plan office furniture systems that would bridge the gap between fully open bullpens and fully enclosed rabbit warrens. These compact, rectangular work stations, framed by vertical panels that rose to various heights short of the ceiling on two to four sides and equipped with work surfaces and storage units, would house the majority of office workers at relatively high densities by the 1980s.

Also setting the stage for new office design concepts after the late 1960s was a trio of other compelling twists in the standard business plot.

- Leading the charge was a flood of Baby Boomers with college degrees who would eventually overwhelm the less educated if no less dedicated clerks. Boomers would upgrade white collar jobs as managerial and professional tasks and the service sector of the economy became more important than clerical tasks and the manufacturing sector.

- In addition, the velocity of organizational change would accelerate as more nations recovered from the devastation of World War II to enter the global economy in the 1960s and raise the competitive barre in the 1970s by introducing their own ideas about management and technology.

- Finally, the appearance of the personal computer in 1981 would scatter once-centralized data processing power across the general office and far beyond its walls, while the explosion in data and communications networks ranging from cellular telephones to the Internet would make the physical office at least theoretically obsolete.

No institution could be constructed to absorb the shock of so many forces of change without being altered in turn, not even the seemingly invincible American business organization. As Charles Handy, a leading British scholar on business management, noted in his celebrated work of 1989, *The Age of Unreason,* modern society has been in the throes of discontinuous change since the 1960s. "Change is not what it used to be," he wrote. "The status quo will no longer be the best way forward. The best way will be less comfortable and less easy but, no doubt, more interesting—a word we often use to signal an uncertain mix of danger and opportunity."

As if in anticipation of this brave new world, architects and industrial designers had been experimenting with furniture since the 1940s that embodied such concepts as modularity and interchangeability so that the results would be seen as a temporary "kit of parts" rather than finished pieces. Starting with residential interiors and then moving into offices, such pioneers as Gilbert Rohde, George Nelson and Robert Propst made possible the first open plan, vertical panel-based office furniture system in 1968. Before long, lighting fixtures were added, wiring was routed through the panels and accessories were attached. Then orthopedically correct or ergonomic seating, a concept last explored in the 1920s, was revived in the mid-1970s by talented young designers eager to infuse ergonomic theory with fresh ideas and new materials. Open planning proceeded

Play ball. La Bouclé, an intriguing textured carpet from Karastan Contract. 800.344.7789.

KARASTAN
CONTRACT

to conquer corporate America, transforming the newly pragmatic, task-driven and endlessly changeable office design into a powerful corporate image of progress.

A LOOK AT TOMORROW'S OFFICE—YOUR GUESS OR MINE

Sooner or later, of course, new revolutions become old regimes. The open plan office showed unmistakable signs of age by the 1990s because it too had become an impediment to change, too costly, too fixed and too confining to respond to business conditions moving at the speed of cyberspace. The United States and other economically advanced societies continued to experience acute pain from what futurist Alvin Toffler called the Third Wave, the movement from industrial society to information society, as the command-and-control model of business administration disentegrated, taking down other institutions with it to make way for something far more fluid, volatile, decentralized and either exciting or frightening, depending on one's personal situation.

Who knows what new business models will supplant the old? Handy has proposed theoretical forms of decentralized business that he calls federal, shamrock and triple-I organizations. Yet the revolution is still a work in progress, marked by rapid advances in business decision making that include multi-disciplinary thinking, concurrent engineering, computer modeling and prototyping, virtual organizations linked by electronics and frequent restructurings in which ad hoc project teams come and go.

Not to be left out of the mix either is the changing composition of the American work force that will spotlight women, minorities and elderly workers as increasingly important factors in human resources and office design, as well as the growing presence of Generation Xers and Yers with work ethics quite unlike those of their parents. Will members of Gen X go on rejecting tradition and conformity while craving achievement and power on their own terms—trying to balance a lack of faith in employers against close, personal relationships and a desire for fun? And what will become of Gen Y's huge cohort, which has acquired its Baby Boomer parents' taste for material abundance but has yet to face the adversities of a global economy in which even high-tech jobs can cross oceans as easily as state lines?

Long before anyone knows the outcome, we are already demanding that our office buildings, interiors and furnishings respond with increasing accuracy to both the physical demands of the tasks we do and the precise time when we must do them. Not everyone actually wants or needs this degree of flexibility, but even the most conservative office occupants may begin to wonder why they're missing out on the revolution. Insurance companies, law firms and banks can now be spotted among the many organizations taking the plunge with new office configurations.

Out in California's Silicon Valley, for example, a vision of the future that is thriving right now fairly approximates Boston architect Robert Luchetti's vision of the "cave and commons," a mix of small, private offices and large group lounges. The concept is working well for software engineers, who like to alternate long hours of intense concentration in physical isolation with informal break times spent in the company of fellow workers. By contrast, growing numbers of accountants, management consultants, sales people and other so-called road warriors in major business centers are experimenting with "hoteling," the assignment of temporary work stations to occupants who spend the bulk of their working hours off premises serving clients. So far, so good for the business "hotels" and their employee

Dauphin

"concierges" and "guests." Yet there seems to be no single "cure" for aging office designs at this time.

CAN THE OFFICE BE MADE FUTURE-PROOF IF PEOPLE CAN'T?

Whether or not we choose to support or oppose the cubicle world's brave or desperate efforts to remain relevant through such innovations as hoteling, free address, group address, cave and commons, satellite office, home office or even virtual office, we will have to cope with the inescapable sense that everyone will be engaged in continous battle just to survive in the competitive economy of the 21st century. How this will affect us is far from clear. No one is likely to collect a gold watch at the end of a lifetime of tomorrow's work. A career of temporary assignments, which Handy predicts as the coming standard, is either discouraging or stimulating, depending on whether you ask aging Baby Boomers or spunky Gen Xers.

Furthermore, the office that houses us in the year 2000 and thereafter will do little to shield us from a global economy that values flexibility over stability, current need over long-term commitment, theoretical knowledge over lifetime experience, and empowerment and teamwork over authority and responsibility. It's a world in which paradoxically all of us and none of us really matter, a point passionately argued by eminent sociologist Richard Sennett in his 1998 analysis of work, *The Corrosion of Character: The Personal Consequences of Work in the New Capitalism.* If organizational membership is belittled to oblivion in so many ways, corporate decision makers may stand to lose much more than they could possibly gain by making tomorrow's office so frugal, anonymous and impermanent that its power to establish an emotional bond with employees is nullified.

Followers of Dilbert, cartoonist Scott Adams' beleaguered office worker of the late 1990s, are reminded daily that we don't have to like our employers or the offices they provide us if we don't want to. Persuading us otherwise should be an interesting challenge in the coming years. Since architecture and furniture were originally created when civilized people had a reason to stay put, the nonstop business world of the Internet age has created a fascinating dilemma for architects, interior designers and the furnishings industry alike.

HOW TO PRODUCE A SUPERIOR WORK ENVIRONMENT RIGHT NOW

Fortunately, developing a superior office facility—a functional, cost-effective, state-of-the-art design structured to carry out the strategy of the organization and shaped in the image of the organization—is within the reach of almost any business or institution regardless of size, wealth or timetable. It's not rocket science. However, like any other serious endeavor involving substantial amounts of time, money and people, the probability that the development of a major facility will succeed increases sharply with the time and interest that senior management commits to the project. Indeed, who will know better than the chief executive officer and the building committee that he or she typically forms and heads just what the organization intends to achieve in the new headquarters?

Delegating the key decision making to lower echelon personnel will not produce the same results because the design of a new work environment is one of the principal ways that an organization can create up-to-date physical order and coherent visual form to support its long-term goals and strategies. Lower echelon personnel are never as familiar with current management philosophy in their organizations as senior management is,

BRINGING ARTISTRY TO LIGHT

LEUCOS LIGHTING

GOCCIA PL2

GOCCIA S2

GOCCIA T2

GOCCIA
design by R. Toso, N. Massari and Associates

LEUCOS USA INC.
11 MAYFIELD AVENUE EDISON N.J. 08837
TEL (732) 225-0010   FAX (732) 225-0250

and even less likely to exercise the power to enforce any significant change in existing operations and standards, which is exactly what a new office represents. Left without the appropriate knowledge and authority to do the job, they can only repeat aging precedents or guess how superiors would act.

Few organizations employ enough in-house staff with the expertise to develop a new facility from scratch, especially after the "downsizings" of the early 1990s, so senior management will need the help of such outside consultants as an architect, an interior designer, a structural engineer, a mechanical and electrical engineer, a general contractor and a real estate broker. It's a formidable project team to manage. Typically certain key outside team members report directly to the organization in what is known as the design-bid-build method of project management, though other forms, such as design-build and construction management, offer different degrees of control, responsibility and involvement that may be better suited to specific organizations and projects.

Regardless of what route an organization takes, office development proceeds in three stages, during which the number of people and the diversity of their backgrounds, the time and money involved, and the number of key decisions to be made rise to a climax only to subside again. The process is generally reversible only at great expense, in that undoing what has been done will not only waste money already spent, but will delay and thus increase the cost of expenditures still pending. Each design decision imposes its own conditions on the choices that remain until the conclusion is all but certain. Here are the three stages that business and institutional decision makers will face: stage I: strategic planning, programming and other pre-design work; stage II: planning and design; stage III: construction and occupancy.

Stage I: Strategic planning, programming and other pre-design work

Stage I of the development process, strategic planning, programming, budgeting, scheduling and project team, represent the earliest and most far reaching thoughts about the new office facility to be developed. Issues addressed at this point include why it is needed, how it will function, what it will cost, when it will be ready and who will develop it. There is no definite concept yet for the physical appearance of the work environment, inside or out, which would be premature.

1) Strategic planning: Why do you need this project?

Strategic planning involves soul-searching questions about why this particular office development is needed, which should be a logical expression of the ongoing and long-term plans of the organization and its management team. Only in probing its innermost thoughts about products, markets, resources, rivals, hopes and realistic chances, current and future, can senior management think logically about the specific need for a major office facility with an actual location, composition, size, work force and operation.

2) Programming: What do you want to do with your project?

Programming is the formal setting of standards by which a facility will be designed. What functions must be performed, for example; how many employees will be needed; what degree of adaptability, privacy, safety and comfort will be provided; what equipment will be used; which

HALCON
A TEKNION COMPANY

507.533.4235
Showrooms: Chicago and New York

geographic region or metropolitan area provides the most beneficial economic, logistic and demographic characteristics, and how long the facility will serve its purpose.

3) **Budgeting: How much will you pay for your project?**

Budgeting deals with estimated and actual construction costs and design fees, tax and financing arrangements, operating costs and contingencies for cost overruns.

4) **Scheduling: When will your project take place?**

Scheduling measures the critical steps in the life of the project that must be conducted smoothly to meet the organization's chosen occupancy date—which may depend on expiring leases elsewhere.

5) **Project team: Who will develop your project?**

Project team is the group assembled from within and without the organization who are asked to advise and assume responsibility for the development of the facility. Team members frequently chosen from within the corporation include: chief executive officer, chief financial officer, director of corporate real estate, director of human resources, and managers of facilities, communications, data processing and purchasing. Team members chosen from outside the organization might comprise some of the following: architect, interior designer, structural, mechanical, electrical and plumbing engineers, general contractor, construction manager, real estate consultant, information technology consultant, lighting designer, acoustician, landscape architect and food service consultant.

It cannot be overemphasized that the organization would be best served by retaining the architect and interior designer before the other outside members of the project team are chosen. Though any specific concepts about the form of a new facility are premature at the start of the development project, the architect and interior designer are fully prepared to assist the organization in exploring all possibilities for the function of the space—including such issues as site selection, applicable zoning, code, ADA, health and safety requirements, building type, base building evaluation, lease analysis, space planning, floor area, budgeting and scheduling. Furthermore, they have no interest in the project besides the wellbeing of the organization itself.

What should the organization look for in selecting an architect and interior designer? Important criteria include: the technical competence to create the type of facility desired; the design talent to transform the vision of the organization into a physical presence; the managerial skills to produce quality projects of this type on time and budget; the personal compatibility to work in a cooperative manner; and the references to demonstrate what is possible through what has already been done. Though these characteristics are fairly self evident, each organization will have to decide for itself where to place the emphasis in making the "right" choice.

Stage II: Planning and design

Stage II, planning and design, bring considerable expertise to focus on the major technical and aesthetic problems of developing a working office environment. At this stage, the chain of command is firmly established from the project manager to the CEO, and from the many outside consultants whose advice will be

**ATHERTON LAMPS
BY BARBARA BARRY**

Available in two sizes to accommodate multiple settings with your choice of fine linen or white pongee silk shades.

The wood base is offered in natural maple or coffee finishes and the metal accents are available in Polished Brass, Boyd Brass, Polished Nickel or Satin Nickel.

Exclusively from the makers of the American Aesthetic® Boyd Lighting ©1999 Tel.415.778.4300 Email info@boydlighting.com www.boydlighting.com Photography: John Sutton Patent Pending

BOYD LIGHTING

solicited by the key consultants reporting to the client's organization. The fact that today's major projects may routinely summon a dozen or more experts makes the assignment of project responsibility more important than ever before.

1) **Site selection: Where will your project be?**

    Site selection is the identification of a suitable property for construction, after proper study of title, zoning laws, building codes and environmental impact.

2) **Space planning: Where will all the functional groups coexist in space?**

    Space planning fits the various functional groups of the organization on given floors of the building while establishing good organizational relationships or "adjacencies," circulation patterns, vertical or "stacking" plans and principal entry points.

3) **Design development: How does the final design look and work?**

    Design development creates the needed structural, mechanical, lighting, power, heating, ventilation and air conditioning (HVAC) and information processing systems within the final architecture and interior design of a specific aesthetic form.

4) **Production: How is the actual facility going to piece together?**

    Production is the preparation of working drawings or "construction documents" to be used to fabricate building components ("shop drawings") and construct the entire building, as well as the precise descriptions or "specifications" of the particular products, materials and construction methods to be used.

Stage III: Construction and occupancy

Stage III, construction, occupancy and post-occupancy, brings the project to climax and close. Specifications and working drawings are submitted to manufacturers, fabricators and contractors for bids. From their replies come contract awards that bind builder and owner to more or less fixed costs and completion dates.

1) **Construction: Can your project actually be built as filed?**

    Construction follows the architect's and interior designer's working drawings with a keen eye for field conditions and for significant change orders instituted by the organization, its consultants and others. Payments are usually made for given percentages of job completion.

2) **Occupancy: When does your project become your facility?**

    Occupancy is the phased moving of the organization's personnel and equipment into the completed or nearly completed facility. This is usually preceded by employee orientation programs to introduce the staff to its new offices.

3) **Post-occupancy services: Will your project work today—and beyond?**

    Post-occupancy services are those supplied by the organization's facilities management or general administrative staff or outside consultants to fine tune the new facility, particularly in such areas as HVAC, lighting and interior design details, and to maintain and update it in accordance with the changing needs of the organization.

Most organizations end up with the offices they deserve. How well suited your new work environment will be to your needs depends on how accurately you want it to reflect prevailing attitudes towards your

Corporate Choice

Novawall®
The Standard for Fabric Wall and Ceiling Systems

Novawall Systems, Inc.   800.695.6682

Architectural Interiors: Camas Associates   Photo: c. Rick Alexander & Associates, Inc.   Ad design: FORMA Design, Washington, DC

business among the various constituencies you involve inside and outside of your ranks. An organization possessing a healthy respect for its people, products and customers plus a strong sense of self-direction will express its confidence in its new facilities as surely as it does in any other important undertaking.

Organizations that realize the power of the visual world to communicate to the public can consciously develop new facilities to reinforce their brand identities with customers, vendors and employees alike. The notion is hardly new, since Metropolitan Life Insurance was portraying its striking New York headquarters building in advertising as "the light that never fails" soon after it was designed by Napoleon LeBrun and Sons in 1907. Among the many practitioners of this art today are such well known names as IBM, Restoration Hardware, Federal Express, Starbucks and Nike.

Good offices are the product of an organization's collective intelligence, cooperation and vision as well as its money, time and manpower. More than we may realize at first, our architecture and interior design act like mirrors by revealing what we are today or would like to be tomorrow. Let's hope that we can honestly like the face that gazes back at us.

written by:
Roger Yee *is currently the editorial director of* Contract Design *magazine. Holder of a master of architecture degree from Yale University, Yee worked in a number of architecture firms, including Philip Johnson & John Burgee, Architects, in New York City, before assuming editorial positions with numerous professional and consumer publications. He has also held the post of marketing advisor to a commercial real estate firm, Cushman & Wakefield. In addition, Yee has chaired a committee of the Mayor's Advisory Council on the Interior Design Industry in New York, lectured at the Dartmouth Institute at Dartmouth College, and received the Jesse H. Neal Award for Editorial Excellence from the Association of Business Publishers.*

The Solutia Doc Awards are an industry benchmark achieved by only the most distinguished designers.

WINNING FIRM: The Environments Group, Chicago, IL

DESIGN TEAM (SHOWN IN PHOTO, LEFT TO RIGHT): Cary Johnson, IIDA, Stephanie Bellus Frey, and Joseph Connell, IIDA

PROJECT: Center for Business Innovation at Ernst & Young LLP

CARPET FIBER: Ultron® VIP Nylon

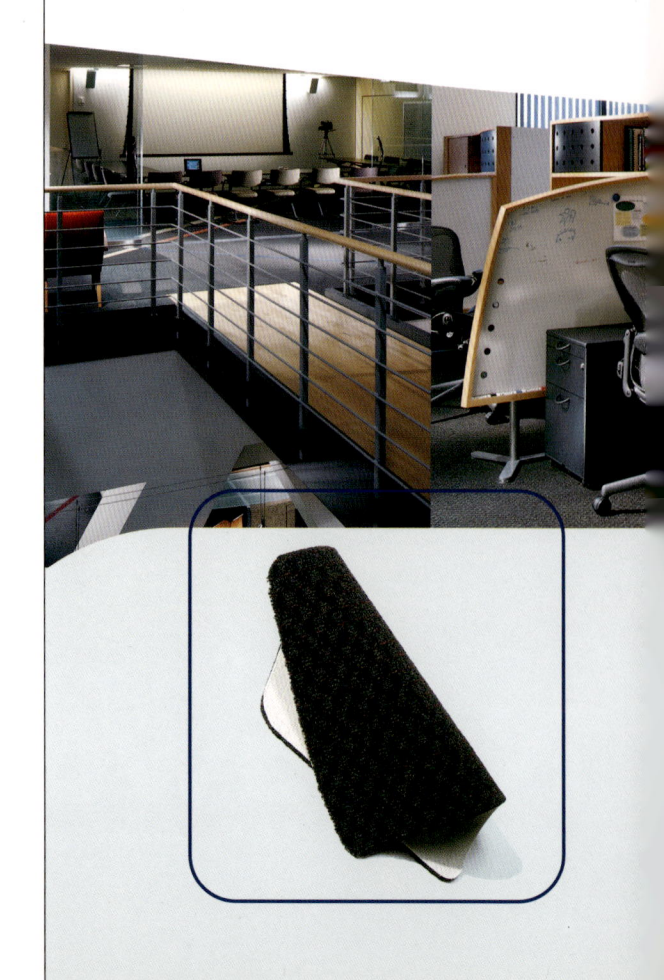

presenting doc award

winner The Environments Group

Imagine a research organization that enhances the creative work process, energized by natural light, a sweeping atrium and carpet colors inspired by the Renaissance. Our Doc winners did. And took top prize.

SOLUTIA
Applied Chemistry, Creative Solutions™

DOC. THE CONTEST.
THE MARK OF EXCELLENCE.
ASK FOR THE 1999 CALL-FOR-ENTRIES.

LET US TELL YOU MORE: 800-543-5377, 770-951-7600 OR WWW.ULTRONVIP.COM.

Project photography by Steve Hall © Hedrich Blessing

Cleator

Battery Park
Designed By: Edward F. Weller III

ELEGANT AWARD WINNING DESIGNS

THAT EMBODY A UNIQUE BLEND OF

FUNCTIONAL AND AESTHETIC FLEXIBILITY

FOR TODAY'S ELECTRONIC OFFICE

B&B Italia. The choice for quality, harmony and modern living.

Diesis, seat system designed by Antonio Citterio and Paolo Nava in 1979.
To reach the dealer nearest you call 1-800-872-1697
B&B Italia U.S.A. INC, 150 East 58th Street, New York, NY 10155.
Internet: http://www.bebitalia.it   e-mail: bbitalia@nyct.net

B&B ITALIA
Timeless and Treasured

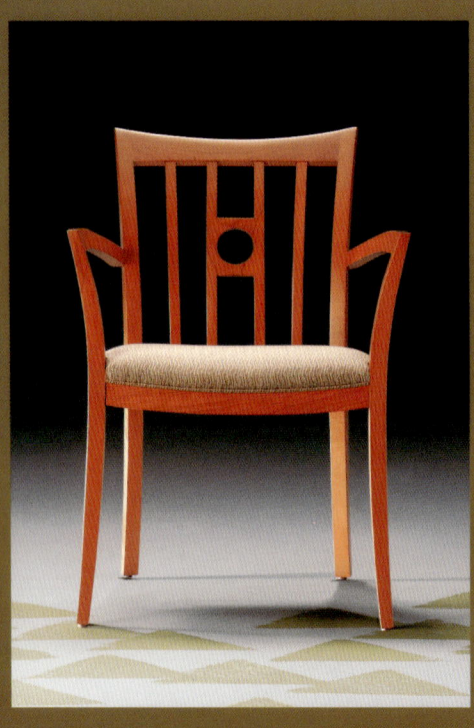

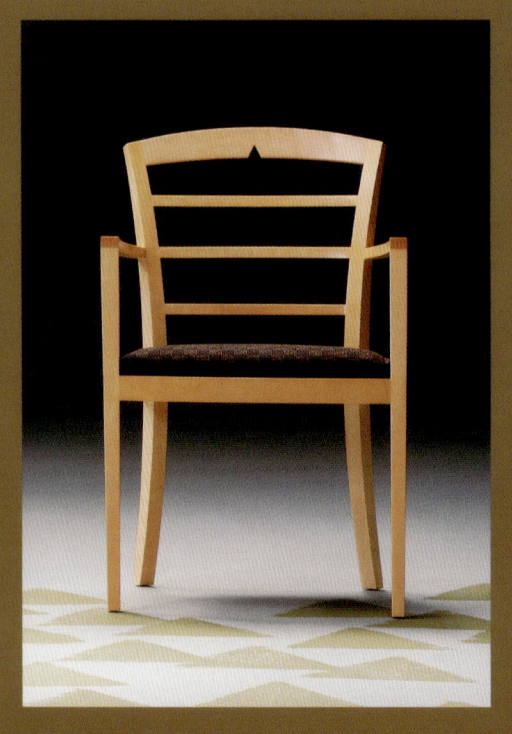

TERRANCE HUNT COLLECTION

TODAY, MORE THAN EVER BEFORE, THE PRODUCT WE SELECT AS CONSUMERS MUST BE EXPRESSIVE OF INDIVIDUAL TASTES, WORK WELL WITHIN ITS ENVIRONMENT, AND PROVE ITSELF AS A WORTHY INVESTMENT.

THROUGH DISTINCTIVE DESIGN, CABOT WRENN'S SEATING, LOUNGE, OCCASIONAL TABLES, AND CONFERENCE TABLES SUPPORT THE INTEGRITY OF TODAY'S BUSINESS INTERIORS. YOU CAN BE ASSURED, THAT THE CABOT WRENN PRODUCT THAT YOU SELECT WILL PROVE ITSELF EFFECTIVE IN A VARIETY OF SETTINGS, WHILE ENDURING THE PASSAGES OF TIME.

CabotWrenn®

Wired
for the future

Computers, telephone lines and power outlets — in today's boardrooms, they're vital.

Imagine a work surface inlaid with flip-up voice/data/power modules for plugging in what you want.

Imagine storage for excess cable in graceful, elliptical legs with easily removable panels.

Imagine a conference table invented for tomorrow.

Imagine VOX®. Designed by Mark Müller.

257 Finchdene Square
Scarborough, Ontario
Canada M1X 1B9

Tel 800.668.9318
Tel 416.298.5700
mail@nienkamper.com

ICF group
ICF · Unika Vaev · Nienkämper · Helikon

nienkämper

Simple, Effective

...And More. Simplicity and function reign throughout the EganSystem. The entire EganSystem has been carefully designed, engineered and tested to provide the highest level of function, appearance and safety. The unique design of the track and the corner mounting blocks allow the panel to lie flat against the wall and prevents components from being accidentally knocked off the track.

Egan Visual Inc.,
1-800-263-2387
Fax 1-905-851-3426
email: Interiors@egan.com
website: www.egan.com

EGAN

Communication...

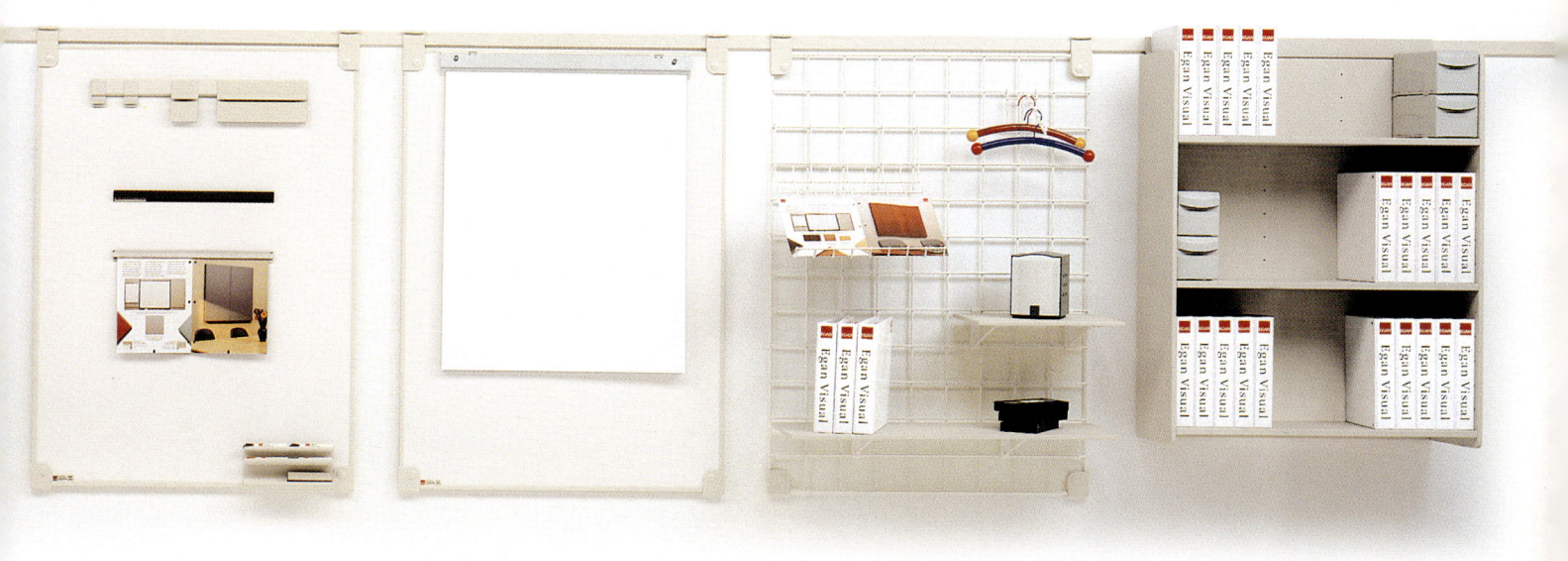

EGAN

For even greater flexibility Egan panels are reversible with a porcelain writing surface on one side and either another porcelain surface or a fabric-covered tackable surface on the other.

The complete line of Egan products includes: EganSystem and Shelving, Egan Cabinets, Lecturns, AV Support, TooGo New Workplace and Training Solutions. And our TeamBoard, the computer interactive whiteboard.

In Stock

Instant Ship

FLOSUSA

Romeo Moon designed by Philippe Starck.   1 800 939 3567 • 1 516 549 2745

Teknion

LEVERAGE™ HAS THE ABILITY TO ADDRESS A COMPLETE RANGE OF PLANNING REQUIREMENTS AND TO ACCOMMODATE CHANGE IN TODAY'S DYNAMIC WORK ENVIRONMENT. ITS COMPONENTS COME TOGETHER EASILY, MAKING LEVERAGE A USER-FRIENDLY SYSTEM WITH SIGNIFICANT COST-SAVING POTENTIAL.

TEKNION   LEVERAGE

® TEKNION 1999. LEVERAGE IS A TRADEMARK OF TEKNION. TEKNION IS A REGISTERED TRADEMARK OF TEKNION. www.teknion.com. 877.TEKNION. IN CANADA CALL 1.416.661.3370.

ARK

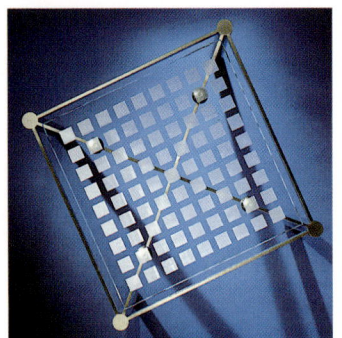

KALYPSO

ARCHITECTURAL RESPONSE KOLLECTION, INC

2918 HALLADAY STREET
SANTA ANA, CALIFORNIA 92705

TEL. 714.241.7100
TOLL FREE 888.241.7100
FAX. 714.241.7600
EMAIL info@ark-inc.com
WWW.ARK-INC.COM

Helios

Elysian

Architectural Response Kollection, Inc

2918 Halladay Street
Santa Ana, California 92705

Tel. 714.241.7100
Toll Free 888.241.7100
Fax. 714.241.7600
Email info@ark-inc.com
www.ark-inc.com

ARK

rhapsody

Rhapsody in cherry. Features include towers with electrical outlets and wire-management channel, bookcase and display shelving, modular upper and lower components, left or right-hinged doors and clear anodized finish for pulls and towers.

Rhapsody in maple. Features include soft-closing doors, stacking and sorting shelves, easy wire routing, paperwork classification trays and tower-mounted screens.

An exalted expression of feeling or enthusiasm.
A reason to jump the fence, explore what lies outside the familiar and pursue
new visions of personal and shared work settings.

PAOLI FURNITURE™
www.paoli.com 800 457 7415

Not Negotiable.

Harter Teso is *uncompromisingly styled* executive seating that lends a touch of continental sophistication to any office environment. Its passive ergonomic design fosters the healthy movement of the seated human body. High-back, mid back, and armless versions available.

Simply put, it's beautifully comfortable. And for that, *there is no substitute.*

HARTER

HOLD OUT FOR HARTER

A Jami Company / Telephone: 800.543.5449 / e-mail: info@harter.com

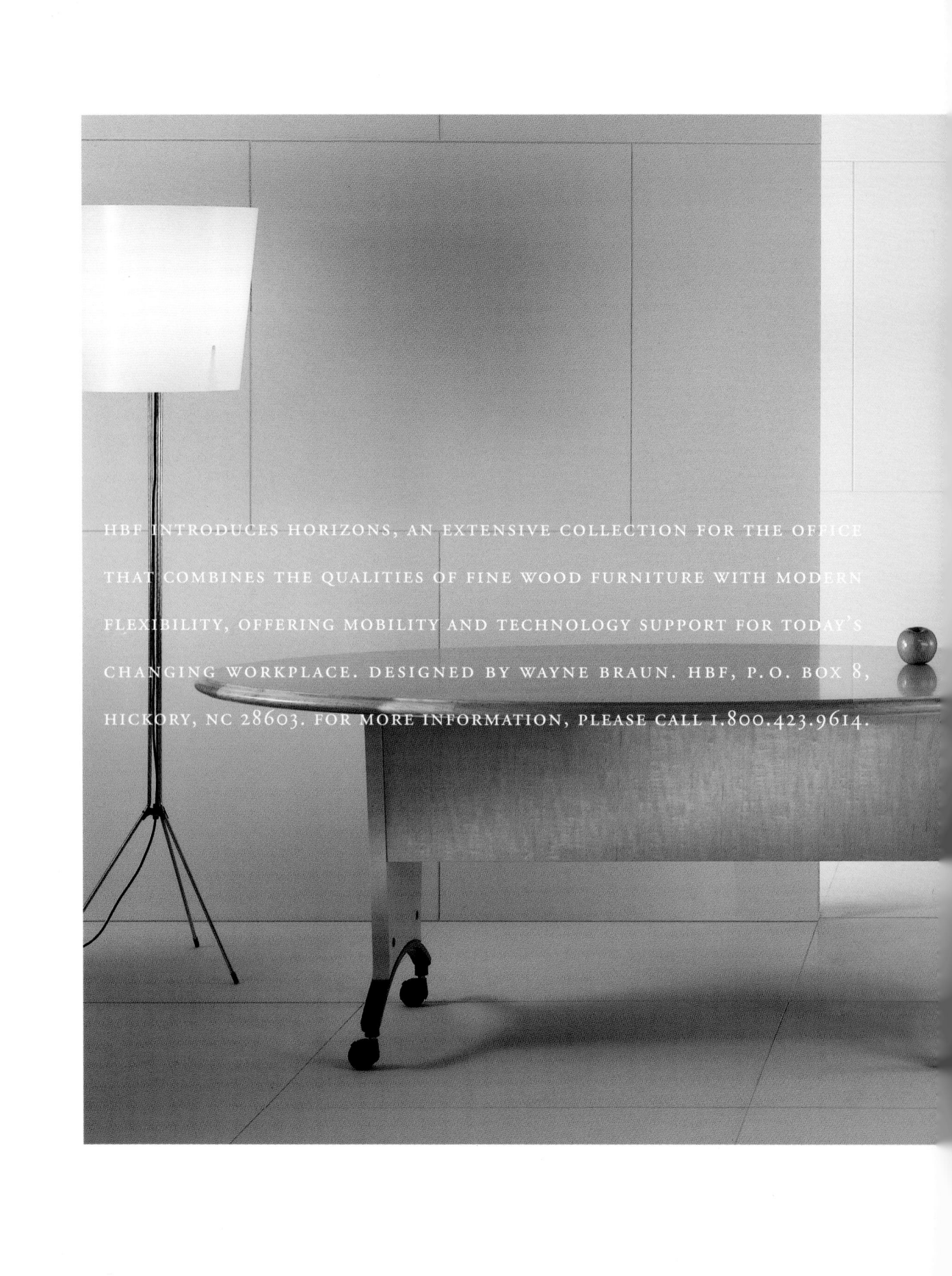

HBF INTRODUCES HORIZONS, AN EXTENSIVE COLLECTION FOR THE OFFICE THAT COMBINES THE QUALITIES OF FINE WOOD FURNITURE WITH MODERN FLEXIBILITY, OFFERING MOBILITY AND TECHNOLOGY SUPPORT FOR TODAY'S CHANGING WORKPLACE. DESIGNED BY WAYNE BRAUN. HBF, P.O. BOX 8, HICKORY, NC 28603. FOR MORE INFORMATION, PLEASE CALL 1.800.423.9614.

H B F

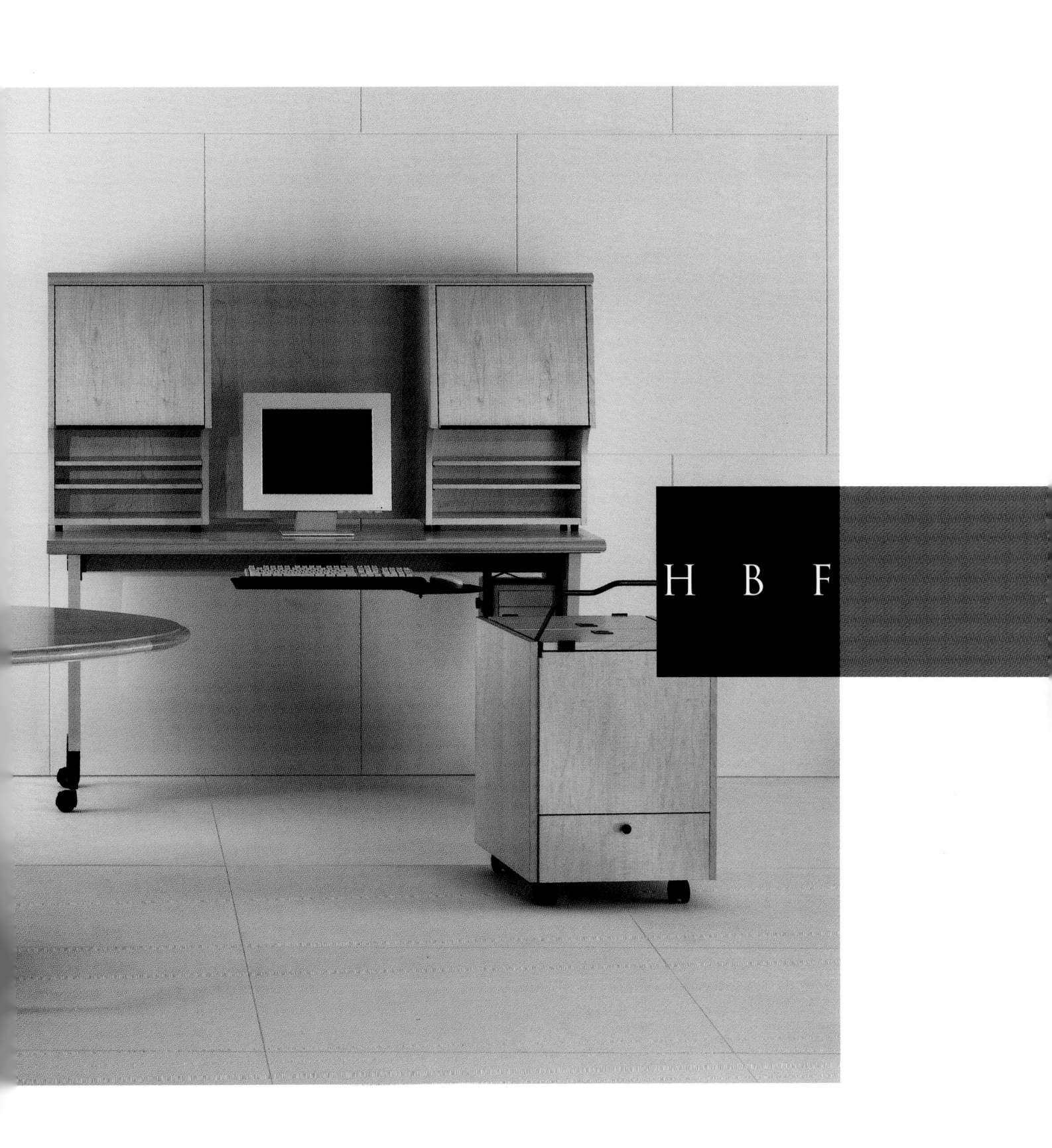

sophisticated

textures

C O N S T A N T I N E

CONSTANTINE COMMERCIAL CARPET • 800.308.4344 • PRODUCT SHOWN LINEN TEXTURE

BASF
Zeftron Nylon

WEBB...
the lounge series

waiting/working

comfortable

mobile

pivoting tablet arm

communication/power

storage

six webbing colors

1, 2 & 3 seats

Designed by
Burkhard Vogtherr

Davis Furniture Ind Inc.
PO Box 2065
High Point, NC 27261-2065
Tel 336 889 2009
Fax 336 889 0031
Email mail@davis-furniture.com
Web www.davis-furniture.com

DAVIS
design *is* a choice

THONET®

A new era in multi-purpose seating.

GOLF 1501

VERTIGO 1605

PAMPLONA 8499

PIUMA P-4200-WS

WAFER 5290

LAMM L1001

LAMM L1001 AUS

LAMM L1001 USB TA

© 1999 Thonet Industries, A Division of Shelby Williams Industries, Inc.

Seating Products Since 1830   403 Meacham Road   Statesville, NC 28677   800.551.6702   Service@Thonet.co

green

(grēn) n.[ME *grene* < OE *grene*.]

1. The hue of that portion of the spectrum lying between yellow and blue. **2.** Something green in color. **3.** greens. Green foliage or growth, esp.: *a)* Branches and leaves of plants used for decoration. *b)* Leafy plants or plant parts eaten as vegetables. **4.** *a)* A grassy lawn or plot. *b)* A putting green. -*adj.-er,-est*. 1. Youthful: vigorous. 2. Fresh: brand-new. *3.* Not aged, <greenwood> **5.** Relating to, or supporting environmentalism. **6. DesignTex Climatex® Lifecycle™ Products designed by William McDonough.**

D E S I G N T E X

Visit our website at **www.dtex.com** or call **1.800.221.1540**

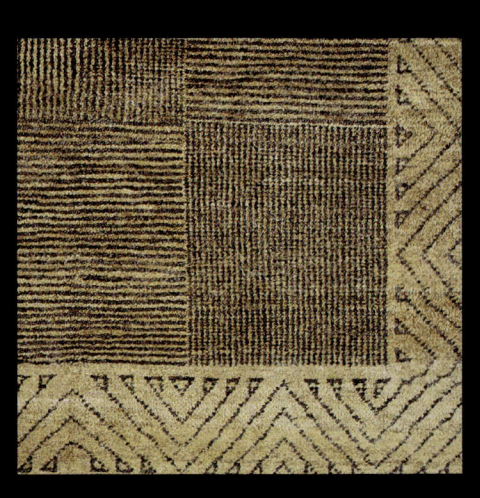

MICHAELIAN & KOHLBERG

Exquisite hand-made carpets to the trade.

578 Broadway, (corner of Prince), Suite 201
New York, New York 10012   (212) 431-9009

tella

introducing...

formula E design: Manfred Petri

Tella (800) 268-0511

Harbinger

Specify Harbinger woven carpet for unequaled craftsmanship and endurance. 1.800.241.4216 www.harbingercarpet.com

Modular Furniture in scenery

Architecture: Ronald Krueck & Olson; Steel and Glass House, Chicago, 1980
Presentation and photography: Balthasar Burkhard, 1999

U. Schaerer Sons Inc., A & D Building
150 East, 58th Street, New York, NY, 10155
Phone 212 371 1230 / Phone1 800 4 HALLER
www.hallersystems.com

Switzerland: USM U. Schärer Söhne AG, CH-3110 Münsingen
Phone ++41 31 720 72 72, www.usm.com

HALLER SYSTEMS™
Modular Furniture

A solid business decision.

Solid Wood Solutions

HARDEN contract

8550 Mill Pond Way
McConnellsville, New York 13401
315-675-3600 • Fax: 315-245-2884
E-Mail: contract@harden.com
Website: http://www.furniture-office.com

Graphic Standards™

Picnic (CS008)

Gumballs (CD002)

Mondrian (CD004)

Boats (CD008)

Kaleidascope (CD011)

a contradiction in Laminate

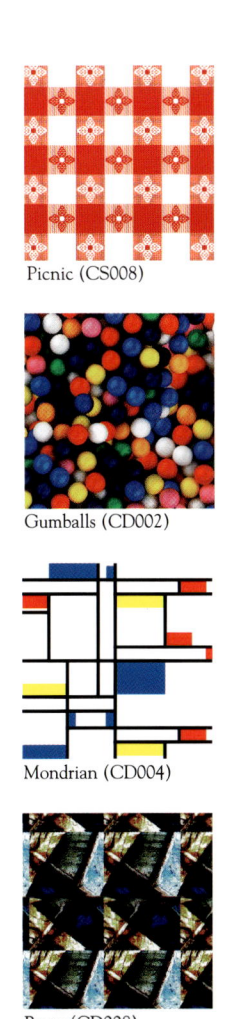

We're pleased to introduce Graphic Standards™, 30 distinctive custom laminate patterns that will change the way you think about high pressure laminate designs.

Using state-of-the-art digital and silk-screen printing processes, Wilsonart brings you a readily available line of off-beat, exciting designs just right for that not-so-standard project.

For the new Graphic Standards™ postcard sample deck, call 800-433-3222.

WILSONART
INTERNATIONAL

The computer sits here.
You sit here.
The client sits here.

Contour Collection
See the client.
See the computer.
Together.
Designed by Archetype.

OFS®

1-800-521-5381   www.ofs.styline.com

Somewhere, someplace you've experienced a MechoShade® hard at work.

It could have been at the office, school, auditorium, hospital or someone's home that you experienced the beauty and functionality of a MechoShade®. Now, more than ever, MechoShade roller shades are being specified for their esthetic and functional design characteristics of visibility, solar protection and low maintenance for homes, offices and corporate spaces. Available in manual, motorized or computerized solar tracking systems, visibly transparent MechoShades are the ideal solar protection solution for typical windows, skylights, greenhouses or atriums where greater use of natural daylight is desired. MechoShade roller shades are also available as room darkening shades or blackout for audio/visual integration and/or privacy.

MechoShade features ThermoVeil®, EuroVeil™ and Soleil™ shade cloths which are available in a broad range of colors, textures weaves and densities which meet or exceed the demands of the most discriminating designer and compliment all types of glazing from clear to reflective.

For more information contact your local MechoShade representative by calling Toll Free 1-877-774-2572 or at our website at http://www.mechoshade.com

MechoShade®

MechoShade Systems, Inc. • 42-03 35th Street, Long Island City, NY 11101

© Copyright 1999, MechoShade Systems, Inc., Long Island City, NY. All rights reserved. MechoShade and ThermoVeil are registered trademarks of MechoShade Systems, Inc. Long Island City, NY. EuroVeil and Soleil are trademarks of MechoShade Systems, Inc., Long Island City, NY.

BALDINGER

Michael Graves	 Modena Michael Graves	 Firenze Michael Graves	 Giulia / ADA Michael Graves	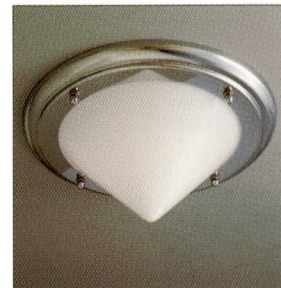 Verona Michael Graves
 Victoire Andrée Putman	 Bertille / ADA Andrée Putman	 Andrée Putman	 Linda Andrée Putman	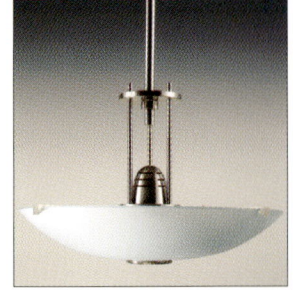 Constantin Andrée Putman
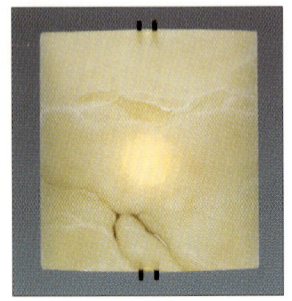 Max / ADA Richard Meier	 Double Joseph Richard Meier	 Ana / ADA Richard Meier	 Richard Meier	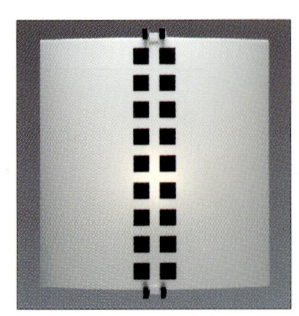 Max / ADA Richard Meier
 Kylix Table Lamp Robert A.M. Stern	 Robert A.M. Stern	 Tassel Robert A.M. Stern	 Kylix Robert A.M. Stern	 Greek Key Robert A.M. Stern

PRODUCED AND DISTRIBUTED BY BALDINGER ARCHITECTURAL LIGHTING INC
19-02 STEINWAY STREET, ASTORIA, NY 11105 TEL: 718-204-5700 FAX: 718-721-4986

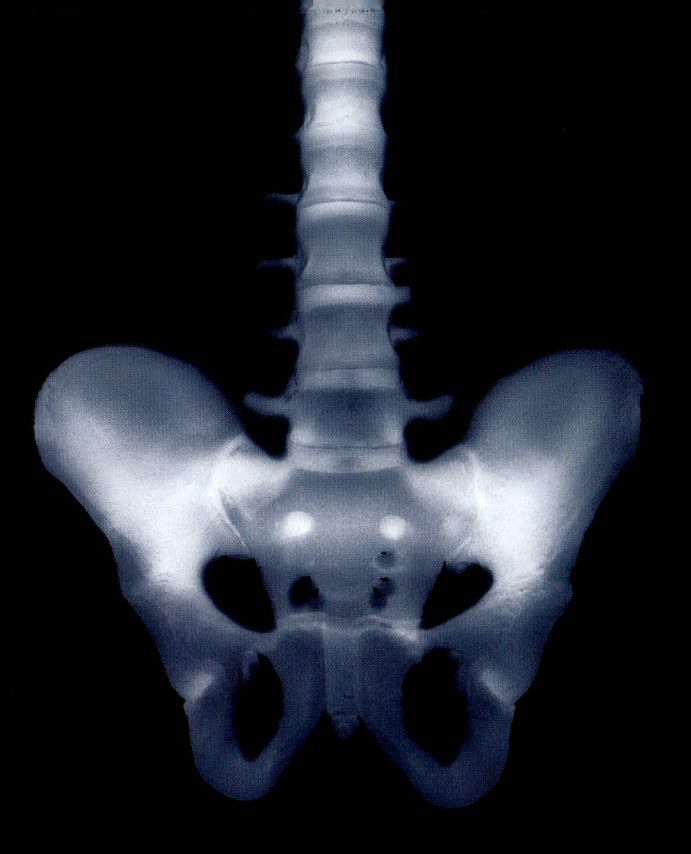

WHICH BONE TO PICK?

The Os Stack and Os Task chairs are good for all your bones. And pretty easy on the eyes too.

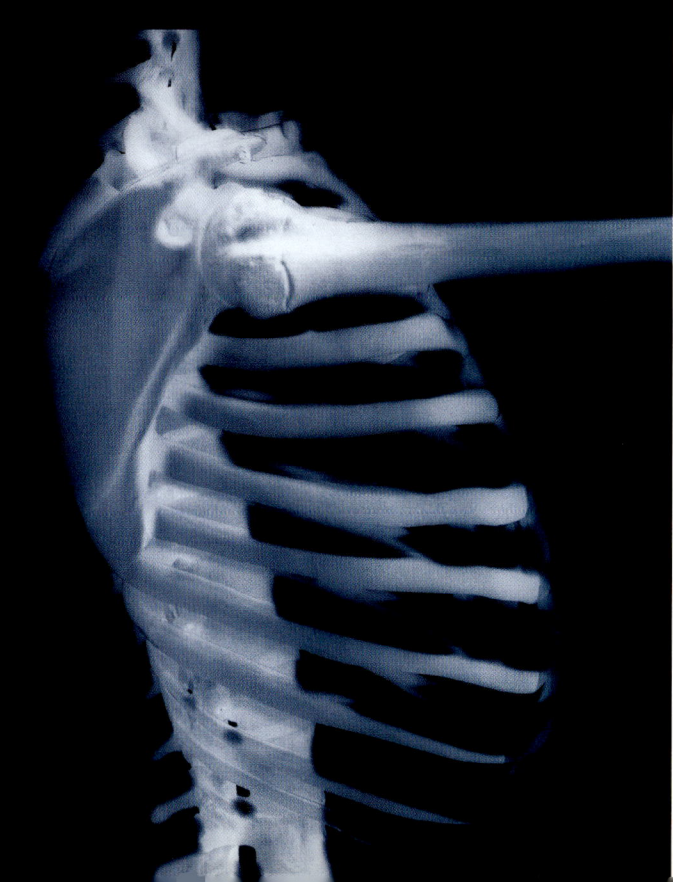

Os^{S+T}

1 800 563 3502 · www.allseating.com

allseating

INDEX BY PROJECTS

3 Arts Enter2000 L Street, NW, Washington, DC **280**

A.T. Kearney, Dallas, TX **318**

Allegiance Healthcare Corporation Headquarters, Deerfield, IL **114**

Allianz Insurance Company, Los Angeles, CA **262**

Allstate F Lobby, Northbrook, IL **248**

American Airlines, City Ticket Office, London, UK **304**

American College of Surgeons, Chicago, IL **98**

Asian Headquarters for an international financial institution, Hong Kong **144**

AutoZone Corporate Headquarters, Memphis, TN **190**

Bank of America, Executive Offices, Interstate Johnson Lane Tower, Charlotte, NC **184**

BB&T Center for Little & Company, Charlotte, NC **178**

Bloomberg, L.P., San Francisco, CA **355**

BMC Software, Inc., Corporate Headquarters, Houston, TX **86**

BMW of Manhattan, Inc., New York, NY **292**

Brillstein-Grey Entertainment, Beverly Hills, CA **20**

Brobeck, Phleger & Harrison LLP, Irvine, CA **18**

BT Office Products International, Deerfield, IL **242**

Caribiner International, Dearborn, MI **110**

Carl Marks & Company, New York, NY **14**

CB Richard Ellis, Memphis, TN **186**

Chase Manhattan Bank, Trading Facility, New York, NY **308**

Citibank Tampa Center, Tampa, FL **134**

Citigroup Corporate Center, New York, NY **334**

Clarks Companies, N.A.,The, Newton, MA **34**

CNA Cafeteria, Chicago, IL **244**

Concert Reston, Concert Global Communications, Reston, VA **278**

Cramer Rosenthal McGlynn Inc., New York, NY **228**

DavisElen Advertising, Los Angeles, CA **264**

Dechert Price & Rhoads, Washington, DC **170**

Deloitte & Touche Consulting Group, Pittsburgh, PA **58**

Deloitte & Touche LLP, Philadelphia, PA **162**

Deloitte & Touche, Consulting Group, Cleveland, OH **238**

Deutsche Telekom, New York, NY **340**

DPR Construction, Newport Beach, CA **68**

Draft Worldwide, New York, NY **30**

EarthShell Corporation Headquarters, Baltimore, MD **118**

EPT Landscape Architects, San Juan Capistrano, CA **198**

Ernst & Young LLP, Austin, TX **324**

Ernst & Young LLP, Dallas, TX **326**

Ernst & Young, LLP, Workplace of the Future, Los Angeles, CA **84**

Eugene du Pont,The, Preventive Medicine and Rehabilitation Institute, Wilmington, DE **214**

Executive Offices Menlo Park, CA **42**

Federal Home Loan Bank, Pittsburgh, PA **60**

Federation Employment and Guidance Service, Inc., New York, NY **230**

FedEx, World Technology Center, Collierville, TN **188**

FileNET, Regional Headquarters, Kirkland, WA **194**

Fina Oil and Chemical Company, Plano, TX **130**

Financial Ideas Exchange, New York, NY **116**

Financial Institution, New York, NY **160**

Financial Institution, New York, NY **306**

Financial Media Services Company, Princeton, NJ **312**

First National Bank, Akron, OH **240**

First Union Corporation, Customer Information Center, Charlotte, NC **180**

First USA Bank, Pennsylvania Railroad Building, Wilmington, DE **216**

First USA Bank, Three Christina Center, Wilmington, DE **212**

Focus Media, Santa Monica, CA **258**

Forbes Silicon Valley Bureau, Burlingame, CA **46**

Fort James, International Headquarters, Deerfield, IL **346**

Fort James, North American Headquarters, Norwalk, CT **350**

Fragrance Resources, New York, New York **231**

Fraser Papers, Stamford, CT **352**

G.G.K. Satellite Offices, Garden City, NY **222**

GE Capital Mortgage Services Inc., Cherry Hill, NJ **164**

General Dynamics, Falls Church, VA **174**

Gillette Company, The, Headquarters, Boston, MA **119**

Goldman, Sachs & Co., Superbooth at New York Stock Exchange, New York, NY **309**

Gruntal & Co., New York, NY **28**

Guidance Solutions, Marina del Rey, CA **92**

Halstead Industries, Inc., Greensboro, NC **254**

Harvest Partners, New York, NY **12**

Hewlett-Packard, Paramus, NJ **224**

HKS Corporate Headquarters, Dallas, TX **132**

Howrey & Simon, Menlo Park, CA **172**

Hudson News, Grand Central Terminal, New York, NY **302**

Hudson News/Euro Café, Washington Dulles International Airport, Washington, DC **300**

ING Baring Furman Selz LLC, New York, NY **208**

Intech Corporation, Philadelphia, PA **122**

Interface Americas' Corporate Headquarters, "Talimeco", Atlanta, GA **90**
Investment Firm, New York, NY **204**
ITG Inc., New York, NY **202**
J. Muller International, New York, NY **294**
Kahunaville, Carousel Center, Syracuse, NY **210**
Kirkland & Ellis Law Offices, New York, NY **310**
KPMG, Mountain View, CA **266**
Kvaerner, Inc., Philadelphia, PA **62**
Lancaster Group Worldwide Inc., New York, NY **252**
Latham & Watkins, Orange County, CA **66**
Lehman Millet Incorporated, Boston, MA **36**
LSG/Sky Chefs Sky Center, JFK International Airport, Jamaica, NY **303**
M. A. Hanna Co., World Headquarters, Cleveland, OH **236**
MacTemps, Boston, MA **35**
Madison Dearborn Partners, Inc., Chicago, IL **102**
Martin Agency, The, Richmond, VA **78**
MBIA (CapMAC), New York, NY **290**
McDevitt Street Bovis, Corporate Headquarters, Charlotte, NC **182**
MCI Telecommunications Corporation, Washington, DC **276**
Media General, Richmond, VA **74**
Merrill Lynch Business Financial Services, Chicago, IL **26**
Merrill Lynch, New York, NY **126**
Mission Imports, Laguna Niguel, CA **196**
Mitsui Trust & Banking Co., Ltd., New York, NY **206**
Mobil Oil Company Limited, Witan Gate House, Milton Keynes, UK **332**
Morgan, Lewis & Bockius, LLP, New York, NY **158**
Motor Parkway Corporate Center, Hauppauge, NY **220**
MTV Networks' West Coast Headquarters, Santa Monica, CA **94**
National Public Radio Headquarters, Washington, DC **64**
Nextlink, Bellevue, WA **70**
Nickelodeon, Burbank, CA **22**
Oaktree Capital Management, LLC, Corporate Headquarters, Los Angeles, CA **82**
Offices for a High-Tech Company, Seattle, WA **72**
Offices for Waters Design Associates, New York, NY **10**
Offices of IA, Interior Architects Inc., Washington, DC **142**
Omni Building, Garden City, NY **218**
Paramount Park School, Paramount, CA **199**
Paul, Weiss, Rifkind, Wharton & Garrison, New York, NY **134**
PeopleSoft Headquarters, Pleasanton, CA **270**

Perfumes Isabell Corporate Headquarters, New York, NY **358**
Pfizer, Inc., New York, NY **54**
PG&E Energy Services, San Francisco, CA **138**
Pillsbury Madison Sutro Law Offices, Palo Alto, CA **44**
Playmates Toys, Inc., Corporate Headquarters, Costa Mesa, CA **200**
PNC Bank, Regional Headquarters, Philadelphia, PA **124**
Polaris Claim Reception Center, Tampa, FL **120**
Prime Group Inc., The, Chicago, IL **140**
Prudential Bank & Trust, Atlanta, GA **250**
RCM Capital Management Executive Offices, San Francisco, CA **48**
Reliance Insurance Co., Philadelphia, PA **166**
Sasaki Associates, Inc., San Francisco, CA **288**
SBC Warburg, New York, NY **330**
Sciens Worldwide, New York, New York **232**
Scudder Mutual Fund Service Center, Salem, NH **284**
Scudder Shareholder Service Center, Norwell, MA **286**
Segrets Showroom, New York, NY **40**
Sharf Information Center, Museum of Fine Arts, Boston, Boston, MA **39**
Sverdrup CRSS Offices, Arlington, VA **322**
Ted Moudis Associates' Own Offices, New York, NY **342**
Temerlin McClain, Las Colinas, TX **314**
Think New Ideas, Hollywood, CA **260**
Tiffany & Co., New York, NY **338**
Tishman Speyer Properties, New York, NY **50**
Tokai Bank of California, Executive Offices and Retail Branch, Los Angeles, CA **88**
Tufts Health Plan, Watertown, MA **282**
Universal Studios Offices, Universal City, CA **146**
US Airways Club, Philadelphia, PA **298**
USG Conference and Training Center, Schiller Park, IL **246**
Viant, Boston, MA **108**
Viant, San Francisco, CA **106**
Virgin Atlantic, Upper Class Departures Lounge, Dulles International Airport, Loudoun County, VA **274**
Wayne Dalton Corporation, World Headquarters, Mt. Hope, OH **234**
White & Case, LLP, Los Angeles, CA and New York, NY **156**
Wilmington Trust, Inc., New York, NY **226**
Winston & Strawn, New York, NY **100**

INDEX OF ADVERTISERS

AGI *375*
American Institute of Architects *361*
Allseating *431*
Arcadia *435*
ARK (Architectural Response Kollection, Inc.) *412-413*
B&B Italia *405*
Baldinger *430*
Bonaventure *380*
Boyd Lighting *399*
Cabot Wren *406*
Carnegie *365*
Cleator *404*
Constantine *418*
Dauphin *393*
Davis *419*
Designtex *421*
Edward Fields *373*
Egan *408-409*
Flos USA *410*
Fixtures Furniture *368*
Geiger Brickel *362-363*
Gianni *376*
Halcon *397*
Haller Systems *425*
HBF *416-417*
Harbinger *424*
Harden Contract *426*
Harter *415*
Herman Miller *382-383*
ICF Group *364*
JM Lynne *366*
Jofco *377*
Karastan *391*
Knoll *367*
Kroin *385*
Lees *369*
Leucos, USA *395*
Masland Contract *381*
MechoShade *429*
Michaelian & Kohlberg *422*
New York Design Center *374*
Novawall *401*
Nienkamper *407*
OFS *428*
Paoli Furniture *414*
Schumacher Contract *372*
Solutia *402-403*
Steelcase *370-371*
Teknion *411*
Tella *423*
Thonet *420*
Tuohy *389*
Unifor *378-379*
Versteel *387*
Wilson International *427*

The
Power of
Individuality

Meos

Arcadia
800-585-5957